o Malachi

Welcome to academia.

Chrispas Nyombi

UK Takeover Law
and the Board Neutrality Rule

UK Takeover Law
and the Board Neutrality Rule

by

Chrispas Nyombi

WILDY, SIMMONDS & HILL PUBLISHING

UK Takeover Law

A catalogue record for this book is available from The British Library

ISBN 9780854902293

Wildy, Simmonds & Hill Publishing
58 Carey Street
London WC2A 2JF
England
www.wildy.com

Contents

PREFACE

Practical and theoretical contribution of the book

Since the turn of the twentieth century, companies have been at the forefront of social and economic development in the UK and around the world.[1] Every country has had its economic profile shaped in some way by corporate organisations. However, UK companies in particular, operate in an increasingly competitive marketplace which places greater demand on attracting investment and generating wealth in order to remain competitive and survive. This has driven companies to look beyond their national borders and seek opportunities in foreign markets.

Access to foreign markets is often achieved through mergers and acquisitions (M&A), also known as takeovers.[2] Statistics on worldwide M&A activity (Figure 1) show a significant increase in M&As between 1985 and 2016.

Figure 1: Worldwide M&A activity between 1985 and 2016

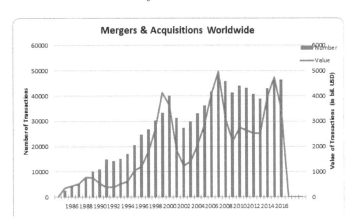

Source: Institute of Mergers, Acquisitions and Alliances (IMAA).[3]

---

[1] See John K Galbraith, *The New Industrial State* (Houghton Mifflin Company: Boston 1967) Chapter 4. He discussed the growing importance of companies in the United States (US) and around the world. Also see his earlier text John K Galbraith, *The Affluent Society* (4th edn, Houghton Mifflin Company: New York 1998) 81-142. He placed companies at the centre of social and economic development in Western economies.

[2] See Helen Berry, *Globalisation and the rise of "economic nationalism": Takeovers and regulation within the European Union* (2009) 1 (2) International Journal of Economics and Business Research 234, 236- 238.

[3] Institute of Mergers, Acquisitions and Alliances (IMAA), 'Statistics on Mergers and Acquisitions worldwide' (2016) available at <http://www.imaa-institute.org/statistics-mergers acquisitions.html#MergersAcquisitions_United%20Kingdom> accessed 17

Based on Figure 1, in 1985 roughly 3000 M&As were taking place worldwide and by 2016 this figure had increased to 46000, averaging 38000 since the year 2000. However, from 2001- 2002, there was a decline in the takeover activity. One of the factors behind the decline was the dot.com bubble in 2000.[4] Despite that, the rapid growth in worldwide M&A activity since 1985 is testament to the important role played by globalisation which has enabled companies to venture into new markets in search of new opportunities.

In the UK, between 2001- 2015, more than one hundred companies were being taken over by foreign companies each year (see Chapter 1, Table 1).[5] The takeover activity saw household names such Cadbury, Thames Water, British Aviation Authority and Manchester United fall into foreign hands. In terms of economic value, the price offered to take over these companies meant that billions of pounds were being spent in the UK during that period. In 2007, at the peak of the takeover activity, £82 billion foreign acquisitions were made (see Chapter 1, Table 1).[6]

The UK economy has proved attractive to foreign companies because of its strong economic profile. Based on the 2016 world economic league table, the UK is the fifth largest economy in the world.[7] However, the UK has many other important attributes such as a robust legal system, political stability and a strong currency which appeal foreign investors.[8]

Due to the high takeover activity in the UK, outgoing shareholders have been able to earn premiums on their investments.[9] This is because target companies are often taken over at a premium and the billions used to acquire the companies go to shareholders to entice them to sell their stock.[10] However, the large premiums paid out by the acquiring company

December 2016.
[4] See Roger Lowenstein, *Origins of the Crash: The Great Bubble and Its Undoing*, (Penguin Books Press: New York 2004) 114–115. He explains how equity value in industrialised nations steadily rose between 1997- 1999 due to growth in the internet sector and eventually burst in 2000.
[5] A foreign company is one registered to do business or incorporated in another jurisdiction.
[6] Office for National Statistics, Mergers and Acquisitions by foreign companies (2012) Available at statistics.gov.uk
[7] Centre for Economics and Business Research, World Economic League Table 2016 (December 26 2016).
[8] Nigel Driffield, Jim Love, Sandra Lancheros and Yama Temouri, How attractive is the UK for future manufacturing foreign direct investment (Foresight: Government Office for Science 2013) 5 and 8-12.
[9] See Tim Koller, Marc Goedhart and Wessels David, *Valuation, Measuring and managing the value of companies* (6th edn, Wiley John & Sons: New Jersey, 2015) 565-592; Marc Goergen and Luc Renneboog, Shareholder Wealth Effects of European Domestic and Cross-Border Takeover Bids (2004) 10 (1) European Financial Management 1, 10- 17.
[10] On takeover and shareholder's wealth, see Chapter 1.3; see Sudi Sudarsanam, *Creating*

could have a detrimental effect on its post-takeover performance. Studies have shown that the acquiring company's stock value declines from the announcement date and up to five years following a takeover.[11] The studies point to increased debt levels as one of the variables behind the decline in stock value.[12]

This can be exemplified by the Royal Bank of Scotland's (RBS) £49 billion takeover of Dutch bank ABN Amro in October 2007.[13] RBS made an offer of three times the book value of ABN Amro. The deal was bad for two reasons: (1) ABN Amro was widely exposed to the subprime mortgage crisis, meaning it was worth only a fraction of what RBS had paid and (2) at the time of the deal, most banks were trading at around book value, making the price paid by RBS look even more inflated.[14] Less than a year later, RBS asked shareholder for an extra £12 billion to shore up its finances following a 5.9 billion write-down of assets. In the end, RBS had to rely on a government bailout package to avoid collapsing. This shows that takeovers do not guarantee positive post-takeover performance.

Given the potential adverse impact on the post-takeover performance of the acquiring company, it is important that the right takeover decision is made by the target company that reflects its long-term value. The acquiring company may need to pay-off the massive debts used to finance the acquisition and this could mean undertaking restructuring activity in its businesses, including that of the acquired company. This creates the danger that accepting the wrong bidder could lead to non-value maximising restructuring in the target company which could damage the long-term financial health of the target company and impact on the interests of stakeholders such as employees and the whole economy whose fundamentals support takeover activity.[15]

value from Mergers and Acquisitions: The challenges (Pearson Education: Prentice Hall, New Jersey 2011) Chaps 14-16.
[11]   See Sara B Moeller, Frederik P Schlingemann and Rene M Stulz, Wealth destruction on a massive scale, a study of acquiring firm returns in the recent merger wave (2005) 60(2) Journal of Finance 757, 775-777; Anup Agrawal, Jeffrey Jaffe and Gershon N Mandelker, The Post-Merger Performance of Acquiring Firms: A Re-examination of an Anomaly (1992) 47 (4) Journal of Finance 1605, 1615-1620.
[12]   Roy D Baker and Robin J Limmack, UK takeovers and acquiring company wealth changes: The impact of survivorship and other potential selection biases on post-outcome performance, (2001) Working Paper, University of Stirling, 19-27.
[13]   RBS was joined by Belgian bank Fortis and Spanish bank Banco Santander in the deal for ABN Amro.
[14]   The Financial Services Authority, The failure of the Royal Bank of Scotland: Financial Services Authority Board Report (December 2011) 21-22.
[15]   Andrei Shleifer and Lawrence H Summers, Breach of Trust in Hostile Takeovers in Alan J Auerbach, *Corporate Takeovers: Causes and Consequences* (University of Chicago Press: Chicago 1988) 50-51. They studied the takeover of a company called Youngstown Sheet and Tube in 1977 and found a total loss of 6,000 jobs between 1977 and 1979. They concluded that

The final decision in a takeover situation is made by shareholders. The target company's shareholders are guaranteed the opportunity to decide the outcome of a takeover bid by the shareholder-centric takeover rules in the UK. The introduction to the Takeover Code 2016 states that the Code is "designed principally to ensure that shareholders are treated fairly and are not denied an opportunity to decide on the merits of a takeover and that shareholders of the same class are afforded equivalent treatment by an offeror."[16]

The Takeover Code 2016, which is administered by the Takeover Panel, regulates takeover activity in England and Wales.[17] The Takeover Panel is an independent body that not only issues and administers the Takeover Code but also supervises and regulates takeovers. As explained in Chapter 6.1.2, the takeover regulation in the UK has developed over time to reflect the interests of shareholders rather than the board and other key stakeholders. As a result, shareholders as a body have been given primacy over the takeover decision making process.

Fundamental to the operation of shareholder primacy during takeovers is Rule 21 of the Takeover Code, the so-called board neutrality rule. It prohibits the board of directors from frustrating a takeover. Thus, the board of directors cannot put in place any defensive measures to fend an unwanted bidder unless they gain the approval of a majority of the shareholders.[18]

Due to Rule 21, the board of directors is deposed as the main controlling organ in the company. This operates contrary to principles of company law which holds that the company's business is controlled by the board of directors appointed by the shareholders.[19] However, a takeover raises questions of ownership and transferability of property which means that the owners of the shares should be able to make the final decision over the destination of their property.[20]

Shareholder primacy under UK takeover law was summed up by Professors Armour, Deakin and Konzelmann: "What can be said with some confidence is that the [Takeover Code] sets up a system that focuses director attention in the conduct of a bid on the immediate question of

---

the debt levels taken on by the acquiring company was the main factor behind the breach of trust post-takeover.
[16] Takeover Code 2016, Section A, at A.1.
[17] Takeover Code 2016 (also known as the City Code on Takeovers and Mergers).
[18] See Chapter 1.1 and 1.2 on the scope of Rule 21 and Chapter 5.2 on takeover defences.
[19] See Companies (Model Articles) Regulations 2013, Article 3; Table A, Article 70.
[20] See the discussion in Chapter 3 on Private property rights and takeovers.

whether it is in shareholders' best interest to accept a tender offer."[21] There was an acknowledgement that "UK takeover regulation has a strikingly shareholder oriented cast."[22] The distinguished scholars clearly points to the discretion target company shareholders enjoy during takeovers, enabling them to focus on serving their own interests before considering other stakeholders.

Due to shareholders primacy during takeovers, directors are pushed to serve the interests of shareholders ahead of other stakeholders. This is because the protection afforded to non-shareholding stakeholders such as employees (including management) is only influential on the outcome of the takeover decision but not binding.[23] Given the lack of sufficient protection to non-shareholding interests during takeovers, the important question is whether shareholders would be willing to overlook their own interests if it conflicts with the interests of other stakeholders.[24]

However, during takeovers, the board of directors does not automatically stand for the interests of employees and this is largely down to the dynamic role they play within the company. Most large public companies have a governance structure that consists of three key constituencies: (i) the shareholders, (ii) the board of governors (also known as the board of directors) and (iii) senior managers. The shareholders have property ownership rights while the board of directors wields controlling powers and senior management manage the company's business on a day to day basis. However, their roles overlap.[25]

This governance structure can be a source of conflict during a takeover because the interests of senior management are likely to clash with those of the board of directors. Senior management are usually full-time employees on high salaries and privileges whereas board members represent certain shareholders who want to sell and make a profit. Thus the group that is most likely to resist a takeover is the senior management group and they are more likely to stand up for the interests of ordinary employees, also being employees in an ordinary sense. Executive directors may lose their jobs following a takeover, as they are part of management, but also

---

[21]   John Armour, Simon Deakin and Suzanne J Konzelmann, Shareholder Primacy and the Trajectory of UK Corporate Governance (2003) 41 (3) British Journal of Industrial Relations 531, 536.
[22]   John Armour and David A Skeel, Who Writes the Rules for Hostile Takeovers, and Why?-The Peculiar Divergence of US and UK Takeover Regulation (2007) 95 Georgetown Law Journal 1727, 1735.
[23]   See Chapter 1.4 on directors' duties to non-shareholding stakeholders.
[24]   See the findings in Chapters 4.1.3 and 5.3 on the role of arbitrageurs such as hedge funds during the Takeover of Cadbury.
[25]   See Chapter 1.5 on company stakeholders.

represent shareholders who placed them there to oversee their investment and make financial gains. Such dynamics make takeovers an information rich event for researchers because it creates a conflict of interest situation; but only for the short term, ultimately shareholder primacy prevails.

However, even though shareholders have greater legitimacy to control the takeover process due to their property claim on the company, corporate social responsibility enters the debate because a company is social institution and it relies on all its stakeholders to function (see the discussion on the economic theories of the firm in Chapter 2.4). Viewing the company as a social institution means that takeovers should be looked at both in terms of their economic but also social value. This means consideration should be given to the interests of non-shareholding stakeholders as well rather than prioritising the financial value to shareholders. These arguments were advanced by stakeholder theorists in the latter half of the twentieth century.[26]

Non-shareholding stakeholders seek protection during takeovers because empirical studies carried out in the 1980s and 90s found a strong relationship between takeovers and a negative impact on non-shareholding stakeholders such as employees and suppliers.[27] However, there are gaps in research literature.

First, studies have shown that employees stand to lose their jobs within a period of ten years following a takeover.[28] However, even though there is strong empirical support for job losses post-takeover, the available evidence is based on takeover cases before 2000. Thus, there is a need for research evidence that tests the relationship between takeovers and job losses in the twenty-first century.

Second, the board of directors typically consists of senior managers whom the bidding company must approach before shareholders can be informed of the takeover offer. Research evidence shows that senior management are at risk of losing their positions when a company is taken over.[29] However, most of the takeover cases studied are American. Thus,

[26]   See Chapter 2.4 on the nexus of contact, agency and team production theories of the firm.
[27]   See Chapter 2.5, for empirical evidence on takeovers and their impact on the interests of non-shareholding stakeholders.
[28]   Andrei Shleifer and Lawrence H Summers, Breach of Trust in Hostile Takeovers in Alan J Auerbach, *Corporate Takeovers: Causes and Consequences* (University of Chicago Press: Chicago 1988) 50-51; Wages also decrease in real terms within ten years following a takeover, see Til Beckman and William Forbes, An examination of takeovers, job loss and wage decline within UK Industry, (2004) 10(1) European Financial Management 141, 157-159.
[29]   See Swarnodeep Homroy, Effect of Mergers and Acquisitions on CEO Turnover in Large Firms and SMES: A Hazard Analysis (2012) Department of Economics, Lancaster University, 16-23; Jeffrey A Krug and Ruth V Aguilera, Top Management Teams turnover in mergers

there is a general lack of research on the impact of takeovers on senior management in the UK.

Last but not least, suppliers want to retain the contractual relations they had with the senior management team before the takeover. They are worried that there could be a renegotiation or non-renewal of contract post-takeover. Empirical research has shown a positive relationship between senior management turnover post-takeover and renegotiation of supplier contracts.[30] However, there is insufficient evidence that directly links takeovers to breach of supplier contacts. Furthermore, the research evidence is mainly based on takeovers in the US.

Thus, although existing research evidence shows a positive relationship between takeovers and the detrimental effect on the interests of non-shareholding stakeholders such as employees, suppliers and senior management, it suffers from two major shortfalls. First, the research evidence is based on takeover cases before the twenty-first century thus there is a need for research on the takeover activity in this century. Second, the research evidence is predominantly American thus there is a need for UK based studies.

In light of existing research evidence on takeovers and their impact on non-shareholding stakeholders' interests, it begs an important question: is the primacy afforded to shareholders during justified? To answer this question, we need to go beyond empirical studies on the extent to which takeovers impact on the interests of non-shareholding stakeholders and enter a debate over shareholders' interests versus other stakeholders' interests. It is generally accepted that the role of a company in a western capitalist system is mainly to create wealth for its shareholders.[31] However, a company depends on all its stakeholders such employees to function. Thus, knowing the role of a company within a western capitalist society will lead a greater understanding of the competing interests within a company.

In order to judge on whether shareholder primacy can be justified, a study on the extent to which takeovers impact on the interests of non-shareholding stakeholders is carried out. These findings will inform the

and acquisitions (2005) 4(1) Advances in Mergers and Acquisitions 121, 146–147.
[30] Vincent J Intintoli, Mathew Serfling and Sarah Shaikh, The Negative Spillover Effects of CEO Turnovers: Evidence from Firm-Supplier Relations (2012), SSRN Working Paper Series, 17-28.
[31] See pro-capitalist commentators such as Milton Friedman, *Capitalism and Freedom* (University of Chicago Press: Chicago 1962) 12-16; Elaine Sternberg, The defects of stakeholder theory (1997) 5 (1) Corporate Governance: An international Review 3, 6-8.

reform proposals which are targeted the board neutrality rule, which is the source of shareholder primacy under UK takeover law.

This study focuses on takeovers rather than mergers for two reasons. First, a merger is a friendly event to which both companies' boards and shareholders are open to the combination of resources. Both companies' stock is surrendered and issued to the new company that combines both into one entity. For example, the 1999 merger of GlaxoWellcome and SmithKline Beecham meant that both companies ceased to exist thus creating a new company called GlaxoSmithKline.[32]

Takeovers, on the other hand, normally occur when an offer for over 50 per cent of the company's stock is accepted by shareholders thus enabling the buyer to take up a controlling stake in the company. The board of the target company, subject to the approval of shareholders, can elect to retain its distinct name and operations. Takeovers place the board of directors in a position of negotiation over shareholders' interests with the long-term interests of the company and its non-shareholding stakeholders. As a result, studies have shown that takeovers have a greater impact on non-shareholding stakeholders' interests as compared to mergers.[33]

Second, UK takeover law hands substantial decision making powers over the outcome of a takeover bid to shareholders which allow them to determine the outcome of a takeover. However, the issue goes beyond priority claims but whether giving shareholders decision making powers undermines and increases the risk on non-shareholding stakeholders such as employees. Mergers, on the other hand, do not involve control issues since it is a friendly undertaking which both parties have negotiated and agreed to undertake. In a takeover situation, some shareholders may approve the bidder with the highest offer and others may reject the bidder despite the high premium due to concerns over the long-term health of the company and its remaining stakeholders. Thus, studying takeovers would provide a good understanding of the competing interests during takeovers and the motivations of shareholders during the offer period.

It seeks to understand the role played by shareholder primacy during the offer period and whether it contributes to the impact on non-shareholding stakeholders' interests post-takeover. Since only the target

[32] Loizos Heracleous and John Murray, The urge to merge in the pharmaceutical industry (2001) 19 (4) European Management Journal 430, 431.
[33] See for example, on senior management turnover Swarnodeep Homroy, Effect of Mergers and Acquisitions on CEO Turnover in Large Firms and SMES: A Hazard Analysis (2012) Department of Economics, Lancaster University, 16-23; on employee jobs see Klaus Gugler and Burcin Yurtoglu, The effects of mergers on company employment in the USA and Europe (2004) 22 (4) International Journal of Industrial Organization 481, 493–497.

company shareholders have primacy in a takeover situation, this study focuses on the target company.

Book layout

This book is broken down into seven main chapters. Chapter one explains the fundamentals of takeovers. The rationale for choosing takeovers is explained. The chapter focuses on explaining shareholder primacy under takeover law and the interests of non-shareholding stakeholders. It also explains the methodologies used in this research and any challenges encountered. This chapter is important because it explains why it was worthwhile to study the impact of takeovers on company stakeholders and what the study aims to achieve.

Chapter two reviews research evidence on takeovers and the impact on employees, senior management and suppliers' interests post-takeover. This chapter is important because it reviews the important literature that has made a significant contribution to the topic. In the end, it highlights the gaps in existing research literature that this study aims to fill. This chapter is important because it provides the foundations of this study.

Chapter three examines the changing role of a company in society from its pre-twentieth century conception to the modern view. It is argued that although shareholders are the legitimate decision makers in law and business practice, a modern company has greater social responsibility as compared to a pre-twentieth century company. Thus, policy makers should intervene and impose social responsibilities, if they cannot be voluntarily achieved. In this chapter, the role and function of a company as an agent of capitalism is discussed. This brings into consideration the financial interests of shareholders and their property rights but also the social role of the company as well as modern challenges such as investor short-termism. This chapter helps us to understand why non-shareholding stakeholders' interests deserve protection despite shareholders being the legitimate decision makers under the western capitalist model.

Chapter four provides two case studies that present findings on the impact of takeovers on employees, senior management and suppliers. The two companies studied are Cadbury and Corus. The takeover cases were selected because shareholders were required to decide on the outcome of a takeover bid despite uncertainty over the long-term interests of other stakeholders such as employees. This chapter also provides evidence on the behaviours of shareholders during the takeover process which is essential to understanding the role of shareholder primacy during takeovers

Chapter five analyses and discusses the findings from the case studies, which is a logical follow up of the preceding chapter. Although chapters four and five should ideally be together, they have been separated to avoid having an extremely long chapter that is too difficult to read. The content and purposes of both chapters is also different; with chapter four presenting the findings and chapter five providing an analysis and discussion. Thus separating them can be justified on those two grounds.

First and foremost, chapter five analyses the evidence from the Cadbury and Corus takeovers to determine the degree of impact on the board of directors, employees (including senior management) and suppliers. It finds that all three stakeholders had their interests negatively impacted on by the takeovers. Second, it analyses evidence from the Cadbury and Corus takeovers on the role of shareholders during the takeover process. The findings from the case studies support established research evidence that target company shareholders earn a premium from takeovers. The findings also show that short-term investors or arbitrageurs buy up the target company's shares in hope of a profit once the deal is finalised. This has a major influence on the ability of the board and long-term shareholders (those who hold shares prior to a public announcement of the takeover offer) to prioritise the long-term interests of the company such as employee jobs. Furthermore, it shows that since short-term shareholders such as hedge funds are set up to make profit for their beneficiaries, this makes it unlikely that they would overlook their core objective when faced with a high premium for their shares despite putting the target company's stakeholders in a potentially risky position.

Chapter six considers the reform proposals. The proposals are targeted at Rule 21 of the Takeover Code 2016, which is the source of shareholder primacy under UK takeover law. In light of the evidence in part one showing a relationship between takeovers and a detrimental effect on the interests of employees, suppliers and senior management, as well as the influence of short-term investors on the outcome of the takeover bid, two alternatives to the current model of takeover regulation are proposed and critically evaluated. These are: (1) disenfranchisement of short-term shareholders' voting rights and (2) adoption of a board centric model of takeover regulation such as the US Delaware model. The latter would mean abolition of Rule 21 and thus allowing the board to put measures in place to frustrate a takeover they believe is not in the long-term interest of the company. The proposal to disenfranchise the voting rights of short-term shareholders was part of the consultation leading up to the 2011 amendments to the Takeover Code but was subsequently rejected by the

Takeover Panel.[34] Variations to this proposal are considered on the basis that they offer a less drastic and more appropriate reform solution.

The chapter concludes that there is insufficient evidence to justify a fundamental change of UK takeover law to either a multi-tier voting rights or a board-centric model. The solution is to give incentives to shareholders to think and act long-term such as strengthening the stewardship obligations under the Stewardship Code 2012.

Finally, chapter seven provides a summary of the book and closing remarks, which is a logical follow up of the preceding chapter. Although both chapters should ideally be together, uniting them would have resulted in a chapter that is too long and unworkable. The content and purposes of both chapters is also different; with chapter six evaluating the reform proposals and chapter seven summarising the findings and putting the research goals into context. Thus separating them can be justified on those two grounds.

Chapter seven brings together the various strands of argument throughout the book. The research questions are examined in light of the findings and remarks over the recommendations for reform are given. The aim is to test whether the goals of this study have been achieved and to explain the contribution the study has made to research literature. The main conclusion reached is that takeovers have a detrimental effect on the interests of employees, the board of directors and suppliers but more empirical work, especially in relation to the interests of suppliers, is needed. Due to a lack of sufficient evidence, reform to shareholder primacy under takeover law is deemed to be unjustified.

[34] Takeover Panel, Response Statement to the Consultation Paper on Review of Certain Aspects of the Regulation of Takeover Bids (RS 2010/22, October 2010) para 4.4.

CHAPTER 1: THE FUNDAMENTALS OF TAKEOVERS

Introduction

Since the turn of the twentieth-first century, the UK has remained a major attraction to foreign companies in pursuit of takeover targets. Statistics from the Office of National Statistics (ONS) covering a period of ten years from 2001 to 2015 indicate that over 2000 UK companies were taken over by foreign companies during that period.

Table 1: Transactions in the UK by foreign companies between 2001 and 2015

	Acquisitions	
Annual	Number	Value
2001	162	24,382
2002	117	16,798
2003	129	9,309
2004	178	29,928
2005	242	50,280
2006	259	77,750
2007	269	82,121
2008	252	52,552
2009	112	31,984
2010	212	36,643
2011	206	32,014
2012	161	17,414
2013	141	10,839
2014	110	15,041
2015	145	31,745

Source: Office for National Statistics (2016)

This means that on average 180 foreign acquisitions were taking place each year in the UK. That is testament to a buoyant takeover market that shows no sign of stopping.

The high interest in the UK companies has resulted in many household brands falling into the hands of foreign companies. Some of these brands include Cadbury which was taken over by Kraft Inc. in 2011 in a deal worth

£11.9 billion.[1] The loss of an iconic British brand with a 186 year heritage to a foreign company brought public outcry, more-so that Cadbury's board of directors stated from the beginning that the takeover would make "no strategic or financial sense."[2]

Despite the loss of iconic brands, the UK has had billions of pounds flowing into its economy due to the foreign direct investment (FDI) made through takeovers. Direct investment is an investment that adds to or acquires a lasting interest in an organisation operating in an economy.[3] FDI normally covers three types of outward investments: (1) a company establishes a branch or subsidiary in a foreign country and injects capital (also known as greenfield investments); (2) a company buys or sells the equity of a foreign company (M&A activity); and (3) a company injects additional capital into an existing foreign subsidiary.[4] Although all three types bring investment into the country, of particular interest in this book, is M&A activity and its contribution to the UK economy.

The Organisation for Economic Co-operation and Development (OECD) study into foreign acquisitions and its impact on economies found that M&A FDI accounts for an estimated 80 per cent of the total FDI among OECD countries.[5] Similarly, it is estimated that in developing countries, the contribution of M&A on FDI had increased from 10 per cent in 1980 to a third by 2000.[6] The increasing influence of M&A FDI on economies was credited to privatisation in developing countries and the opening up of domestic sectors to foreign investors.[7] In the UK, a significant proportion of FDI flow is accounted for by large multinational acquisitions. For example, in 2005, a transaction involving Shell between the Netherlands and UK accounted for 45 per cent of the FDI inflow in the UK that year.[8]

---

[1] Graham Ruddick, Kraft agrees to buy Cadbury for 11.9bn, *The Telegraph* (19 October 2010).
[2] David Jones, Cadbury stresses Kraft bid makes no strategic sense, *Reuters* (25 September 2009).
[3] Definition taken from the Office for National Statistics (*Foreign Direct Investment: Background notes*, First Released, 2005).
[4] Richard H Kreindler, The Law Applicable to International Investment Disputes (The United Nations Conference on Trade and Development (UNCTAD), 2003) 3 EDM/Misc.232/Add.5; Nigel Driffield, Jim Love, Sandra Lancheros and Yama Temouri, How attractive is the UK for future manufacturing foreign direct investment (Foresight: Government Office for Science 2013) 5 and 8-12.
[5] Stephen Thomsen, International Investment Perspectives: Freedom of investment in a changing world' (2013) OECD, ch 4.
[6] Calderon Cesar, Norman Loayza and Luis Serven, Greenfield foreign direct investment and mergers and acquisitions: feedback and macroeconomic effects (2004) World Bank Policy Research Working Paper 3192, Washington, DC. 15.
[7] Basu Parantap, Chandana Chakraborty and Derrick Reagle, Liberalization, FDI, and Growth in Developing Countries: A Panel Cointegration Approach (2003) 41(3) Economic Inquiry 510, 513-515.
[8] Grahame Allen and Aliyah Dar, Foreign Direct Investment (House of Commons Library

However, there is no evidence that FDI through M&A activity brings in money which contributes to economic growth.[9] This is because most of money used to takeover companies ends up in the hands of shareholders, who in most cases, widely dispersed all over the world.[10] Thus, dispersed share ownership damages the relationship between inflow and growth. Despite that, foreign M&A activity benefits the economy through technological spillovers that help local firms to create a more competitive business environment, promotion of total factor productivity and capital investment in local firms. [11]

Takeovers are often the preferred form of investment for entering foreign markets particularly in markets with high barriers to entry. For example, before Tata Steel decided to make a takeover offer for Corus Steel in 2007, they were locked in merger negotiations.[12] This is because being a much smaller company as compared to Corus, Tata Steel had estimated that it would take them longer to realise the economic benefits sought by operating in Europe as compared to buying a company that is already established in the region.[13]

There are many motives for choosing to take over an overseas company. The most often cited motives include access to a wider customer base, diversification of investment and financial stability.[14] This is likely to create synergies by combing the resources of the two firms and as a result generating more wealth for shareholders. Furthermore, operating in different markets could give the company more financial security in case its domestic market experiences instability or becomes saturated due to factors such as high competition.[15] Foreign acquisitions could also be driven by a need to get new technologies.[16] This commonly arises when a foreign investor acquires a local firm specifically for its technological capabilities.

briefing paper, London 2013) SN/EP/1828 at 3.
[9]   Miao Wang and Sunny Wong, What Drives Economic Growth? The Case of Cross-Border M&A and Greenfield FDI Activities (2009) 62 (2) Kyklos 316. The researchers conclude that: "Based on data for 84 countries from 1987 to 2001, our results indicate that the growth effect of M&As is negative" at 328.
[10]   See Chapter 4.1.3 on share ownership in Cadbury.
[11]   Hans Christiansen and Mehmet Ogutcu, Foreign Direct Investment for Development: Maximising Benefits, Minimising Costs (2002) OECD working paper. 4-8.
[12]   Rajesh B Kumar, *Mega Mergers and Acquisitions: Case Studies from Key Industries* (Hampshire: Palgrave Macmillan, Basingstoke 2012) 207.
[13]   However, sometimes takeovers are preferred even in the absence of barriers to entry for logistical or financial reasons, Jrisy Motis, Mergers and Acquisitions Motives Toulouse School of Economics (2007) University of Crete: Working Paper, 8-11.
[14]   *Ibid* 3-9.
[15]   Miklos Koren, Financial Globalization, Portfolio, Diversification, and the Pattern *of* International Trade (2003) Department of Economics, Harvard University, 28.
[16]   Shireen Alazzawi, Foreign direct investment and knowledge flows: evidence from patent citations (2004) University of California, working paper, 6.

Due to the benefits of foreign acquisitions, the UK has seen its companies venturing overseas in pursuit of foreign targets. ONS statistics in Table 2 indicate that over 100 foreign takeovers were being made each year by UK companies between 1987- 2013.

Table 2: Outward: Number of acquisitions by UK companies between 1987 and 2015

Year	
1987	431
1988	648
1989	681
1990	586
1991	550
1992	679
1993	521
1994	422
1995	365
1996	442
1997	464
1998	569
Date 1999	590
2000	557
2001	371
2002	262
2003	243
2004	305
2005	365
2006	405
2007	441
2008	298
2009	118
2010	199

2011	286
2012	122
2013	58
2014	113
2015	136

Source: Office for National Statistics (2016)

However, based on Table 2, since the peak of 1989 when 681 acquisitions were made abroad, the number of foreign acquisitions has been on a gradual and sustained downward trend. In 2013, only 58 foreign acquisitions were made by UK companies, marking a record low. In contrast, Table 3 shows that during the same period, acquisitions of UK companies by overseas companies were stable, averaging 184 acquisitions per annum.

Table 3: Acquisition of UK companies by foreign companies between 1987 and 2015

Year	Inward : Number of acquisitions
1987	61
1988	99
1989	168
1990	143
1991	146
1992	210
1993	267
1994	202
1995	131
1996	133
1997	193
1998	252
1999	252
2000	227

2001	162
2002	117
2003	129
2004	178
2005	242
2006	259
2007	269
2008	252
2009	112
2010	212
2011	237
2012	161
2013	141
2014	110
2015	145

Source: Office for National Statistics (2016)

Thus Table 3 illustrates that the UK continues to be an attractive location for foreign companies in pursuit of takeover targets while fewer UK companies are targeting their foreign counterparts.

Given the rising number of UK companies being taken over each year by foreign companies, it is important to appreciate the important role played by takeover law in regulating the conduct of the target companies during the takeover process.

The Takeover Code: The source of shareholder primacy

Takeovers in the UK are regulated by the Takeover Code 2016, which is administered by the Panel on Takeovers and Mergers (the Takeover Panel). The Panel is charged with overseeing and regulating transactions that the Takeover Code governs, including the bidding process. As the regulatory watchdog on M&A, the Takeover Panel has a powerful voice with companies and the government, thus giving substantial weight on its recommendations for any changes to the Takeover Code.[17] Furthermore, since its founding in 1968, it has maintained the view that shareholders are the owners of the company and should be entitled to receive bids and make a decision over them. However, being a statutory body, it does not have the legal power to enforce its decisions thus they are subject to judicial review.[18]

The Takeover Code is based on six General Principles, which are essentially statements on standards of commercial behaviour. These are:

General Principles 1: *All holders of the securities of an offeree company of the same class must be afforded equivalent treatment; moreover, if a person acquires control of a company, the other holders of securities must be protected.* Shareholder equality is reflected throughout the Code.

General Principle 2: *The holders of the securities of an offeree company must have sufficient time and information to enable them to reach a properly informed decision on the bid; where it advises the holders of securities, the board of the offeree company must give its views on the effects of implementation of the bid on employment, conditions of employment and the locations of the company's places of business.* The code sets a bid timetable designed to allow sufficient time for all particulars to be discussed while at the same time deterring companies from being subject to an unduly long periods of siege.

General Principle 3: *The board of an offeree company must act in the interests of the company as a whole and must not deny the holders of securities the opportunity to decide on the merits of the bid.* This is essentially an articulation of the board neutrality rule.

General Principle 4: *False markets must not be created in the securities of the offeree company, of the offeror company or of any other company concerned by the bid in such a way that the rise or fall of the prices of the securities becomes artificial and the normal functioning of the markets is distorted.* The Financial Conduct Authority (FCA) the principal regulator of the securities market in UK but from the beginning of a takeover bid until it becomes unconditional, the Panel works with the FCA to avoid the creation of false markets for the securities of the bidder and target.

---

[17]   Mathew Curtin, Evolution, Not Revolution, for U.K. Takeover Rules (2010) Wall Street Journal, October 21.
[18]   *R v. Panel on Take-overs and Mergers, ex p Datafin plc* [1987] QB 815

General Principle 5: *An offeror must announce a bid only after ensuring that he/she can fulfil in full any cash consideration, if such is offered, and after taking all reasonable measures to secure the implementation of any other type of consideration.* The Code seeks to ensure that bidders have sufficient resources to complete the bid and therefore committed to the cause.

General Principle 6: *An offeree company must not be hindered in the conduct of its affairs for longer than is reasonable by a bid for its securities.* The takeover code establishes a rigid timetable which is 109 days from posting an interest in taking over the target company.

These principles reflect the collective opinion of those professionally involved in the field of takeovers in regards to appropriate business standards. In addition, the Takeover Code contains a series of rules that govern the conduct of both the target and bidding company. The 38 rules are effectively expansions of the general principles.

Following the implementation of the Takeovers Directive[19] by means of Part 28 of the Companies Act 2006, the rules set out in the Takeover Code achieved a statutory basis. The statutory changes brought about by the Takeover Directive were much expected for two major reasons: (i) the Takeover Panel was heavily involved in the formulation of the Takeover Directive and the UK Takeover Code was seen as a blueprint on which other Member States should develop their laws,[20] and (ii) by 1987, the government was already considering putting the takeover panel on a statutory footing.[21] Due to the Takeover Panel's involvement, the Directive ended up reflecting the takeover regime in UK at the time of its implementation.

For example, when Article 9 of the Takeover Directive (on the board neutrality rule) received statutory basis under section 943, it was already established under rules 2 and 8 of the Takeover Code 2002. After implementation of the Directive, the rules were reinstated under General Principles 4 and 5 of the Takeover Code 2006 (now General Principles 3 of the Takeover Code 2016 following the 2011 reforms).

Prior to the implementation of the Takeover Directive, the Takeover Panel's powers did not derive from any statute and the Takeover Code did not have the force of law. Now the Takeover Code works in conjunction

---

[19] Takeover Directive (2004/25/EC). The Takeover Directive came into force on 6th April 2007. It replaced The Takeovers Directive (Interim Implementation) Regulations 2006 (IS 1183/2006).
[20] Geoffrey Morse, *Charlesworth's Company law'* (17th ed, Sweet & Maxwell, 2005) 676.
[21] Takeover Panel on Takeovers and Mergers, Report on the Year ended 31 March 1987.

with the Companies Act 2006. The Takeover Code comes into play at the onset of any M&A, to regulate the conduct of the target company and the bidder.

The Takeover Code permits shareholders to determine the outcome of a takeover bid. This right is enshrined under Rule 21 of the Takeover Code, the so-called board neutrality rule.

Rule 21.1(a) states that:

"During the course of an offer, or even before the date of an offer, the board must not, without the approval of the shareholders in general meeting, take any action which may result in any offer being frustrated or in shareholders being denied the opportunity to decide on its merits"

Rule 21 requires directors not to do anything with the effect of frustrating a takeover bid, unless shareholders approve it by a majority at the time of the takeover. The board neutrality rule stands even when the board has reasons to believe that a takeover is not good for the company in the long-run. Directors must rely on their consultation powers to persuade shareholders through informed and reasoned arguments that the offer is too low or the bidder may have ulterior motives that are bad for the company.[22] However, there are no guarantees that shareholders will abandon the opportunity to sell their shares to the bidder based on the advice of the board.

Due to Rule 21, shareholders are elevated from their position as financiers to decision makers. Although a takeover is essentially a decision over ownership in the company to which shareholders in the general meeting should have a final say, it is also a strategic management decision that would have an impact on the long-term interests of the company and other stakeholders. Thus, if a company is viewed as a purely economic entity set up to serve the interests of its members then shareholders' decision making powers enshrined under Rule 21 should not be challenged. However, if viewed as a social entity then this calls for a more stakeholder friendly approach to takeovers.

As a result, Rule 21 is the source of shareholder primacy under UK takeover law because it invites shareholders to make a decision on the strategic direction of the company.[23] By having the power to decide on such

---

[22] Takeover Code 2016, Rule 3.1.
[23] David Collison, Stuart Cross, John Ferguson, David Power & Lorna Stevenson, Shareholder Primacy in UK Corporate Law: An Exploration of the Rationale and Evidence' (2011) ACCA Research Report 125, 77.

an outcome, shareholders find themselves in control over the company's immediate fate. For example, in 2004, the American businessman Malcolm Glazer made an attempt to buy Manchester United Football Club but the bid was resented by the board because of the large amount of borrowing attached to it.[24] Since the club's board had refused to recommend the bid to their shareholders, the Glazers pursued a hostile takeover by approaching the club's shareholders directly for their shares. The shareholders agreed to sell despite the recommendations of the board not to sell. The shareholders were able to ignore the board's advice because when a takeover is successful, it is a private contract between individual shareholders and the acquiring company that takes place rather than an agreement between the decision makers in the company. Thus, the board neutrality rule places directors in a difficult position in regards to the protection of non-stakeholders' interests.

Furthermore, the prohibition against takeover defences applies only to takeover defences in relation to an imminent takeover. This means pre-bid defensive tactics fashioned by the target board are not caught by Rule 21. However, directors' duties under the Companies Act 2006 would limit the effectiveness of such defences.[25] Directors must make sure that their actions promote the success of the company and are conducted for a proper purpose.[26] In regards to the latter, the articles of association of large companies normally give directors broad discretionary powers. The proper purpose rule serves to limit their discretionary powers in cases where they go against the interest of the company. Case law demonstrates that takeover defensive actions could be caught by the proper purpose rule if their purpose is illegitimate or not in the interest of the company.[27] Thus, company law rules make it difficult for boards to fashion takeover defences pre-bid.

However, despite the continued operation of the board neutrality rule under takeover law, academic scholarship is divided on the issue of takeover defences. Those in support of non-frustration rules argue that a system that prevents the board from frustrating a takeover bid can be justified on two grounds. First, it supports the principle of free transferability of shares[28] and second, directors' actions may be tainted by self-interest instead of

---

[24] Bose Mihir, *Manchester Disunited: Trouble and Takeover at the World's Richest Football Club* (Aurum Press, London 2007) 81.

[25] Companies Act 2006, Sections 171-177.

[26] Section 172 the duty to promote the success of the company and Section 171(1) the proper purpose rule.

[27] The two leading cases on allotment of shares to defeat a takeover are *Hogg v. Craphorn* [1967] Ch. 254 at 265; [1966] 3 W.L.R. 995 and *Howard Smith v. Ampol Petroleum Ltd [1974]* A.C. 821 PC (Australia).

[28] Paul Davies, *Gower and Davies' Principles of Modern Company law* (Sweet & Maxwell, London, 2008) 962.

maximising shareholder value.[29] The two justifications are grounded in the management entrenchment hypothesis which centres on the view that any takeover defence is likely to increase managerial job security and control in the company at the expense of shareholder value.[30] On those grounds, it supports shareholder primacy during takeovers. Professors Easterbrook and Fischel argue that it is fundamental to the efficient workings of the takeover market that shareholders should be able to sell their shares without managerial intrusion.[31] This is premised on the view that takeover defences in the UK are heavily restricted by what seems to be a prevailing attitude by businesses and lawmakers that takeovers are beneficial and even if not actually encouraged, they should not be stifled.[32]

The shareholder agent hypothesis, on the other hand, supports adoption of takeover defences as a means of increasing shareholder value by putting trust in the board of directors.[33] Professor Kershaw provides three justifications for the shareholder agent hypothesis.[34] First, the board may be in a better position to understand the true value of the company, which may not be reflected in the share price, such as research and development (R&D) projects, as compared to shareholders. Second, takeover defences would give time and power to the board to find alternative bidders thus increasing competition and the offer price. Third, takeover defences would enable to board to deter bidders who may not have the company's best interests at heart and at the same time serve the interests of all company stakeholders.

Furthermore, although academic scholarship provides a case for the removal of the takeover defence prohibition, the arguments are overshadowed by the issue of directors' self- interest. It is difficult to guarantee that armed with the defensive powers, the directors would not use them to serve their own interests by negotiation high severance payments with the bidders before approving the bid or rejecting a value maximising bid due to the risk of being ousted from their positions.

---

[29]   The High Level Group of Company Law Experts, Report of the High Level Group of Company Law Experts on a Modern Regulatory Framework for Company Law in Europe (Brussels, 4 November, 2002) 21 <http://www.ecgi.org/publications/documents/report_en.pdf> accessed 2 July 2016.

[30]   George O Barboutis, Takeover defence tactics: Part 1: the general legal framework on takeovers (1999) 20 (1) Company Lawyer 1, 2-3.

[31]   Frank H Easterbrook and Daniel R Fischel, The Proper Role of a Target's Management in Responding to a Tender Offer (1981) 94 (6) Harvard Law Review 1161, 1195-1199.

[32]   See Company Law Committee of the Law Society, Response to the Department of Trade and Industry Consultation (April 1996) on the Thirteenth Directive on Company law concerning takeover bids, para 1.5 and 9.3.

[33]   *Ibid* para 93.

[34]   David Kershaw, *Company law in context: Text and Materials*, (2nd edn, Oxford University Press, Oxford 2012) 107. Chapter on The Market for Corporate Control.

11

Given the discretion enjoyed by shareholders during takeovers, it is not surprising, therefore, that the takeover of Cadbury in 2010 raised important questions over shareholder primacy under UK takeover law. The public outcry that accompanied the takeover brought a debate on whether takeover rules in the UK are biased towards the needs of shareholders.[35] The questions surrounded the continued imposition of a rule which prevents the board from frustrating takeovers, even ones which the board unanimously agrees is in direct conflict with the long-term interests of the target company.

Shareholder primacy and the growing policy concern

After carrying out a review of the Takeover Code in 2009, the Takeover Panel concluded that it had become "too easy" for takeovers to succeed, and that "hostile offerors have, in recent times, been able to obtain a tactical advantage over the offeree company and its shareholders."[36] This led one American scholar to question: "why is the United Kingdom so married to the idea of the board neutrality rule if its own takeover watchdog unequivocally states that it places companies at a disadvantage?"[37]

The role of shareholders during takeovers was reviewed in Parliament by the Business, Innovation and Skills Committee following the takeover of Cadbury, and it reported that:

"[T]he takeover of Cadbury by Kraft has highlighted a number of important issues in respect of the way in which foreign takeovers of UK companies are conducted. It has been the catalyst for a wider debate, both in government and in the City, about how takeovers are conducted... Recent experience of the behaviour of boards and shareholders in situations ranging from....the Kraft acquisition of Cadbury indicate that it is time to reconsider many aspects of corporate governance".[38]

---

[35] Michael R Patrone, Sour Chocolate? Cadbury/Kraft and the 2011 Proposed Amendments to the UK Takeover Code - A Call for Further Research (2011) *8 BYU International Law & Management Review 64*, 64-65; Rhys Pippard, A Takeover Too Far Can the UK prohibition on board defensive action be justified any longer? (2011) SSRN Working Paper, 4.

[36] The Takeover Panel, *Consultation Paper Issued by the Code Committee of the Panel: Review of Certain Aspects of the Regulation of Takeover Bids* (RS 2010/22, October 2010).

[37] Michael R Patrone, Sour Chocolate? Cadbury/Kraft and the 2011 Proposed Amendments to the UK Takeover Code - A Call for Further Research (2011) *8 BYU International Law & Management Review 64*, 83.

[38] House of Commons, *Business, Innovation and Skills Committee, Mergers Acquisitions and Takeovers: the Takeover of Cadbury by Kraft, Ninth Report of Session 2009-2010* (HC 234, Published 6 April 2010) 27.

The Deputy Secretary General of the trade union Unite, Jack Dromey, told the Business, Innovation and Skills Committee BIS Committee that:

"[I]t simply cannot be right that in the way the market works good companies can be subject to predatory bids that put at risk the real economy and the public interest with no regard for workers, local communities and suppliers. Instead of responsible shareholder capitalism what we have now at its most obscene is nanosecond trading"[39]

Similarly, the Takeover Panel concluded in their response to a public consultation on takeovers in 2010 that "the outcome of offers, and particularly hostile offers, may be unduly influenced by the actions of so-called short-term investors".[40] Short-term investors were criticised for investing in companies merely to make a quick profit and paying little regard to non-price related factors such as employee jobs. Thus, there is a general concern among policy makers and some academics that shareholder primacy increases undue risk on non-shareholding stakeholders.

Due to concern over shareholder primacy, in March 2011, the Takeover Panel published and invited comments on its proposed changes to the Takeover Code 2006. Following a response paper published in July 2011, the amendments to the Takeover Code took effect on 19 September 2011.[41] Despite putting a number of safeguards to protect the interests of employees,[42] Rule 21 was not reformed. Thus shareholders continue to enjoy primacy over the takeover process and the perceived disadvantages of the board neutrality rule still prevail.

There were mixed responses to the proposed amendments to the Takeover Code in 2011. Vince Cable, the Business Secretary, observed that the Takeover Panel's recommendations did not go far enough in restricting the influence of shareholders such as hedge funds who tend to be interested in short-term gain with little regard to the interests of non-shareholding stakeholders.[43] However, the Institute of Directors welcomed the approach taken by the Takeover Panel that it "erred on the side of

---

[39] *Ibid* 22.
[40] The Takeover Panel, *response statement to Public Consultation Paper PCP 2010/2: Review of certain aspects of the regulation of takeover bids* (London, October 2010).
[41] The Takeover Panel, *Reviews of Certain Aspects of the Regulation of Takeovers Bids: proposed amendments to the Takeover Code* (March 2011); The Takeover Panel, *A review of the 2011 Amendments to the Takeover Code* (November 2012).
[42] See the discussion in Chapter 5.4.1.3 on employee protection following the 2011 amendments to the Takeover Code.
[43] Elizabeth Rigby, Vince Cable plans to toughen up takeover rules, *Financial Times* (13 July 2014).

caution" by not reforming Rule 21.[44] Thus, reform to shareholder primacy is not supported by everyone, especially the business community. This has major implications for the law reform proposals on reducing shareholder primacy advanced in Chapter 6.

Given the growing concern amongst academics and policy makers over shareholder primacy, it is important to obtain evidence on the actions of shareholders during takeovers and its influence the takeover. Such evidence is provided in Chapter 5 while the views of the business community are explored in Chapter 6 before discussing the reform proposals. The next step is to explore three important aspects: (1) the motivations behind takeovers, (2) whether shareholders make substantial gains from takeovers and (3) why a company may become a takeover target.

Takeovers: risks and gains

Takeover deals for UK companies often involve large sums of money. The Cadbury takeover, worth £11.9 billion, was one of the biggest takeovers in the past decade.

Table 4: Ten biggest takeovers of UK listed companies in terms of value by foreign companies between 2001 and 2011

Target	Acquirer	Nationality	Year	Value (Billions) £
O2	Telefonica	Spain	2005	18
Cadbury Plc	Kraft Inc	USA	2011	11.9
Alliance Boots	KKR	USA	2007	11.1
British Aviation Authority (BAA)	Ferrovial	Spain	2006	10
Powergen	E.on	Germany	2002	9.6
ICI	Akzo Nobel NV	Dutch	2008	8
Thames Water	RWE	Germany	2001	4.8
Corus Steel	Tata Steel	India	2006	4.3

---

[44] Institute of Directors, IoD reacts to review of Takeover Code (Press Release, 21 October 2010).

| P&O | Dubai Ports World | United Arab Emirates (UAE) | 2006 | 3.9 |
| Jaguar | Tata | India | 2008 | 1.15 |

Source: Office for National Statistics (2012)

As shown in Table 4, the Cadbury deal is dwarfed by the £18 billion takeover of a UK based company called o2 by Telefonica, a Spanish media company. The smallest of the top ten deals was the £1.15 billion takeover of Jaguar by an Indian company called Tata. The sheer size of these deals begs three important questions: What are the motivations behind these takeover deals? Who stands to gain? And when is a company at risk of a takeover?

a)   Motivations behind takeovers

First and foremost, in regards to motivations behind takeovers, neo-classical theorists believe that takeover activity is motivated by synergy benefits. Synergy is characterised as the ability of two or more entities to generate greater value by working together than when operating separately. As a result, the value of the merged firm would be greater than the sum of two individual firms. However, other studies have found that synergy effects are sought after in 30 per cent of cases. This is because factors such as job security and motivational perks play an important role in the decision to undertake restructuring action such as a takeover.

Behavioural finance theorists offer support to the neo-classical argument that the motive behind takeover activity is a search for new technology and financial resources. The theory posits that managers are not rational in their decision making and often seek to benefit themselves by taking over other companies. This is supported by the agency theory which is premised on the view that managers do not always act in the best interest of their shareholders due to the separation of ownership and control in public companies (the agency theory is subject to further analysis in Chapter 2.4.2).

b)   Managerial performance and the takeover risk

Second, in regards to the risk of a potential takeover, empirical evidence has shown that companies face a higher risk of being taken over if their performance lags behind industry benchmarks. This disciplinary mechanism is referred to as the market for corporate control because it theoretically pushes management to work for the benefit of the company in order to avoid a situation where the company becomes a takeover target due to poor performance. It also deters management from pursuing their own interests through the threat of job loss and damage to their reputation. This makes the market for corporate control a good supplement to failing internal governance structures.

However, the monitoring role of the market for corporate control is subject to question. A UK based study found that takeovers do not perform their disciplinary role because directors from both badly performing and well performing companies are ousted from their positions indiscriminately following a takeover. Another UK based study concluded that there is limited evidence that takeovers "play an important role in reversing the non-value maximizing behaviour of target companies." They examined pre and post takeover performance of companies taken over in the UK between 1985 and 1996. They found that 70 per cent of the acquired companies were not badly managed or underperforming. They also found that the acquiring companies were not necessarily better performers as compared to the target companies in terms of profit levels. Thus, the research evidence shows that all companies are subject to the market for corporate control regardless of their performance.

c)   Takeovers and shareholders' wealth

Third and lastly, it is important to determine whether takeovers create value for shareholders. Existing empirical evidence shows that takeovers deliver lower shareholder value to the acquiring company's shareholders as compared to the target company's shareholders. A study conducted in the US reviewed 13 previous studies on shareholder returns around the takeover announcement date. They found excess returns of 30 per cent to the target company's shareholders in successful takeovers but only 4 per cent for the bidding company's shareholders.

Another American based study reviewed the results of 663 takeovers made between 1962 and 1985. They found that premiums for target company shareholders averaged around 30 per cent. However, the study found a decline in excess returns to the acquiring company's shareholders from 4.4 per cent in the 1960s to 2 per cent in the 1970s and finally to -1 per cent in the 1980s. This clearly indicates that the target company's shareholders stand to gain more from takeovers as compared to those of the bidding company.

Two studies published at the turn of the twenty-first century on shareholders' returns during takeovers support the conclusions reached in the 1980s and 1990s. A study of takeovers cases between 2000 and 2004 found that takeovers fail to deliver value for the acquiring company's shareholders while the target company's shareholders earn substantial returns. Another study found that the acquiring company's outgoing shareholders expected returns were negative as compared to 9 per cent expected returns for the target company's shareholders. Other studies also found a strong relationship between takeovers and negative long-run returns to the acquiring company.

The strong empirical evidence which shows that acquirers' returns are significantly reduced post-takeover led some researchers to conclude that takeovers destroy shareholder wealth because outgoing shareholders leave with windfalls while the acquiring firm is left financially badly off. Some researchers went as far as questioning the rationale behind takeovers by concluding that the "acquiring firm's strategy of growing through acquisitions seems no longer sustainable".

Both the acquired and acquiring company have to shoulder the excess gains of outgoing shareholders through greater debt which directly impacts on the interests of all remaining company stakeholders. For example, an increase in debt levels could threaten the job security and financial contribution to the community. As one researcher concludes, "it comes as no surprise that about 50 percent of acquisitions ultimately end up in divestitures". This is because research evidence shows that takeovers fail to serve the purpose of value creation leading to a quick realisation of the new acquired firm to avoid further losses.

On that background, although target company shareholders make substantial gains from takeovers, there is strong empirical evidence which shows that the acquiring company experiences negative returns in the long-run following a takeover. This makes the choice of bidder very important because if their motivation is not value maximising for the target company, it is likely that the bidder would need to restructure the huge debts taken on to acquire the company and this could mean employee redundancies among other cutbacks.

The risks attached to takeovers mean that making the right decision is critically important for the long-term success of the company. Both the Takeover Code 2016 and the Companies Act 2006 require directors to consider the long-term interests of the company and its stakeholders before recommending a bid to shareholders. However, with shareholders holding the decision making powers, discharging these duties becomes difficult.

Directors' duties to non-shareholding stakeholders

In 2006, the UK enacted a new Companies Act that brought wholesale changes to company law and the protection of non-shareholding stakeholders in the company. Among the major changes was the restatement and codification of the general duties of directors now set out under sections 171 to 177 of the Companies Act 2006.

The most relevant directors' duties during takeovers are found under section 171, the proper purpose doctrine, and section 172, the duty to act in good faith in promoting the success of the company. Both duties were originally formulated in *Re Smith & Fawcett Ltd*, where Lord Greene MR. explained that: "directors must exercise their discretion bona fide in what they consider, not what a court may consider, is in the interests of the company, and not for any collateral purpose."

The proper purpose doctrine operates so as to prohibit directors from fettering their discretion by contracting with an outsider as to how a particular discretion conferred by the articles of association will be exercised except, possibly, where this is to the company's commercial benefit. On when the duty should be discharged, Neil LJ in *Fulham Football Club Ltd v. Cabra Estates Plc* endorsed the view of Kitto J in the Australian case *Thornby v. Goldberg* that:

> "[T]here are many kinds of transaction in which the proper time for the exercise of the directors' discretion is the time of the negotiation of a contract and not the time at which the contract is to be performed ... If at the former time they are bona fide of opinion that it is in the interests of the company that the transaction should be entered into and carried into effect I see no reason in law why they should not bind themselves."

The proper purpose doctrine is relevant during takeovers because it requires directors not to have any ulterior motive in their decision to recommend or resent a takeover bid. For example, in *Teck Corporation Ltd v. Millar*, the British Columbia Supreme Court held that an allotment of shares designed to defeat a takeover was proper, even though it was made against the wishes of the majority shareholder. In that case, Berger J stressed that provided that directors act in good faith, they are entitled to consider the reputation, experience and policies of anyone seeking to take over the company and use their powers to protect the company, if they decide on reasonable grounds that a takeover will cause substantial damage to the company.

The proper purpose doctrine is an incident of the central fiduciary duty of directors to promote the success of the company found under section 172 of the Companies Act 2006. It reads as follows:

> "A director...must act... in good faith... to promote the success of the company for the benefit of its members as a whole, and in doing

so have regard to… (a) the likely consequences of any decision in the long term, (b) the interest of the company's employees, (c) the need to foster the company's business relationships with suppliers, customers and others, (d) the impact of the company's operations on the community and the environment, (e) the desirability of the company maintaining a reputation for high standards of business conduct, and (f) the need to act fairly as between members of the company."

The duty does not shift the primacy away from shareholders rather it requires the board "in doing so (to) have regard" to the interests of other stakeholders in the company. This "enlightened shareholder value approach" is premised on the belief that the rise of shareholder primacy has shifted the balance of corporate power toward shareholders, making their priorities more important to corporate boards, at the same time, movements across the economy favouring long-term investment strategies, sustainable business practices, and broader conceptions of corporate accountability, have created an environment in which shareholder and stakeholder interests are more likely to align. Thus section 172 reaffirms shareholder primacy while recognising that well managed companies operate on the basis of enlightened shareholder value.

As a matter of fact, enlightened shareholder value, although it is the statutory basis for stakeholder protection, it prioritises shareholder interests above those of other stakeholders. Despite that, it provides scope stakeholder related action by requiring directors to have regard to these interests. Thus, section 172 stakeholder protection is merely a discretionary requirement premised on economic rationality rather than legal mandate.

However, in the consultation document on takeovers, General Principle 3 of the Takeover Code requires "the board of the target company (to) act in the interest of the company as whole" and (to) provide an independent view on the general effect of the bid on "employment, conditions of employment and the locations of the company's places of business." This principle works in conjunction with section 172 of the Companies Act 2006, which requires directors to take into consideration the interests of stakeholders such as employees, the environment and communities. Thus directors are required by the Companies Act and the Takeover Code to consider the interests of a wide range of company stakeholders when advising shareholders on the merits of a bid. The board of directors therefore will need to demonstrate that a full range of stakeholder interests informed their deliberations when recommending or criticising a takeover bid.

However, despite the adoption of enlightened shareholder value under General Principle 3, shareholders in the UK retain control over the takeover process and directors are required to consider shareholder interests ahead of other stakeholders. Despite that, neither the Takeover Code nor Companies Act imposes a duty on directors to recommend a bid on price alone if it is not in the best interest of the company. Directors are required to have regard as well to the interests of non-shareholding stakeholders during takeovers.

Having explored the protection afforded to non-shareholding stakeholders during takeovers, the next stage is to explain the various stakeholders in the company and their interests during a takeover.

Target company stakeholders and their interests

A company has many "stakeholders" that directly or indirectly play a role in its operations and eventual success. Stakeholder as a concept is very broad and may include any group or individual who can affect or is affected by the achievement of a company's objectives. The narrow view focuses only on those stakeholders who have a contractual relationship with the company. A narrow approach is taken in this book thus only those stakeholders that have a contract with the company are studied. The two main factors behind the selections are proximity and economic loss.

Figure 2 shows the various stakeholders in the company and their proximity, in terms of the nature of their relationship. This proximity is portrayed under three levels, with level one depicting those stakeholders that have a contract with the company and level three showing those stakeholders who merely influence or are influenced by the actions of the company.

Figure 2: Company stakeholders

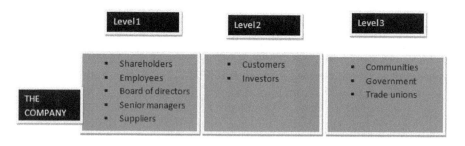

Stakeholders under level one include shareholders who provide start-up capital for the company through a share purchase agreement, employees who provide labour through an employment contract, directors who are the controlling organ, senior management who act company managers and suppliers who provide essential input into the company's processes through the supply contract.[45] The important terms which set out the nature of their relationship with the company are stated in the contract.

It is important to appreciate the importance of their contractual relationship with the company. First, shareholders contract with the company for financial investment in form of shares. Shareholders hope to make a return on their investment when the company is a going concern. Second, suppliers want to maintain good contractual relations and payment of money due to them.[46]

Third, the board of directors, senior management and employees have contractual and economic interests to protect during a takeover. Typically, the major shareholders (usually institutional shareholders) will be represented on the board of directors, which creates an overlap between shareholders and the board. Similarly, it is common to find board members employed as senior managers (executive directors). The executive directors join senior managers (typically heads of departments) in the day to day management of the company (as opposed to non-executive directors who work on a part-time basis). Again, this creates an overlap between the board of directors and senior management. Although senior managers are employees of the company, they are different from ordinary employees at the bottom, who are not senior managers, nor part of the board or part of shareholders. Thus members of the board may be wearing three hats during a takeover: i) executive directors (answerable to shareholders) ii) senior managers, and iii) employees.

There are two stakeholders under level two; customers and investors. These stakeholders are not selected for this study. Customers do not have a contract with the company but are directly affected by the company's activities and decision making. However, the company depends on customers to buy their goods or services on a come and go basis but with no contractual obligation. Potential investors would base their decisions over investment on the financial performance of the company. Thus, any decision making or event in a company of interest would have an influence on investors but would not directly impact on them.

---

[45]   Edward Freeman and Reed David, Stockholders and Stakeholders: A new perspective on Corporate Governance (1983) 25 (3) California Management Review, 88, 93-94.
[46]   Gilles Chemla, Hold-up, Stakeholders and Takeover Threats (2005) 14 (3) Journal of Financial Intermediation 376, 387-395.

The third category of stakeholders has no direct relationship with the company. These stakeholders are merely influenced by or do influence the actions of the company.[47] For example, communities do not have a contract with the company but expect the company to live up to its social responsibilities. These stakeholders are not directly impacted on by the decision making in the company. Research that looks into how takeovers affect the interests of these stakeholders falls outside the scope of this study and will serve future research ambitions.

Thus, this book focuses only on employees, suppliers and senior managers. The three stakeholders are chosen because of their contractual relationship with the company. Shareholders naturally form part of the study because they have decision making powers under takeover law and they are the owners of the company. Empirical studies have shown that target company shareholders stand to gain substantially from takeovers (see 1.3 above). In fact, shareholder primacy under takeover law is one of the reasons why non-shareholding stakeholders demand more protection during takeovers in order to minimise the impact on their interests. Thus studying shareholders' behaviours during takeovers is essential for understanding how non-shareholding stakeholders' interests may be impacted on by takeovers.

Before carrying out research on how non-shareholding stakeholders are impacted on by takeovers, it is important to appreciate some of the interests senior management, employees and suppliers want to protect during takeovers. First, while the interests of shareholders can be characterised in financial terms, the interest of employees include financial and non-financial components.[48] Financial compensation can be characterised as the firm specific investment in the company while non-financial components are physical and psychological, reflecting the status of employees as citizens in a welfare state.[49]

Employee contracts entitle them to remuneration and other agreed upon payments. These entitlements are protected under the Employment Rights Act 1996 and the Transfer of Undertakings (Protection of Employment) Regulations 2006. These payments serve as compensation for their labour. The contracts can however, be terminated post-takeover in order to cut

---

[47] James E Post, Lee E Preston and Sybille Sachs, *Redefining the Corporation Stakeholder Management and Organizational Wealth* (Stanford University Press, Stanford CA 2002) 270.
[48] Til Beckman and William Forbes, An examination of takeovers, job loss and wage decline within UK Industry, (2004) 10 (1) European Financial Management 141, 157-159.
[49] Virginie Perotin and Andrew Robinson, Employee Participation in Profit and Ownership: a Review of the Issues and Evidence (2003) Working paper, Social Affairs Series, Luxembourg Parliament, Directorate- General for Research, 2-5.

costs or for other strategic reason. Without sufficient legal safeguards during takeovers, employees' interests end up dependant on the decision making of shareholders and the persuasion powers of directors who are heavily restricted by Rule 21 of the Takeover Code.

Secondly, board members are fearful of the market for corporate control because the acquirers are likely to make changes to the board of the acquired company in favour of their own. A study on senior management turnover post-takeover found that takeovers destroy leadership continuity in target companies' top management teams for at least a decade following a takeover deal.[50] The target companies lost 21 per cent of their executives each year for at least 10 years following a takeover. This is because the acquiring company may elect to have one Chief Executive Officer (CEO) and Chief Finance Officer (CFO) and to fill most executive positions with their own personnel.[51]

Last but not least, through their supply contracts, suppliers forge relations that are instrumental to their continued operation and survival. Suppliers want to have these contractual relations protected during takeovers. The Takeover Code does not permit suppliers in the takeover decision making process, rather they must rely on the consultation provided by directors, who are guided by section 172 of the Companies Act 2006 to influence the outcome of a takeover.

Having explored the major concerns surrounding shareholder primacy and the interests of all non-shareholding stakeholders during takeovers, three main questions have been raised: (1) to what extent takeovers impact on the interests of company stakeholders, (2) what role does shareholder primacy play in the outcome of takeover bids, and (3) how can takeover law be reformed to give more safeguards to non-shareholding stakeholders. Thus, if takeovers have a detrimental effect on the interests of employees, senior management and suppliers yet shareholders are able to walk away with substantial gains, then questions should be raised over the continued imposition of Rule 21 of the Takeover Code.

This study seeks to add empirical support on the extent to which takeovers impact on the target company's non-shareholding stakeholders post-takeover. This information is harnessed from case studies on two UK companies which were taken over by foreign companies in the past decade. The takeover deals studied are Kraft's takeover of Cadbury in 2010 and

---

[50] Jeffrey A Krug and Walt Shill, The big exit: executive churn in the wake of M&As (2008)29 (4) Journal of Business Strategy 15, 18-20.
[51] Anup Agrawal and Ralph A Walkling, Executive Careers and Compensation Surrounding Takeover Bids (1994) 49 (3) Journal of Finance 985, 997-99.

Tata Steel's takeover of Corus Steel in 2007. This study is original because it provides an examination of the role played by the board neutrality rule during the takeover process and how limiting the involvement rights of the board of directors affects the interest of other stakeholders. It also considers specific reform proposals for Rule 21.

CHAPTER 2: THEORETICAL FOUNDATION OF TAKEOVER LAW AND THE PROTECTION OF NON-SHAREHOLDING STAKEHOLDERS

Introduction

This chapter reviews research literature which has made a significant contribution to our understanding takeovers and shareholder primacy in the company. This literature review will determine whether the goals of this book have a strong empirical and conceptual foundation. It identifies what previous scholars have contributed and the gaps in existing literature on shareholder primacy and takeovers. Thus, it provides a benchmark for measuring whether this book advances literature.

The scholarly work in this chapter is divided into five parts. Significant research on shareholder primacy in the company is reviewed. Second, key research on the market for corporate control and agency costs. Third, significant research on economic theories of the firm is reviewed. It largely consists of research that supports the protection of all stakeholders' interests in the company. Fourth, key research on the impact of takeovers on employees, senior management and suppliers is reviewed. Finally, the gaps in existing research literature which this study aims to fill are identified.

Adam Smith (1776) The wealth of nations

Shareholder primacy under UK takeover law has its roots in the joint stock company,[1] which is the modern day equivalent of a company formed under the Companies Act 2006. The ability to sell its stock, in the form of shares, to individual shareholders distinguished the company from other business structures such as partnership. Those who bought shares in a joint stock company were only entitled to involvement rights such as voting and dividends. The day to day running of the company was left in the hands of professional managers.

In 1776,[2] a British economist Adam Smith became the first scholar to study shareholder primacy in companies.[3] He observed that:

"[T]he trade of a joint stock company is always managed by a court of directors... frequently subject, in many respects, to the control of a general court of proprietors. But the greater part of these proprietors

---

[1] It was formed under the Joint Stock Companies Act 1847 (19 & 20 Vict. c.47)
[2] The book was reprinted in 1976.
[3] Adam Smith, *An Inquiry into the Nature and Causes of the Wealth of Nations* (Clarendon Press, Oxford 1976).

seldom pretend to understand anything of the business of the company; and ... give themselves no trouble about it, but receive contentedly such half yearly or yearly dividend, as the directors think proper to make to them."[4]

He added that the board of directors and not shareholders, managed companies. This was largely due to shareholders' lack of skill and knowledge to manage companies. Adam Smith advanced literature on shareholder primacy in the company by calling for shareholders to be given greater protection to monitor managers. He warned that a lack of control and monitoring creates a danger that management will serve their own interests at the expense of the owners:[5]

"[T]he directors of such companies, however, being the managers rather of other people's money than of their own, it cannot well be expected, that they should watch over it with the same anxious vigilance with which the partners in a copartnery frequently watch over their own ..."[6]

The unchecked freedom enjoyed by directors in companies raised concern because they were dealing with other people's money. Thus, unless some form of control was imposed, directors were not expected to always serve the owners' interests.

However, Adam Smith left a number of unanswered questions on the position of shareholders and other stakeholders in the company. The scholar predicted that "negligence and profusion...must always prevail"[7] in such companies and as a form of guidance, he suggested that optimal market efficiency depended on owners of capital being directly involved in its management. Thus, the emphasis was largely on empowering shareholders to monitor and control the actions of managers. However, Adam Smith did not recognise the interests of other company stakeholders as deserving protection simply because they had no capital investment in the company.[8] He supported shareholder primacy on the basis that owners of capital were more likely to exercise greater diligence when dealing with their assets than management or other stakeholders.[9] However, subsequent

---

[4] *Ibid* 741.
[5] *Ibid* 741.
[6] *Ibid* 741.
[7] *Ibid* 741.
[8] Adolf Berle and Gardner Means, *The Modern Corporation and Private Property* (Commerce Clearing House, New York 1932) 340.
[9] *Ibid* 344.

researchers not only questioned the position of shareholders as owners but also supported the protection of all stakeholders' interests (see 2.2 below).

Adam Smith's contribution to the development of theory on shareholder primacy was largely ignored in research literature until the early twentieth century due to two factors. First, at the time the wealth of nations was published, corporate form was a relatively new phenomenon and capital markets were not as developed as they are today. As a result, there was no dispersal of ownership and this made it easier to monitor management and exert governance in companies. Second, there were few registered companies and their size and role in society was not as significant as it is today. Guided by a growing economy and greater establishment of companies, twentieth century researchers tried to fill the gaps in literature left behind by Adam Smith.

Berle and Means (1932) The modern corporation and private property

The next significant academic contribution to shareholder primacy came in 1932. Two American scholars, Adolf Berle and Gardner Means, set out to investigate the growing economic and political challenges posed by public companies.[10] Their book focused on the separation between company owners and management in public companies.

The researchers collected statistical data on the ownership structure of public companies in America. Between 1929 and 1930, they studied the 200 largest non-financial companies. They found that 44 per cent of the companies had no individual ownership stake equalling 20 per cent of the company's stock.[11] Only 11 per cent of the companies had a large owner with a majority of the company's shares. The researchers estimated that roughly 65 per cent of public companies in America did not have a majority owner and their stock was widely-held by thousands of shareholders. Ownership was becoming vested in individual investors with small-scale wealth.

Based on these findings, Berle and Means argued that the dispersal of ownership had "destroyed the unity that we commonly call property."[12] Since those who hold minority shareholding in public companies are so widespread, they are not in position to be organised to hold those who handle their investment to account. According to the researchers, physical

---

[10] Adolf Berle and Gardner Means, *The Modern Corporation and Private Property* (Commerce Clearing House, New York 1932) 6.
[11] 20 per cent is deemed as an approximate minimum for a control stake in the company.
[12] Adolf Berle and Gardner Means, *The Modern Corporation and Private Property* (Commerce Clearing House, New York 1932) 7.

property such as land could bring direct satisfaction regardless of its market value and thus represents an extension of the owner's personality. Within public companies, those attributes of physical property had been lost and replaced by passive share ownership, which offers no satisfaction other than dividends and gains after selling their shares. This argument is important in understanding why shareholders may opt to sell their shares when approached by a bidder during a takeover because shares theoretically offer no other satisfaction apart from profitable gain.[13]

Furthermore, the unwillingness of shareholders to intervene in the management process was criticised for having enhanced the status managers and altered the nature of property. According to Berle and Means, the dispersed shareholders lacked both the resources and incentive to effectively monitor and control management in the use of their investment. They were unwilling to engage in activism because it required both financial commitment and information resources.[14] As a result, the dispersal of share ownership in public companies left shareholders uninterested in the day to day management of the company yet the company was largely made of similar shareholdings. This left the body which is directly interested in the day to day affairs of the company, the board of directors, free to manage the resources of the company to their own advantage, without effective shareholder oversight.

Berle and Means advanced literature on shareholder primacy by arguing that shareholders had "surrendered the right that the corporation should be operated in their sole interest"[15] and could no longer be called company owners. Shareholders were now the owners of passive rather than active property and the traditional view of property was no longer applicable to them. Thus, shareholder primacy in the company was no longer justifiable given the passive nature of their property.

After rejecting the notion of shareholder ownership, Berle and Means turned to the concentration of economic power within public companies for answers on the constituent that deserves primacy. They observed that "... companies form the very framework of American industry. The individual must come in contact with them almost constantly. He may own an interest in one or more of them, he may be employed by one of them, but above all he is continually accepting their service."[16] Thus the huge economic power

---

[13]   See John Christman, *The Myth of Property: Towards an Egalitarian Theory of Ownership* (Oxford University Press: New York, 1994) 8.
[14]   Adolf Berle and Gardner Means, *The Modern Corporation and Private Property* (Commerce Clearing House, New York, 1932) 8.
[15]   *Ibid* 312.
[16]   Adolf Berle and Gardner Means, *The Modern Corporation and Private Property* (Commerce

of public companies places them in a position of influence and power over society at large. This gives public companies an important role in society because employment and availability of services or products depends on their continued success.

Berle and Means highlighted some of the challenges posed by the concentration of economic power in large public companies:

"[T]he economic power in the hands of the few persons who control a giant corporation is a tremendous force which can harm or benefit a multitude of individuals, affect whole districts, shift the currents of trade, bring ruin to one community and prosperity to another. The organizations which they control have passed far beyond the realm of private enterprise - they have become more nearly social institutions."[17]

Thus, concentrated economic power helped to promote public companies as social-economic institutions, which can affect the functioning of entire communities and industries. On that background, Berle and Means believed that companies should serve the interests of all stakeholders rather than focusing solely on shareholders.

Furthermore, Berle and Means contributed to research literature by suggesting ways of controlling management. They believed that legal restraints on management were the answer. They argued that legal restraints had "become increasingly the only reason why expectations that corporate securities are worth having" and "the strength of law in this regard is the only enforceable safeguard which a security owner really has".[18] They saw common law fiduciary duties as the best way to entice management to promote the success of the company. Thus, despite a rejection of shareholders' property ownership status, Berle and Means supported shareholder primacy through their common law solution to managerial control.

However, the common law fiduciary duties were aimed at protecting shareholders' interests rather than all the company's constituents. This was criticised by Merrick Dodd who argued that a company is "an economic institution which has a social service as well as a profit-making function."[19] He believed that a company had wider social obligations and it must serve

Clearing House, New York 1932) 19.
[17] *Ibid* 46.
[18] Adolf Berle and Gardner Means, *The Modern Corporation and Private Property* (Commerce Clearing House, New York 1932) 132.
[19] Merrick Dodd, For Whom Are Corporate Managers Trustees? (1932) 45 (7) Harvard Law Review,1145, 1148.

society rather than individual members. According to Dodd, the culture of profit first and other responsibilities second was no longer sustainable. In his view, common law fiduciary duties limited the scope of the company and undeservedly gave primacy to shareholders at the expense of other stakeholder groups.

Furthermore, Berle and Means ignored the role of stock markets as a means through which managers can be controlled. According to Alchian, a renowned financial economist at the time, "ignoring or denying the force of open competitive market capitalization is…a fundamental error in the writing about ownership and control and about the modern corporate economy."[20] The market for corporate control, which gained prominence in the latter half of the twentieth century (see 2.3 below), is a market-based device that forces managers to work in the long-term interest of the company or risk market discipline in the form of a takeover.

Henry Manne (1965) The market for corporate control

In 1965, American economist Henry Manne investigated whether takeovers can act as a form of managerial discipline.[21] His research was conducted at a period when takeovers were becoming increasingly common in the US. For example, a study which examined hostile takeovers in the US during the late 1950s and 1960s found 79 hostile takeovers from 1956-1960 and twice as many during the period of 1964-66.[22] Manne responded to the increase in hostile takeover activity by arguing that market control mechanisms are an effective way of monitoring and controlling corporate behaviours as well as preserving the traditional profit maximising goal of companies post-takeover.

To explain how stock markets can act as a managerial disciplinary tool, Manne relied on capital rather than product markets. Theoretically, both product and capital market mechanisms can be used to control company managers.[23] The product market pushes the company to deliver quality goods otherwise consumers would not buy the products and that could

---

[20] Armen Alchian, *Corporate management and property rights*, in Henry Manne, (ed.), *Economic policy and the regulation of corporate securities* (Washington, D.C.: American Enterprise Institute, 1969); reprinted in Erik Furobotn and Svetozar Pejovic, *The economics of property rights*, (Cambridge, MA: Ballinger, 1974) 136.

[21] Henry G Manne, Mergers and the Market for Corporate Control (1965) 73 (2) Journal of Political Economy 110, 112-114.

[22] Notes, Cash Tender Offers, (1969) 83 (2) Harvard Law Review, 377, 377.

[23] Mark Roe, Corporate Law's Limits (2002) 31 (2) Journal of Legal Studies 233, 257; John Coffee, The Rise of Dispersed Ownership: The Roles of Law and the State in the Separation of Ownership and Control (2001) 111 (2) Yale Law Journal 1, 4; George Triantis and Ronald Daniels, The Role of Debt in Interactive Corporate Governance (1995), 83 (4) California Law Review, 1073, 1085.

threaten the positions of managers in the company because the company would struggle to meet sales targets. The product market also pushes the company to act in a socially responsible manner since dissatisfied customers could switch to another brand or product and this would affect sales figures and eventually lead to the dismissal of managers for underperformance.[24] On the other hand, the stock market does not necessarily rely on consumer patterns; it is linked to the share price performance of the company. Theoretically, if a company does not perform well, it would be reflected in the share price and this would lead to less investment in the company.[25] Directors would also risk not being re-elected to the board if the company's share price is not growing. Thus, managers have an incentive to ensure that the share price of the company is constantly growing by working in the economic interest of the company.

Manne argued that stock markets can regulate managerial conduct because a large-scale sell of shares by dissatisfied shareholders has the potential to depress a company's share price.[26] If a group of shareholders sell their shares, it sends a signal to other shareholders that something is wrong within the company. Being passive and largely reactive, other shareholders will follow the outgoing shareholders. This would lead to the share price of the company falling. The threat also exists when a large shareholder opts to sell their shares. Both the market and other shareholder would react to this news. To avoid a situation in which dissatisfied shareholders elect to leave the company, managers would need to serve the interests of shareholders. Thus, shareholders' lack of commitment to the company and readiness to sell their shares at any time, acts as a threat to errant managers.[27]

Manne advanced literature on takeovers by arguing that such a large-scale sale of shares makes the company vulnerable to a takeover bid.[28] This is because underperforming companies can be seen as takeover targets due to their falling market share. This invites prospective buyers who view underperforming companies as easier targets because shareholders would most likely jump at the opportunity of being offered more money

---

[24] Azizjon Alimov, Does product market competition discipline managers? Evidence from exogenous trade shock and corporate acquisitions (2014) City University of Hong Kong Department of Economics and Finance Working Paper, 13.

[25] Eugene F Fama, Efficient capital markets: a review of theory and empirical work (1970) 25 (2), Journal of Finance 383, 383-384; Lynn A Stout, The Mechanisms of market inefficiency (2003) 28 (3), Journal of Corporation Law 635, 637.

[26] Henry G Manne, Mergers and the Market for Corporate Control (1965) 73 (2) Journal of Political Economy 110, 112.

[27] Frank H Easterbrook and Daniel R Fischel, *The Economic Structure of Corporate Law* (Harvard University Press: Cambridge, MA, 1991) 171.

[28] Henry G Manne, Mergers and the Market for Corporate Control (1965) 73 (2) Journal of Political Economy 110, 113.

for their shares. Manne called this market-based disciplinary mechanism the market for corporate control.

According to Manne, the market for control acts as a disciplinary mechanism by ousting underperforming managers from their positions. As a result, managers would try to limit the risk of a takeover bid by ensuring that the company performs well.[29] Manne argued that the threat of a hostile takeover "condition(s) managers to a specific point of view perfectly consistent with the shareholders' interest...keeping the price of the company's shares as high as possible."[30]

However, the market for corporate control as a managerial disciplinary mechanism suffers from a number of shortfalls. First it is based on the assumption that companies which are subject to takeovers are inefficiently run thereby restructuring the company and removing the inefficiency would result in gains for the acquiring firm. However, an empirical study carried out in the UK found that target companies are not always poorly performing or run inefficiently.[31] This shows that the market for corporate control is indiscriminative and acts as a threat to both well performing and underperforming managers.

Secondly, the market for corporate control does not apply to all cases of company mismanagement.[32] For corporate mismanagement to affect the share price, it must be both major and longstanding. Thus only cases of serious mismanagement are likely to trigger a takeover because it would be reflected in the company's share price. Badly mismanaged companies could also deter potential bidders because they may view the damage as irreversible. Thus, the takeover threat is not enough to discipline management because it depends on the availability of another company that is willing to take over the underperforming one.

Furthermore, since takeovers are infrequent, they are unlikely to be a plausible disciplinary tool in all cases of company mismanagement. A study of takeover activity and managerial turnover found that the disciplinary effect also depends on the levels of takeover activity.[33] This means that for the mechanism to work as a disciplinary tool, takeovers must be frequent.

---

[29]   *Ibid* 112.
[30]   Henry G Manne, Our Two Corporation Systems: Law and Economics (1967) 53 (2), Virginia Law Review 259, 265-66.
[31]   Julian Franks and Colin Mayer, Hostile takeovers and the Correction of Managerial Failure (1996) 40 (1) Journal of Financial Economics 163,171-177.
[32]   Blanaid Clarke, Articles 9 and 11 of the Takeover Directive (2004/25) and the Market for Corporate Control (2006) 26 (2), Journal of Business Law 355, 360-362.
[33]   Wayne H Mikkelson and Megan M Partch, The decline of takeovers and disciplinary managerial turnover (1997) 44 (2) Journal of Financial Economics 205, 225-227.

Last but not least, an active market for corporate control may encourage managers to pursue empire-building tactics to shield themselves from the disciplinary effects of the market-based mechanism.[34] Empire building tactics enable the management team to approve acquisitions that may make the company too expensive to take over. This harms shareholders wealth and protects inefficient managers.

Similarly, the cost of completing a takeover, taking into consideration the need for premium offer, limits the effectiveness of the market for corporate control. Few companies would have the financial capacity or be willing to use large financial resource to take over another company. However, despite the limitations, managers may seek to reduce the risk of takeovers due to fears that it may cost them their jobs or their reputation in the market could be stained as poor managers.[35]

Although the market for corporate control can function as a tool for managerial discipline, there were two major gaps in Manne's work. First, after explaining the significance of the market for corporate control, Manne did not identify any limitations to this mechanism. He did not consider the possibility that management could put in place defensive strategies that may deter a potential bidder. Thus, the issue of how to regulate the market for corporate control was left unresolved but subsequent researchers have explored it at length.[36]

Second, the interests of other company stakeholders such as employees and creditors were not considered in the discussion on whether the market for corporate control can discipline managers. The role of the market for corporate control was seen as protecting shareholders' wealth without regard to the interest of other company stakeholders. This is however surprising, given that research literature treats shareholders as mere investors with similar characteristics to other company stakeholders such as creditors.[37] This led Professor Parkinson to conclude that "since the shareholders are not owners, there is no reason to suppose that that they should behave in an owner-like way."[38]

---

[34] Andrei Shleifer and Robert W Vishny, A Survey of Corporate Governance (1997) 52 (2) The Journal of Finance 737, 756.
[35] Eugene F Fama, Agency Problems and the Theory of the Firm (1980) 88 (2), Journal of Political Economy 288, 298.
[36] Roberta Romano, A Guide to Takeovers: Theory, Evidence, and Regulation (1992) 9 (1), Yale Journal on Regulation 119, 129-131.
[37] See the discussion in Chapter 2.1 and 2.2.
[38] John E Parkinson, The Contractual Theory of the Company and the Protection of Non-Shareholder Interests in David Feldman and Franklin Meisel (eds.) Corporate and Commercial Law: Modern Developments (London: Lloyds, 1996) 123.

During the 1970s and 80s, a number of American economists sought to explain why all company stakeholders interests should be considered by the board of directors when making strategic company decisions (see 2.4 below).

Economic theories of the firm

Researchers in the 1970s and 80s devised economic theories of the firm in a bid to find a trade-off between shareholder primacy and the interests of other company stakeholders. The theories were premised on the view that the interests of all company stakeholders should be considered in the decision making. These economic theories are important in our understanding of why the board of directors should consider the interests of all stakeholder groups since they all have interests that are tied up in the company and all contribute to the eventual success of the company.

Easterbrook and Fischel (1991) Nexus of contract theory

Two American economists, Easterbrook and Fischel, classified the company as a nexus of contracts.[39] Being a nexus of contracts, company constituents such as employees and creditors are deemed to have provided the company some form of asset in return for compensation. Thus, the contract is formed through a process of bargaining over the terms of their compensation and arrangements that would guarantee protection for their compensation. The firm is the main entity that unites all constituents to form a nexus.

The aim of Easterbrook and Fischel's study was to influence legal development in embracing a social model that protects the interests of all company constituents rather than following a purely economic model premised on maximising shareholders' wealth. The nexus of contract theory is both descriptive and normative because it explains why organisations are structured the way they are but also tries to explain how they ought to be structured. While the descriptive aspect has dominated financial economics literature, the normative aspect has been largely neglected in research literature. The openly normative objective of their book was to "preach to legislatures and judges about what the law ought to be if it is to promote social welfare."[40]

Despite that, Easterbrook and Fischel believed that shareholders are more deserving of protection than other company constituents. They relied on the residual claimant argument as support for shareholder primacy in

---

[39] Frank H Easterbrook and Daniel R Fischel, *The Economic Structure of Corporate Law* (Harvard University Press: Cambridge, MA, 1991).
[40] *Ibid* vii–viii.

the company.[41] The argument is based on the assumption that shareholders are the primary risk-bearing group in the company having made equity investments. Thus, the company has the discretionary authority to allocate the equity to the end user through the objects set out in the company's constitution and strategic decisions made at the general meeting. Shareholders can vote in the general meeting to determine the outcome of their investment and elect directors to control it. However, despite their equity investment, shareholders are last in line during insolvency. For those reasons, Easterbrook and Fischel argued that their primary risk-bearing status and position during insolvency qualifies shareholders as the residual claimants that are entitled to have the board of directors exclusively accountable to them.

They offered support to shareholder primacy by recognising that stakeholders such as creditors and employees have explicit contracts, which entitle them to fixed payments whereas shareholders have implicit contracts that only entitle them to leftovers after deducting fixed claims. As a result, they classified shareholders as residual claimants and they suggested that the main goal of the company should be shareholder wealth maximisation.

Easterbrook and Fischel advanced literature by uniting the social and economic view of the firm. They argued that rather than purely giving primacy to shareholders, management should take into consideration the interests of other company stakeholders.[42] They believed that the interests all company stakeholders can be considered alongside those of shareholders during decision making process.

The researchers also supported legal protection, with duties imposed on directors for shareholders but also consideration given to non-shareholding stakeholders.[43] According to Easterbrook and Fischel, a company is a nexus of two sets of contracts. The first contract is negotiated between the company and the stakeholder. The second is a contract created by law. The presence of these two forms of contracts implies that each contracting party is governed by a system of rights and obligations achieved through fair bargaining. For stakeholders such as communities without a negotiated contractual agreement with the company, they argued that corporate law would act as a standard form contract and would protect their interests. Legal protection comes in the form of employment law, consumer law, and

---

[41]   Armen A Alchian and Harold Demsetz, Production, information costs and economic organization (1972) 62 (5), American Economic Review 777, 782.
[42]   Frank H Easterbrook and Daniel R Fischel, *The Economic Structure of Corporate Law* (Harvard University Press: Cambridge, MA, 1991) 310.
[43]   *Ibid* 16.

tort law among others. Thus, the legal duties of directors would extend to protecting the interests of all company stakeholders.

The nexus of contract theory received support from stakeholder theorists who believed that shareholder primacy was not well grounded because many other constituents had a legitimate claim on the company.[44] Giving primacy to the interests of shareholders went against the idea that the "interests of all stakeholders are of intrinsic value."[45] Thus, shareholder primacy is supported by nexus of contract theory because of their equity investment in the company but to be limited by including the interests of other stakeholders in the decision making process.

Jensen and Meckling (1976) Agency theory

In 1976, Jensen and Meckling devised the agency theory in a bid to find a solution to the problem of managerial control and to show that managerial mismanagement affects all company stakeholders. According to Jensen and Meckling, managers are in an agency relationship with the company. They defined the agency relationship as a contract under which one or more persons (the principal(s)) engage another person (the agent) to perform some service on his or her behalf which involves delegating some decision-making authority to the agent.[46] Thus, the principal delegates some decision-making authority to the agent in order to enable them to perform the service.

The main assumption behind agency theory is that interests of the principal may sometimes conflict with those of the agent.[47] According to agency theorists, managers are imperfect agents thus they worry not only about the company but also their own interests. The solution to such a problem would be to write a complete contract and for the principal to engage in monitoring the agent to ensure that they serve their interests.

Agency theorists recognised that it is impractical and inefficient to write a contract that covers all managerial actions.[48] It is inefficient because it limits managerial discretion, which may be needed to promote the success of the company. It is impractical because writing a contract that exhausts all future actions of the manager is extremely difficult, especially

---

[44] Edward Freeman, Andrew C Wicks and Bidhan Parmar, Stakeholder theory and the corporate objective revisited (2004) 15 (13) Organization Science 364, 366.
[45] Thomas Donaldson and Lee E Preston, The stakeholder theory of the corporation: concepts, evidence and implications (1995) 20 (1), Academy of Management Review 65, 67.
[46] Michael C Jensen and William H Meckling, Theory of the Firm: Managerial Behaviour, Agency Costs and Ownership Structure (1976) 3 (4), Journal of Financial Economics 305, 308.
[47] *Ibid* 306.
[48] *Ibid* 306.

given the regularly changing internal structures and systems in companies. Thus, due to the incompleteness of the managerial contract, self-interested actions may sometimes prevail over the interests of the company and shareholders. This may be in the form of shirking or even stealing from the company.

In regards to monitoring the agent, this is more likely to work in an organisation such as a partnership where there is no separate legal personality. In such an organisation, the principal is often the general manager and they can physically monitor the actions of the agent. However, a public company has a separate legal personality, which means that the principal is a fictional being. Thus, the company has to hope that managers adhere to their contract due to its inability to physically monitor or enforce it.

Jensen and Meckling advanced literature by arguing that the company is not in a position to control or monitor management thus it needs protection from its managers. According to the scholars, the company is a "legal fiction which serves as a focus for the complex process in which the conflicting objectives of individuals ... are brought in equilibrium within a framework of contractual relationship."[49] Thus, agency problem is an issue for all company stakeholders. Taken as a collection of individual groups, agency theory does not support shareholder ownership assumptions.

Despite that, Jensen and Meckling saw the company as a collection of contracts between shareholders, managers and other stakeholder groups. They observed that, "contractual relations are the essence of the firm, not only with employees but with suppliers, customers, creditors, etc."[50] They agreed that, "most organizations are simply legal fictions which serve as a nexus for a set of contracting relationship among individuals."[51]

Although agency theory is applied primarily to shareholder and managers, Jensen and Meckling argued that it can be applied to other stakeholders too and "will lead to a rich theory of organizations which is now lacking in economics and the social sciences generally."[52] Their contribution to research literature was later remarked upon by Australian academics Corbett and Spender that since "Jensen and Meckling in the late 1970s, corporate law theory has been dominated by economic analysis which posits that the corporation is a nexus of contracts."[53]

---

[49] *Ibid* 312.
[50] *Ibid* 311.
[51] *Ibid* 310.
[52] *Ibid* 309.
[53] Angus Corbett and Peta Spender, Corporate Constitutionalism (2009) 31 (1) Sydney Law Review 147, 147.

Thus, through agency theory, Jensen and Meckling attempted to explain the contractual relationships that exist between a company's non-shareholding stakeholders groups such as creditors and employees. Stakeholder groups that have a legitimate claim on the company are affected by the agency problem. The legitimacy is largely based on the existence of an exchange relationship between stakeholders and the company. To agency theorists, non-shareholding stakeholders such as suppliers make contributions to the company by supplying resources and they expect their interests to be taken into consideration in exchange. For example, financial creditors provide the company with finance and expect the company to honour the loan repayment agreement. Employees and managers provide the company with skills and human capital investments and expect adequate working conditions and fair remuneration in return. Suppliers generally provide companies with inputs and expect dependable buyers and fair prices in return.

However, agency theory continues to support shareholder primacy in the company. They warn that "a stakeholder measure of managerial accountability could leave managers so much discretion that managers could easily pursue their own agenda, one that might maximize neither shareholder, employee, consumer, nor national wealth, but only their own."[54]

This book extends Jensen and Meckling's work on agency theory by testing it on cases of takeovers. The aim is to find out whether support for shareholder primacy under takeover law can lead to agency costs for employees, the board of directors and creditors. This would provide evidence that takeovers affect all company stakeholders and the agency costs that arise from company mismanagement do not only affect shareholders' interests but also those of other stakeholders.

Debates over the stakeholder group that deserves legal protection led to the reinvigoration of team production theory, which is also premised on protecting stakeholders' interests to the same extent as shareholders' interests (see 2.4.3 below).

Blair and Stout (1999) Team production theory

Shareholder primacy continued to be challenged in subsequent research literature. Professors Margaret Blair and Lynn Stout mounted one of the most influential challenges in their team production theory of the firm.[55]

---

[54]   Mark J Roe, The Shareholder Wealth Maximization Norm and Industrial Organization (2001) 149 (6), University *of* Pennsylvania Law Review 2063, 2065.
[55]   Margaret Blair and Lynn Stout, A team production theory of corporate law (1999) 85 (2),

Team production theory developed out of the need to mobilise inputs from different actors.[56] The aim was to unite all the company contributories, bound by different contracts, to a single objective. Team production is defined as "production in which 1) several types of resources are used . . . 2) the product is not a sum of separable outputs of each cooperating resource . . . 3) not all resources used in team production belong to one person."[57] The team production problem affects all companies because they have a range of stakeholders that contribute to meeting its objectives.

Team production theory challenges the principal-agent framework. Agency theory takes the shareholder risk bearing argument as a justification for shareholder primacy. Thus, the central problem, in regards to the governance of companies, is getting directors to be faithful agents of shareholders. Although agency theory rejects the idea of shareholder ownership, it treats them as principals whose interests deserve primacy over other company stakeholders. Blair and Stout challenged this interpretation.

Through team production theory, Blair and Stout advanced literature by rejecting the assumption that one stakeholder group can have primacy over others. The rejection was premised on the view that all the stakeholders contribute to the general welfare of the company and none should be given primacy above others. Thus, team production theory carries the assumption that all participants want to benefit from their participation in the company and are interested in finding the most appropriate governance mechanism that would enable support and cooperation among all company participants.

For team production to work, there would need to be a hierarchical structure where one team overlooks and monitors all other members to ensure that they are contributing equally and adequately.[58] The incentive to monitor would come from having greater authority over other members and while other members are compensated for their opportunity costs, the monitors would receive all the benefits accruing from the teamwork. This solution is functional when the monitoring group has ownership and control over the company. Thus, this cannot be replicated in a company where the group with decision-making authority is different from the one with ownership interests.

Virginia Law Review 247, 248.

[56]   Armen A Alchian and Harold Demsetz, Production, information costs and economic organization (1972) 62 (5), American Economic Review 777, 782.

[57]   *Ibid* 779.

[58]   *Ibid* 781.

According to Blair and Stout, directors should be the monitors who control internal proceedings, but all the profitable gains should go to the company not shareholders. This is because shareholders are not the owners of the company and they only have property rights over the company. Thus, shareholders would be given limited powers such as the right to hire executive members. This is because the owner may deem a sale of assets as a more valuable solution than long-term gains from team production.

Team production was criticised for ignoring the influence of market forces on the company.[59] Blair and Stout believed that a company can serve all company constituents' goals and the profiteering body would be the company.[60] However, public companies rely on investment from the public as a major source of finance. Thus, a lack of support for shareholder value maximisation could affect companies because it may deter equity investment. Furthermore, markets can be a source of managerial discipline by encouraging management to serve shareholders' interests in order to invite more equity investment. Thus, market forces limit the potential effectiveness of a team production model.

At the turn of the twenty-first century, shareholder primacy received support from American legal economists Henry Hansmann and Reinier Kraakman, in their paper entitled "The end of history for Corporate Law."[61] They argued that, "there is no longer any serious competitor to the view that corporate law should principally strive to increase long-term shareholder value."[62] This is because "academic, business, and governmental elites (shared a consensus) that ultimate control over the corporation should rest with the shareholder class; the managers of the corporation should be charged with the obligation to manage the corporation in the interests of its shareholders; …and the market value of the publicly traded corporation's shares is the principal measure of the shareholders' interests."[63] In other words, a shareholder-oriented model dominated corporate governance discussions. They concluded that, "the triumph of the shareholder-oriented model of the corporation (around the world) is now assured."[64]

However, Hansmann and Kraakman gave support to balancing shareholders' interests with those of other stakeholders. They recognised

---

[59]   Oliver E Williamson, *Markets and Hierarchies: Analysis and Antitrust Implications* (New York: The Free Press, 1975) 45.
[60]   Margaret Blair and Lynn Stout, A team production theory of corporate law (1999) 85 (2), Virginia Law Review 247, 319.
[61]   Henry Hansmann and Reinier Kraakman, The End of History for Corporate Law (2000) 89 (2), Georgetown University Law Review, 439-468.
[62]   *Ibid* 439.
[63]   *Ibid* 440-41.
[64]   *Ibid* 468.

that shareholder primacy lost momentum in the 1970s and 80s due to the emergence of stakeholder-oriented theories that questioned its legitimacy. On that basis, they argued that the law does not follow a standard shareholder-oriented model and that stakeholder-oriented thinking would lead to legal reform. Thus, despite the dominance of shareholder primacy, acceptance of stakeholder-oriented approaches around the world was predicted to be the next stage of legal development.

This book contributes to this literature by examining the role of shareholder primacy during takeovers and whether it has a detrimental effect to the interests of other company stakeholders. And if it has a detrimental effect, stakeholder-oriented reforms would be considered. The next part reviews existing research literature on stakeholders' interests during takeovers.

The impact on stakeholders' interests post-takeover

Existing research literature supports the view that all company stakeholders are affected by agency costs which means all stakeholders deserve some level of protection. This part reviews key research carried out on the impact of takeovers on employees, senior management and suppliers post-takeover.

Shleifer and Summers (1988) The breach of trust hypobook

In 1988, two American scholars, André Shleifer and Lawrence Summers, published their influential paper titled "Breach of Trust in Hostile Takeovers."[65] It came at a time when many US companies were being subject to takeover bids and taken over at a premium price. They studied the takeover of a company called Youngstown Sheet and Tube in 1977 and found a total loss of 6,000 jobs between 1977 and 1979. The researchers explained the loss of jobs using their breach of trust hypobook .

The main factor behind the breach of trust hypobook is the relationship between implicit contracts and takeovers. According to the researchers, employees make firm specific human capital investments in the company, with a promise of job security in return for their investment. Firm specific human capital includes the "skills or knowledge or networks of personal relationships that are specialized to a given enterprise and that are more valuable in that enterprise than they would be in alternative uses."[66] Due to

[65] Andrei Shleifer and Lawrence H Summers, Breach of Trust in Hostile Takeovers in Alan J Auerbach, *Corporate Takeovers: Causes and Consequences* (University of Chicago Press: Chicago 1988) 50-51.
[66] Margaret Blair, *Wealth Creation and Wealth Sharing* (Washington, D.C: Brookings, 1996) 8.

41

firm-specific investments, employees become 'locked in' the company. The researchers argued that this leaves employees highly vulnerable to future renegotiation of contract.

Takeovers may deter employees from making firm specific investments due to worries over downsizing and renegotiation of implicit contracts.[67] In regards to the former, takeovers may result in downsizing in order to cut costs and create more efficiency. Thus, any income stream accruing from employees made redundant are converted into takeover premiums for outgoing shareholders. Downsizing also amounts to a wealth transfer from employees to shareholders. According to Professor Margaret Blair, "firms that focus solely on share value will have an incentive to shut down operations that are not generating profits for shareholders even though these operations may still be generating substantial real economic rents... over time such policies are likely to discourage further investments by employees in firm-specific human capital."[68]

Shleifer and Summers advanced literature by arguing that a wealth transfer from employees to shareholders mainly occur due to a change in management after a takeover. According to the researchers, if management is not replaced after a takeover, implicit contracts are less likely to be breached for fear that the company's reputation may be damaged. However, following a successful takeover bid, a new management team would need to realize short-term gains in order to recoup the costs of the takeover through asset disposal and downsizing of labour force.

They summed up the wealth transfer argument as follows: "takeovers are external means of removing managers who uphold stakeholder claims. Takeovers then allow shareholders to appropriate stakeholders' ex post rents in the implicit contracts. The gains are split between the shareholders of the acquired and the acquiring firms. At least in part, therefore, the gains are wealth redistributing and not wealth creating."[69]

Furthermore, they argued that although shareholders are not the owners of the company, there are fundamental differences in the treatment of their shareholding contract as compared to an employment contract.[70] Both employees and shareholders have an implicit contract but shareholders claims are protected by corporate law to a greater extent than employee

---

[67] Andrei Shleifer and Lawrence H Summers, Breach of Trust in Hostile Takeovers in Alan J Auerbach, *Corporate Takeovers: Causes and Consequences* (University of Chicago Press: Chicago 1988) 53.
[68] Margaret Blair, *Wealth Creation and Wealth Sharing* (Washington, D.C: Brookings, 1996) 12.
[69] *Ibid* 44.
[70] *Ibid* 43.

claims. This is unjustified since shareholders are being treated as company owners.

In the UK, three empirical studies tested the breach of trust hypobook . First, a study was carried out on 433 companies involved in 240 takeovers between 1983 and 1996.[71] The researchers found a 7.5 per cent decline in employment in those firms. In a follow up study, covering the period of 1967 to 1996, a 9 per cent decline in employment was found.[72] In support of the breach of trust hypobook , the researchers concluded that:

"[I]f the observed employment reductions constitute a reneging on the implicit terms of the labour contract, in the sense of...there may be associated costs generated through the subsequent reductions in firm-specific human capital investment by employees. These will be manifested in lower output levels but any such changes would be very hard to identify".[73]

Second, a qualitative empirical perspective on the effect of takeovers on employees was provided in a study of 15 takeovers during the period of 1993- 1996. The researchers reviewed reports and conducted interviews in a bid to find evidence of a breach of trust. The researchers found employee redundancies in all the takeover cases. One of the case studies was the Glaxo takeover of Wellcome in which 7500 jobs were lost in a bid to cut costs by £340 million. The unions involved argued that "there had been no prior consultation and it was a unilateral decision by an arrogant management."[74]

The researchers found that successful takeovers result in large-scale job losses and asset disposals. This study provides strong empirical support to wealth transfer from employees to shareholders since most of the acquired companies had to take on cost saving measures in order to recoup the money used to pay for the high premium.

Third, the breach of trust hypobook in the UK was tested in a study which investigated the effect of takeovers on employment and wages between 1987 and 1995.[75] The aim was to test whether takeovers result in

---

[71]   Martin Conyon, Sourafel Girma, Steve Thompson and Peter Wright, Do hostile mergers destroy jobs? (2001) 45 (4), Journal of Economic Behaviour and Organization 427, 438.
[72]   Martin Conyon, Sourafel Girma, Steve Thompson and Peter Wright, The impact of mergers and acquisitions on company employment in the United Kingdom (2002) 46 (1), European Economic Review 31, 38.
[73]   *Ibid* 40.
[74]   *Ibid* 32.
[75]   Til Beckman and William Forbes, An examination of takeovers, job loss and wage decline within UK Industry, (2004) 10 (1) European Financial Management 141, 157-159.

a wealth transfer from employees to shareholders via the bid premium. They found that total employment decreased by 11 per cent over a period of five years pot-takeover. The study also found a substantial decline in wages following takeover. As a result, the researchers concluded that the destruction of employee contracts is likely to be related to the bid premium that had to be paid to outgoing shareholders.

However, even though there is strong empirical support for the breach of trust hypobook in the UK, the studies did not refer to takeover cases after 2000. Since the turn of the twenty-first century, no UK based study has investigated job losses pot-takeover.

Krug and Aguilera (2005) Top team management after a takeover

The effect of takeovers on senior management has been extensively studied in research literature since the 1980s. However, only a few studies have investigated managerial turnover after a takeover and most of these studies have been conducted in America. Krug and Aguilera reviewed these studies in their 2005 research paper.[76] The researchers set out to review empirical evidence on the performance of acquired companies and on the turnover of senior management after a takeover. The aim of the research paper was to bring greater awareness on the effect of takeovers on management teams in acquired companies.

On the performance of acquired firms, Krug and Aguilera reviewed 93 empirical studies. They found that target and acquiring company's stock values increased significantly upon the announcement of a takeover. They also found that future returns to the acquiring company were generally negative. They concluded that M&As often fail to realise expected returns and that, "acquisitions, on average, do not improve performance of the firms they acquire."[77]

Furthermore, Krug and Aguilera reviewed seven studies that measured turnover among target company executives post-takeover. The studies were conducted between 1975- 1990. They found that on average 24 per cent of the top management depart during the first year following a takeover. The post-takeover turnover rate of senior management was nearly three times higher than the industry turnover rate of senior executives. Furthermore, more than 30 per cent of the original management team was often gone by the end of the third year, and 60 per cent of the pre-takeover management team was often gone after the sixth year.

---

[76] Jeffrey A Krug and Ruth V Aguilera, Top Management Teams turnover in mergers and acquisitions (2005) 4(1) Advances in Mergers and Acquisitions 121, 146–147.
[77] *Ibid* 122.

In regards company performance prior to the takeover bid, Krug and Aguilera referred to a study which investigated managerial autonomy and status and the link to the high executive turnover rate.[78] The study found that poor financial performance by the target company was associated with high executive departure in the first two years after the acquisition. Krug and Aguilera relied on these findings to conclude that high turnover rates are associated with a perception that the management team was underperforming before the takeover.

After surveying the theoretical and empirical literature on top management turnover following a takeover, Krug and Aguilera concluded that, "our own research indicates that executives who join target companies after the acquisition experience high turnover rates up to nine years after the acquisition."[79]

However, all the studies reviewed by Krug and Aguilera investigated executive turnover rates during the 1970s and 80s. The studies were also based on takeover cases in the US thus there is a need for studies on the turnover rate of executives using UK based takeover cases in the twenty-first century.

Homroy (2012) Effect of mergers and acquisitions on CEO Turnover

Given the lack of empirical evidence on managerial turnover post-takeover within the twenty-first century, Homroy sought to fill this gap by investigating Chief Executive Officer (CEO) exit and firm performance.[80] The study covered the period of 1992-2010. The probability of CEO exit after an M&A and the effect of M&A on firm performance were the two factors studied. The researcher relied on a sample of 2814 American companies.

The researcher found that M&A increased the 'hazard' of CEO turnover. First and foremost, in terms of gender, the study found that female CEOs had an 8 per cent lower turnover rate in the industry but the turnover rate went up by 3 per cent in the event of an M&A. Second, the turnover rate of CEOs was found to be higher in cases involving takeovers as compared to mergers. In the case of mergers, they documented a 37.7 per cent increase in CEO turnover whereas a 141 per cent increase was documented in

[78] Donald C Hambrick and Albert A Cannella, Relative standing: A framework for understanding departures of acquired executives (1993) 36 (4), Academy of Management Journal 733, 759.
[79] Jeffrey A Krug and Ruth V Aguilera, Top Management Teams turnover in mergers and acquisitions (2005) 4(1) Advances in Mergers and Acquisitions 121, 146.
[80] Swarnodeep Homroy, Effect of Mergers and Acquisitions on CEO Turnover in Large Firms and SMES: A Hazard Analysis (2012) Department of Economics, Lancaster University, 16-23.

takeovers. Third, CEOs involved in cross-border M&As were 54.23 per cent more likely to leave the company as compared to domestic acquisitions. Thus, CEO turnover was more documented in cross-border M&As than domestic M&A. Last but not least, the researcher estimated that in the event of an M&A, CEO turnover increases by 132 per cent. These increases were documented in the first two years of an M&A. The study provides empirical support that M&As increase the CEO turnover rate.

Homroy's findings provide strong empirical support to Krug and Aguilera's findings that a strong relationship exists between managerial turnover and M&A activity. However, the study was based on US takeover cases and measured only CEO turnover. Thus, there is a dearth of empirical research on executive turnover following the takeover of UK companies. This book contributes to research literature by examining the effect of takeovers on managerial turnover using UK takeover samples.

Intintoli, Serfling and Shaikh (2012) CEO turnover and suppliers' interests

The relationship between CEO turnover and the renegotiation of suppliers' contracts was studied by Intintoli, Serfling and Shaikh.[81] The aim was to identify whether the replacement a CEO had an economic impact on the company's suppliers.

The researchers studied 743 cases where companies replaced their CEOs. They compared the suppliers' sales rates during the turnover year and the rates in the years without turnover. They found a 20 per cent drop in sales during the turnover years as compared to other years. The researchers also found that the stock price of suppliers was affected by announcement of a CEO removal. They provide evidence that the removal of senior management such as the board of directors directly impacts on suppliers. The findings support the view that CEO replacement has a negative economic effect on company suppliers.

Furthermore, the researchers found that appointment of a new CEO often results in a renegotiation of contract and relations with suppliers are usually affected. This is because agreements between suppliers and companies are governed by implicit contracts, which can be renegotiated without legal ramifications. These findings can be relied on as evidence that the removal of senior management following a takeover can affect suppliers.

---

[81] Vincent J Intintoli, Mathew Serfling and Sarah Shaikh, The Negative Spillover Effects of CEO Turnovers: Evidence from Firm-Supplier Relations (2012), SSRN Working Paper Series, 17-28.

Even though the study provides evidence linking CEO turnover to a drop in suppliers' sales and renegotiation of contracts, research that directly links takeovers and renegotiation of suppliers' contracts is missing.

Summary

Having carried out a theoretical review on shareholder primacy during takeovers and the impact on the interests of employees, senior management and suppliers, two main gaps have been identified. First, most of the research was conducted in the twentieth century, thus few scholars have contributed to the topic since the turn of the twenty-first century. This book contributes to research literature by providing evidence on takeovers cases in the UK covering the period of 2001-2015.

Second, most of the empirical research is from the US and there seems to be a scarcity of UK scholarship on the topic. Thus, this book contributes to research literature by providing research evidence on shareholder primacy and the impact on senior management, employees and suppliers in the UK following a takeover. The aim of this study is to find a relationship between shareholder primacy and its effect on non-shareholding stakeholders post-takeover. The results will help to determine whether the continued imposition of the board neutrality rule, which is the source of shareholder primacy under UK takeover law, is still justified.

CHAPTER 3: ENLIGHTENED SHAREHOLDER VALUE AND THE MODERN CORPORATION

Introduction

The previous chapter has discussed the impact of takeovers on stakeholders' interests and supporting literature for shareholder primacy. It has found that shareholders who are the owners of the company, make substantial earnings during takeovers and their actions could operate to the detriment of other stakeholders. This raises questions over property ownership and stakeholder protection, in particular, should company directors owe their statutory duties towards all company constituents. This chapter focuses on private property and enlightened shareholder value (ESV). The latter is a product of section 172 of the Companies Act 2006 which requires directors to accommodate the interests of non-shareholding stakeholders during the decision making process.

This chapter begins by discussing the roots of the debate on private property rights within a liberal capitalist society. Much of the early literature is rooted in philosophical debates over the property rights which fed the twentieth century conception of the company. However, the direction of the debate had changed at the conclusion of the twentieth century with the emergence of stakeholder theory that underpins collective administration of company resources and decision making. This chapter also discusses the forces that have shaped the development of ESV. Two forces are considered in this chapter: conception of company property and investor short-termism.

Liberal capitalism and private property rights

Before discussing the treatment of company property during takeovers, it is important to appreciate the role played the economic system in the UK towards our understanding of private property. The UK is characterised as liberal capitalist state. Capitalism is a system of societal organisation underpinned by core principles such as property rights, especially private ownership of the means of production and liberalism.[1] The latter is an approach to government premised on individual rights, balance of power and scientific rationality. It is at the centre of a western capitalist society because it underpins the notion of private property. Thus a capitalist society should permit people to pursue their own ends and arrange their resources in a manner that maximises individual benefit. In theory, this

---

[1] Milton Friedman, *Capitalism and Freedom* (University of Chicago Press: Chicago 1962) 8–21.

eliminates coercion by any central authority and makes trade voluntary and mutually beneficial.

Private property rights have been a source of academic debate since the seventeenth century. In the seventeenth century, John Locke, a political philosopher, explored some of the fundamental values that underpin a liberal capitalist society. He observed that "every man has a property in his own person" and that capitalist values such as liberty and property have a foundation independent of laws of any society.[2] He believed that the state was formed by social contract and had an obligation to protect the interests of private property owners.

While recognising that individuals had property rights to which the state was contracted to protect, Locke argued that when an individual adds their own labour or property to a foreign good, they acquire ownership rights in that asset. Locke felt that ownership of property was a result of labour and wanted to see more equity in terms of labour expended and how it is rewarded. Although his ideas came before the industrial revolution, he still saw the prospect of labour being exploited thus violating the social contract.

Karl Marx's class inequality ideas challenged Locke's conception of property that labour has a claim on what they have produced.[3] Karl Marx argued that the working class and upper class cannot be treated equally. It was only natural that the working class which oversees the production would be exploited by the upper class. Of the two early political thinkers, Karl Marx's ideas became more accepted in the twentieth century as they underpin the core values of a western capitalist society.[4]

However, liberal western capitalist states should be distinguished from authoritarian capitalist states such as Russia.[5] In such states, private choice may exist but in limited form. In other words, an authoritarian capitalist environment provides for economic control shared by the people and the government, with a greater share of control in the hands of the government. While the interference by the state may be more or less limited to the rule of law in liberal western economies, in such countries, interference begins once the company acquires substantive economic power. Thus, the

---

[2] John Locke, *Two Treatises of Government, II, 27* (The works of John Locke (10th edition, London Johnson J et al., 1801) V, 353.
[3] Karl Marx, "Capital" Volume 1 translated by Ben Fowkes, David Fernbach (New York: Vintage, 1977-1981) 15.
[4] North C Douglass, *Institutions, Institutional Change and Economic Performance* (Cambridge University Press, 1990) 174-204.
[5] Paul Le Blanc, *Revolution, Democracy, Socialism: Selected Writings of Lenin* (Pluto Press, London, 2008) 83.

difference between liberal capitalism and authoritarian capitalism is the extent to which companies must align their behaviours with the state plan for the economy.

For a system of free market capitalism to work, growth in economic entrepreneurial skills is necessary.[6] This is because in a purely capitalist system, the main method of building up assets is through voluntary acquisition of labour and physical capital that is owned by other people. Since liberal capitalism requires acquisition of assets, this raises questions over whether the acquired assets would still be classified as an extension of the owner and if not, does it create multiple stakeholders with ownership rights over the same property? With the emergence of stakeholderism in the mid-twentieth century and labours' claim for greater protection during takeovers, an answer to the question of company property ownership became ever more important.

Private property rights and the Takeover Directive

In the UK, the strongest line of defence for shareholder sovereignty in the context of takeovers, which exists by virtue of Rule 21 of the Takeover Code 2016, would doctrinally be the fact that shareholders enjoy absolute proprietary rights over the stock they own. This protection was extended across the European Union (EU) in May 2004 following decades of negotiations that culminated in the European Directive of Takeover Bids (Takeover Directive).[7]

The Takeover Directive had two objectives: first, to harmonise takeover regulation in the EU and second, to protect shareholders. Indeed, these objectives are fundamental to free movement of capital which is essentially at the heart of private property rights and community law.[8] To domesticate the various articles, the UK passed the Takeovers Directive (Interim Implementation) Regulations 2006 which gave a statutory mandate to the provisions of the Takeover Code.[9] The regulations were subsequently replaced by part 28 of the Companies Act 2006 which placed both the Takeover Panel and Takeover Code on statutory footing.[10]

---

[6] Monica Prasad, *The Politics of Free Markets: The Rise of Neoliberal Economic Policies in Britain, France, Germany and the United States* (University of Chicago Press, 2006) 328.

[7] Directive 2004/25/EC [2004] OJ L142/12.

[8] Article 63 Treaty on the Functioning of the European Union (Lisbon Treaty).

[9] Statutory Instrument 1183/2006. Article 21 of the Directive required Member States to bring into force laws implementing the Directive by 20 May 2006.

[10] Prior to 2006, UK Takeovers had operated under a so-called 'self-regulation' regime which 'connote a system whereby a group of people, acting in concert, use their collective power to force themselves and others to comply with a code of conduct of their own devising,' *R v The Panel on Takeovers and Mergers ex parte Datafin* (1987) 3 BCC 10, 13.

Despite reflecting the diverging legal cultures and economic systems across the EU, the Takeover Directive has an overwhelmingly shareholder-oriented cast. The Takeover Directive endorses a liberal economic approach by providing adequate safeguards for private property, in this case shareholding, but at the same time allowing them the liberty to sell their shares during a takeover. This is largely enshrined under article 9 of the Takeover Directive, which sets out the non-frustration principle. The article prohibits the board from adopting takeover defences without shareholder approval. The underlying reason behind Article 9 is to protect the property interest of shareholders by giving them the opportunity to decide on the merits of the bid. For employees, the directive merely requires Member State directors of the target company to give sufficient information to employees on the potential impact of the bid on employment.[11] Again, this points to a change in corporate culture where directors are deemed to owe their duties to shareholders and not to employees or the company itself.

Although the UK implemented Article 9 through Rule 21 of the Takeover Code, the approach to protecting shareholders' interests taken under the Takeover Directive is markedly different from that of the UK. The EU perspective treats the board of directors as agents of shareholders whereas[12] traditionally, English law has treated directors as owing their duties to the company as opposed to shareholders. Thus, management decision making is often not aligned to the interests of shareholders. Fundamentally, it is the takeover code's desire to remedy the misalignment by requiring shareholder approval before launching any frustrating measure. This is also reflected in Rule 21 of the Takeover Code, which is contrary to the traditional approach under English company law but aligns with the EU perspective. Arguably, despite being contrary to traditional English company law, Rule 21 offers companies a better chance of protecting themselves against value destroying takeover bids that are ultimately not in the interest of the target shareholders.

However, Article 12(1) of the Takeover Directive creates controversy by allowing Member States to opt out of Article 9.[13] Besides being a failure of harmonisation, it is allows countries to limit the effect of the non-frustration principle thus allowing the board of directors the right to deny shareholders the right to decide on the merits of the bid. In this regard, the Takeover directive fails to secure private property rights for shareholders across

---

[11] Articles 9(5) of the Takeover Directive, Recital number 23 of the Takeover Directive.
[12] Report of The High Level Group of Company Law Experts on Issues Related to Takeover Bids (the "Winter Report") Brussels, 10 January 2002, at 19.
[13] Scott V Simpson, EU Directive fails to harmonise takeovers (2005) A Special IFLR Supplement 15 available at <http://www.iflr.com> (accessed 03 January 2016).

the EU. For example, France adopted the Loi Florange Act in 2014, which reverses the Article 9 of the Takeover Directive, requiring the boards of French companies to frustrate takeovers.[14] Thus, it appears that the decades of negotiation over the core provisions of the Takeover Directive watered-down its goal of harmonisation and protection of target shareholders.

The failure of the Takeover Directive to harmonise rules on shareholder property rights leads us back to the debate on whether shareholders are the residual owners of company property and thus all property rights should be exercised by them. Professor Horrigan summed up this position by stating that: "much of the conventional economic, contract-based and business thinking in support of shareholder primacy is predicated on the idea that those who invest in a company are its true 'owners' and thus should have the final say over the destination of their property."[15] Considered in conjunction with the permeating principle of free tradability of shares, it is difficult to put a convincing argument in support of restrictions on share purchase. Decision-making powers cannot also be given to directors to advance shareholder primacy during takeovers because a takeover is not an asset or business of the company that needs management.

However, company law scholarship has long been at pains in determining the proprietary rights of shareholders. The shareholder as a residual claimant is a term that has much been referred to and the perception that share ownership constitutes an entitlement to corporate profits became conventional wisdom in the twentieth century.[16] However, in order to better understand the ownership rights of shareholders, it is better to conceive the share itself as a bundle of rights;[17] designed to facilitate investment in equity and enforceable against the company. Thus, shareholders do not absolutely own the corporation or part of it; what they own instead is a financial instrument, a "chose in action" *vis a vis* the company, which constitutes property in its own right.[18] This leaves a hole in the shareholder property defence.

---

[14] See the editorial by Professor de Beaufort, Ne pas casser l'équilibre actuel del la legislation sur les OPA, La Tribune February 17, 2014, available at www.latribune.fr (accessed 18/06/2016).
[15] Bryan Horrigan, *Corporate Social Responsibility in the 21st Century: Debates, Models and Practices Across Government, Law and Business* (Cheltenham: Edward Elgar, 2008)104.
[16] Frank H Easterbrook and Daniel R Fischel, Voting in Corporate Law (1983) 26 (2), Journal or Law and Economics 395, 403.
[17] Antony M Honoré, *Ownership* in Anthony G. Guest (eds) Oxford Essays on Jurisprudence (Oxford University Press, 1961)107.
[18] John Parkinson, *Corporate Power and Responsibility: Issues in the Theory of Company Law* (Oxford: Oxford University Press, 1993) 34; Paddy Ireland, Defending the Rentier: Corporate Theory and the Reprivatization of the Public Company, in John Parkinson, Andrew Gamble and Gavin Kelly (eds), *The Political Economy of the Company* (Hart Publishing: Oxford, 2001) 163.

Theoretical foundations of Enlightened Shareholder Value

The debate over corporate property ownership and the protection of non-shareholding stakeholders' interests in the UK has its roots in the eighteenth century philosophical thinking. Eighteen century scholars advanced the classical view of the firm premised on shareholder value maximisation (SVM) to which corporate property was owned by shareholders thus making them the sole beneficiaries of managerial decision making. Enlightened shareholder value (ESV), on the other hand, received statutory force in the early twenty-first century as a response to the emergence of stakeholder theory that underpins the protection of non-shareholding stakeholders' interests.

The debate was started by Adam Smith in his 1776 treatise on capital markets in which he identified morality as one of the essential constraints on corporate entities from engaging in self-interested activities in respect to the welfare of society.[19] However, moral responsibility and its application to companies is severely limited. The fact that law imputes a personality on companies for the purposes of establishing legal responsibility does not satisfy the conditions of moral responsibility. Moral responsibility requires a state of consciousness sufficient to form intention in regard to performing an act and to have reasonable knowledge of the nature and consequences of such action.[20]

Despite having legal personhood, a company does not possess any of the human capacity for compassion, reason or self-restraint that are preconditions to moral consciousness.[21] As a result, companies are limited only by the standards and boundaries established by law and the moderating force of market based competition.

Adam Smith argued that the pursuit of self-interest can sometimes also contribute to the common good, in what he termed the 'invisible hand'.[22] A capitalist economy operates to direct the individual participants to pursue their own economic interests in such a manner that also advances the public good. He observed that: "the prudent man is ever tendful to his reputation, and he therefore seeks to advance his own interests through achieving social

---

[19] Adam Smith, Theory of Moral Sentiments, in Robert L Heilbroner, *The Essential Adam Smith* (3rd Edn, New York: WW Norton & Company, 1987) 107-108.
[20] Michael Phillips, Corporate moral personhood and three conceptions of the corporation (1992) 2 (2) Business Ethics Quarterly 435, 436.
[21] Christopher D Stone, *Where the law ends: The social control of corporate behaviour* (Waveland Press Inc: Illinois, 1991) 35.
[22] For a discussion of the invisible hand see Samuel Fleischacker, *On Adam Smith's Wealth of Nations* (Princeton, NJ: Princeton University Press, 2004) 138-142.

esteem. It is in this way that selfish behaviour can produce social benefits."[23] Thus, free market competition would prompt the business community to an "unremitting exertion of vigilance and attention"[24] leaving the policy makers the responsibility of enabling progressive market competition.

The debate leading up to the twentieth century was on the purpose of a company within society and for whose benefit should a company operate. Milton Friedman made a major contribution to this debate by arguing that "the social responsibility of business is to increase its profits."[25] Friedman observed that social responsibility is "an inappropriate use of the corporate funds in a free-enterprise society."[26] Social distributions by the company prevent shareholders from themselves deciding how they should dispose of their money. He recognised that although shareholders may want the company to give a gift on their behalf, and this could result in more profit, as long as a company pays corporation tax, there is no justification for giving out any more money.

Professor Berle, an advocate of SVM, emphasised the importance of shareholder primacy: "… now I submit that you cannot abandon emphasis on the view that business corporations exist for the sole purpose of making profits for their stockholders until such time as you are prepared to offer a clear and reasonably enforceable scheme of responsibilities to someone else…"[27]

Sternberg argues that running a company for the common good of all its constituents encourages unresponsive management.[28] Similarly, law and economics theorists Easterbrook and Fischel argue that company law should be designed to help the market reach a wealth maximisation outcome.[29]

Contemporary supporters of SVM maintain that although a company has many constituencies, it cannot balance the interests of stakeholders with those of shareholders.[30] Whereas shareholders want profit, stakeholders

---

[23] Adam Smith, *An Inquiry into the Nature and Causes of the Wealth of Nations* (Clarendon Press, Oxford 1976)107.

[24] *Ibid* 192.

[25] Milton Friedman, *Capitalism and Freedom* (University of Chicago Press: Chicago 1962) 12 and 16.

[26] *Ibid* 135.

[27] Adolf Berle, For whom corporate managers are trustees: A Note (1932) 45 (7) Harvard Law Review 1365, 1367.

[28] Elaine Sternberg, The defects of stakeholder theory (1997) 5 (1) Corporate Governance: An international Review 3, 6-8.

[29] Frank H Easterbrook and Daniel R Fischel, *The economic structure of corporate law* (Cambridge MA: Harvard University Press, 1991) 18-23.

[30] James Wallace, Value Maximisation and Stakeholder Theory: Compatible or Not? (2003) 15 (3) Journal of Applied Corporate Finance 120, 121.

such as communities seek investment in local projects and this creates a conflict of interest. For example, an airline would need to increase flights to maximise revenue for the benefit of shareholders but they would be damaging the environment due to increased emissions. Similarly, a tobacco company would need to sell as many cigarettes as possible to maximise revenue but they would be damaging the health of smokers which goes against the interests of communities. On that background, they maintain that balancing the interests of shareholders with those of other stakeholders is unsustainable and impractical. One prominent adversary of stakeholder theory concluded: "[i]n fact, the sooner we get rid of the word "balance" in these discussions, the better we will be able to sort out the solutions."[31]

The economic rise of Japan and Germany in the 1970s and the growing perception that the US and UK were losing ground on both countries led to a change in academic opinion.[32] Scholars began to view the stakeholder friendly approach in Japan and Germany as a more economically sound approach. It accompanied the development of a new theoretical ground; agency theory. An agency relationship is a contract under which one or more persons (the principal(s)) engage another person (the agent) to perform some service on his or her behalf which involves delegating some decision-making authority to the agent.[33]

Agency theorists argued that there are agency relationships within the company, the principals being the management of the latter. Despite not having any grounds on the law of agency and being rather a perception of corporate governance from an economics point of view, agency theory gained support in legal scholarship as an explanatory mechanism for intra-corporate relations and became the starting point for formative suggestions. However, agency theory in its narrowest sense is everything but incompatible with the SVM approach; on the necessary precondition that the only identified group of principals are shareholders.[34] However, from the point of view that managers are agents of a broader array of constituencies, the paradigm shifts. A more inclusive approach of corporate

---

[31] Michael C Jensen, Value maximization, stakeholder theory, and the corporate objective function (2002) 12 (2) Business Ethics Quarterly 235, 251.
[32] Joan Cox and Herbert Kriegbaum, *Innovation and Industrial Strength: A study in the UK, West Germany, the United States and Japan* (Policy Studies Institutive, London, 1989) 54.
[33] Michael C Jensen and William H Meckling, Theory of the Firm: Managerial Behaviour, Agency Costs and Ownership Structure (1976) 3 (4), Journal of Financial Economics 305, 308.
[34] As stated by John Coffee: "The modern theory of the firm sees the corporation as essentially an agency relationship in which shareholders are the principals and management their agents." John Coffee, Regulating the market for Corporate Control: A Critical. Assessment of the Tender Offer's Role in Corporate Governance (1984) 84 Columbia Law Review1154, 1154.

law emerges whereby strong legal protection for all company constituents and market forces (such as takeovers could provide) become necessary.

Stakeholder theory and Enlightened Shareholder Value

Agency theory provided the building blocks for stakeholder theory, without a firm theoretical and conceptual grounding, however. One of the first scholars to make a major contribution to stakeholder theory was Edward Freeman.[35] He argued that stakeholders such as employees, suppliers and communities should be recognised as having significant stakes in the company and the company depends on their participation in its enterprise in order to function and survive.[36]

Thus, recognising the interests and contributions of these stakeholders is important in order for the company to uphold its responsibilities and serve the interests of shareholders. As a matter of fact, stakeholder theory does not challenge shareholders claim as principals but seeks a "broader range of assumptions about how wealth is created, captured, and distributed in a business enterprise."[37]

As supporters of stakeholder theory demanded more control over the company, supporters of shareholder primacy responded with the development of intellectual responses to those demands. They criticised more inclusive approaches for undermining the influence of stock markets on management.[38] They argued that if shareholders were not given greater control over their investment, there would be a general unwillingness to invest in companies. To SVM theorists, stakeholders such as employees have no investment in the company that warrants protection whereas shareholders invest their money, which they deserve greater control and monitoring over.

A relatively novel approach in legal and economics literature, which I view as an attempt to strike a middle ground between stakeholder theory and SVM, is that of ESV.[39] The respective theory supports that managers should run the company with the sole objective of maximising firm value and long-term sustainability of corporate business; thereby avoiding the

---

[35] Edward Freeman, Strategic management: A stakeholder approach (New York: Harper Collins, 1984) 52-69.
[36] *Ibid*, 53; see Gavin Kelly, Dominic Kelly and Andrew Gamble, Stakeholder capitalism (London: Macmillan Press, 1997) 244.
[37] Margaret Blair, Ownership and control: Rethinking corporate governance for the twentieth-first century (Washington DC: Brookings Institution, 1995) 15.
[38] Ismail Erturk, Julie Froud, Sukhdev Johal, Adam Leaver and Karel Williams, *Financialization at Work* (Abingdon: Routledge, 2008) 47.
[39] James Wallace, Value Maximisation and Stakeholder Theory: Compatible or Not? (2003) 15(1) Journal of Applied Corporate Finance 120, 125.

pitfall of having to balance multiple conflicting interests and addressing the points of criticism to stakeholder theory.[40]

At the core of ESV is the perception that firm value in turn results to an efficient allocation of wealth amongst the company's constituencies. A closer examination of this approach reveals that, essentially, it constitutes a response to the problematic effect of short-termism. On the one hand, it does not deny shareholders of their property as members of the company; on the other hand, it advocates that managers should not be under pressure to create short-term shareholder value at any cost. Under ESV, managers are agents of the company as a whole and thus have to consider the interests of all related constituencies. Shareholders maintain their primacy status in the company but with consideration being given to other stakeholders' interests where necessary.

Enlightened Shareholder Value in the twenty-first century

In 2001, when the Company Law Steering Group issued its final report on company law review leading up to the Companies Act 2006, it took an enlightened modern view of the company:

> "[I]t sets as the basic goal for directors the success of the company in the collective best interests of shareholders. But it also requires them to recognize, as the circumstances require, the company's need to foster relationships with its employees, customers and suppliers, its need to maintain its business reputation, and its need to consider the company's impact on the community and the working environment."[41]

As a result, section 172(1) of the Companies Act 2006 brought the concept of ESV into UK company law. It requires the board to consider the interests of a wide range of stakeholders when devising company objectives. The board of directors merely set objectives but do not manage the company except for executive directors. Thus, although not included, executive directors are directly impacted on by takeovers as they have to balance their jobs with shareholders' interests during a takeover situation.

Two studies examined the changing objectives of companies and concluded that ESV had eclipsed SVM theory. First, a study on company objectives in the US found that since the late 1990s, companies were

---

[40] A similar point is made by Professor Andrew Keay, Ascertaining the Corporate Objective: An Entity Maximisation and Sustainability Model" (2008) 71 Modern Law Review 663, 679.
[41] Department of Trade and Industry, Modern Company Law for A Competitive Economy, Final Report, (2001), at para 3.8.

incorporating social responsibility into their objectives and it was increasingly being linked to corporate success.[42] The researcher concluded that a twenty-first century company cannot follow a SVM approach alone because a company plays a social role which ties in the interests of many company constituents. Another study contrasted shareholder primacy with stakeholder value perspectives.[43] The researchers found a gradual shift from shareholder primacy to stakeholder value occurring in the 1990s onwards.

Both studies provide support that ESV, an approach inextricably linked to stakeholder value, has become a key feature of large public companies' objectives. They also indicate that policy changes in the UK since the 1970s had been changing from shareholder value to stakeholder value. In particular, the researchers referred to the ESV approach in the UK as a clear policy move in that direction. The researchers concluded that a company could no longer be viewed as a 'money maker' rather; the role had shifted to serving the wider interests of society.[44]

The mixed support for Enlightened Shareholder Value

Despite the acceptance of ESV in research literature and policy, shareholders in the UK continue to enjoy absolute sovereignty during takeovers. It begs the question: why do policy makers continue to support shareholder primacy under takeover law?[45] This is the next line of our inquiry.

In law, the concept of "the interest of the company" has been interpreted as shareholder primacy by maximising the wealth of the shareholding body.[46] Legal practitioners tend to take SVM as the primary objective of the company.[47] The explanation often advanced for the dominance of SVM is the relationship between shareholders' interests and those of the company. It follows that a company is an artificial entity and thus it would

---

[42]   Michael C Jensen, Value maximization, stakeholder theory, and the corporate objective function (2002) 12 (2) Business Ethics Quarterly 235, 244.
[43]   Yuri Biondi, Arnaldo Canziani and Thierry Kirat, T *The Firm as an Entity: Implications for Economics, Accounting and the Law* (Abingdon: Routledge, 2007) 4–5.
[44]   *Ibid* 5.
[45]   The same question was asked by Michael Patrone: "Why is the United Kingdom so married to the idea of the board neutrality rule if its own takeover watchdog unequivocally states that it places companies at a disadvantage?" Michael R Patrone, 'Sour Chocolate? Cadbury/Kraft and the 2011 Proposed Amendments to the UK Takeover Code - A Call for Further Research' (2011) 8 *BYU International Law & Management Review 64*, 83.
[46]   *Brady v. Brady*(1998) BCLC 20, CA, at 40 per Nourse L.J; Section 172 of the Companies Act 2006; Thomas Clarke, *International Corporate Governance: A Comparative Approach*, (Abingdon: Rutledge, 2007) 281.
[47]   See Hampel Committee, The Hampel Report on Corporate Governance-Final Report (London: Gee,1998) paragraph. 1.16.

be impractical to determine its best interests without having regard the interests of its shareholders.[48] They have invested their money and have value priority when the company is solvent. For example, it was stated in *Brady* v. *Brady* during the 1980s by Nourse L.J that: "the interests of the company as an artificial person cannot be distinguished from the interests of the persons who are interested in it."[49] The phrase "the persons who are interested" refers to shareholders who are treated as 'residual claimants' because of their unfixed claims.[50]

Furthermore, instructing directors to exercise their powers for the benefit of the company without indicating its scope would give imprecise guidance to directors on what the law expects. This led Professor Clark to conclude that company law is "simply defined to deal only with the relationships between shareholders and managers."[51] The law takes SVM as a good measure for firm value since it is quantifiable and shareholders have a residual claim on the company's property.[52] Thus, the main objective for directors has been articulated by the courts as maintaining financial accountability to shareholders.[53]

In theory, the legal mandate has been challenged. Scholars such as Armour and Whincop have questioned shareholder primacy as an economically sound business approach.[54] Research evidence suggests that the black letter description in company law with regard to the characterisation of company and its purposes is not adequate,[55] simply because real world practice is different from the principle in books.[56]

---

[48] Jill Fisch, Measuring efficiency in corporate law: The role of shareholder primacy, . (2006) 31(3) The Journal of Corporation Law 637, 652; See *Gaiman v. National Association for Mental Health* (1971) Ch 317 at 330 per Megarry J.
[49] (1998) BCLC 20, CA, at 40 per Nourse L.J
[50] Paul Davies, Sarah Worthington and Eva Micheler, *Gower and Davies: Principles of Modern Company Law* (8th Edn, London: Sweet and Maxwell, 2008) 507.
[51] Robert Clark, *Corporate Law* (Boston: Little, Brown Book Group, 1986) 30.
[52] Alan Dignam and John Lowry, *Company Law* (Oxford: Oxford University Press, 2012) 644.
[53] Cynthia Williams and John Conley, An Emerging Third Way? The Erosion of the Anglo-American Shareholder Value Construct (2005) 38 (2) Cornell International Law Journal 493, 500.
[54] See a proprietary nature of the company in John Armour and Michael Whincop, The proprietary foundations of Corporate Law (2005) Cambridge: ERC Centre of Business Research Working Paper No 299, 6; see also Paddy Ireland, Property and Contract in contemporary Corporate Theory, (2003) 23(3) Legal Studies 453, 455.
[55] CLRSG, Modern Company Law for a Competitive Economy: The Strategic Framework, (London: Department of Trade and Industry, 1999) 40; Mark Goyder, *Living Tomorrow's Company*, (Aldershot: Gower Publishing Ltd, 1998) Chapter 7.
[56] Brian Cheffins, Using Theory to Study Law: A Company Law Perspective, (1999) 58 (1) Cambridge Law Journal 197, 206; Patrick Atiyah and Robert Summers, Form and Substance in Anglo American Law: A Comparative Study of Legal Reasoning, Legal Theory and Legal Institutions, (Oxford: Clarendon Press, 1987) 405.

The law requires directors to take into consideration a number of factors when discharging their section 172 duty yet in practice there is ignorance towards this approach.[57] As a matter of fact, the Company Law Review Steering Group (CLRSG) endorsed the view that directors are not obliged to overlook the interests of non-shareholding stakeholders:

> "We do not accept that there is anything in the present law of directors' duties which requires them to take an unduly narrow or short-term view of their functions. Indeed they are obliged to take account of all the considerations which contribute to the success of the enterprise."[58]

The CLRSG recognised that a company has evolved beyond a legal construct for conducting business. Its influence goes beyond the business sphere to the extent that companies now wield considerable socio-political power. These changes mean there should be effective restraints on their unchecked and largely privately regulated power, if exercised in anti-social manner.

Furthermore, in the twenty-first century, it is difficult to convince a western liberal democratic society that the public costs of absorbing damage to the economy and society as a result corporate malpractice are merely unfortunate and necessary costs of doing business. For example, leading up to the takeover of Cadbury Plc by the American foods company Kraft Inc in 2010, the Cadbury board was pressured to recommend Kraft's increased offer to shareholders on no other ground other than the offer representing "good value for Cadbury shareholders."[59] The consequences were felt by society at large due to the massive job losses following the closure of Somerdale plant.

Similarly, from 2007-2009, the world experienced arguably the most far reaching financial crisis in modern history.[60] It caused economic and social damage across the world. Studies on the circumstances leading up to the crisis exposed failures of governance and ethics in business. It also revealed

---

[57] See Michael Porter, Capital Choices: Changing the Way America Invest in Industry, (2005) 5(2) Journal of Applied Corporate Finance 4, 6; Kurt Lewin, Field Theory in Social Science: Selected Theoretical Papers, (London: Tavistock, 1952) 169; Robert Hayes and William Abernathy, Managing Our Way to Economic Decline, (1980) Harvard 58 (4) Business Review 67, 71.
[58] CLRSG, Modern Company Law for a Competitive Economy: The Strategic Framework, (London: Department of Trade and Industry, 1999) 40.
[59] Kraft's Press Release, Recommended final offer by Kraft Foods Inc (January 19, 2010).
[60] OECD, Corporate Governance and the Financial Crisis: Key findings and main message (OECD Corporate Governance Committee, 2009); See Hector Sants, The crisis: The role of investors, Speech at the NAFT Investment Conference, March 11, 2009-UK Financial Services Authority).

shortcoming on behalf of parties responsible for overseeing governance such as regulatory authorities and shareholders. While respecting that shareholders are the residual company owners, both examples show that the government has a stake in ensuring that companies not only maximise shareholder value, but also to limit its adverse impact on society.

In the modern economy, it is clear that capitalism cannot be permitted to work without any restraints by relying on the 'invisible hand' because the world has changed significantly. Most individuals in Adam Smith's time could not afford to get a reputation of untrustworthiness or cast out for behaving opportunistically because of their dependence on the community. The market in Adam Smith's conception operates as an integral part of the network of institutions such as church and community that promote public good. However, in our globalised world, the influences that would historically restrain individuals from acting contrary to community norms have been weakened. Electronic communication has distanced individuals from their community without altering their identity.[61]

In the community-based world, social and physical significance safeguarded moral responsibility. In today's globalised world, social institutions such as community and church have to an extent been replaced by powerful social forces promoting individual and corporate interests. As a result, individual and corporate success is today defined in monetary terms and material worth rather than moral worthiness.[62] Thus, the social restraints placed on individuals and companies in past centuries have largely diminished. One cannot expect the 'invisible hand' to have the same influence as it did in Adam Smith's time. This places more responsibility on government to look into the unchecked powers of companies and impose restraints for the common good.

Investor short-termism and Enlightened Shareholder Value

One of the biggest drivers for ESV under takeover law is the issue of investor short-termism. It refers to corporate and investment decision-making based on short-term earnings expectations rather than long-term value creation for all stakeholders.[63] In 1965, the average holding period of

[61] Douglas Smith, *On values and values,* (New Jersey, USA: Pearson Education Inc, 2004) 54, 21, 73-76. Douglas Smith relates the changes from societal values and common good that imposed limits on self-interest in a capitalist society to the transition from a place-based world to a purpose-based world that took shape in the latter half of the twentieth century within growth in technological development.
[62] *Ibid* at 115-18; See Ronald Dworkin, *Is wealth a value? In a Matter of Principle,* (Cambridge, MA: Harvard University Press, 1985) 237-266.
[63] CFA Institute, Breaking the Short-Term Cycle, (Centre for Financial Market Integrity and Business Roundtable Institute for Corporate Ethics, 2006) 3.

shares on the FTSE was between six and eight years. By 2010, the average period had declined to between seven months and one year.[64] Thus, in less than fifty years, there has been a major shift in how shares are traded on stock markets in the UK.

Short-termism became an issue in the late 1960s when individual equity ownership in the UK public companies was increasingly moving into institutional shareholders' hands. Institutional shareholders were able to afford bulk buying of stock which gave them a controlling stake in investee companies and power to influence their strategic direction. As illustrated under Table 1, individual share ownership is a fifth of the fraction it was in 1963.

Table 1: Individual share ownership in the UK by value between 1963 and 2014

	Date	
	1963	54
	1969	47.4
	1975	37.5
	1981	28.2
	1989	20.6
	1990	20.3
	1991	19.9
	1992	20.4
	1993	17.7
Date	1994	20.3
	1997	16.5
	1998	16.7
	1999	15.3
	2000	16
	2001	14.8
	2002	14.3
	2003	14.9
	2004	14.1
	2006	12.8
	2008	10.2

[64] Ian King, Buyout leaves a bad taste, *The Times* (September 1, 2010).

2010	10.2
2012	10.1
2013	10.3
2014	11.9

Source: Office for National Statistics (2016)

Table 1 shows that in 1963, 54 per cent of the UK equity was in the hands of individual shareholders and by 2012 this figure had declined to a mere 10.1 per cent. This indicates that public companies today are run primarily for the benefit of institutional shareholders.

However, the issue is not the replacement of individual shareholders but the manner in which institutional shareholders conduct themselves in the market. The majority of institutional shareholders are long-term investors and these include pension and insurance funds.[65] Other institutional investors such as hedge funds tend to prioritise short-term gain over long-term value. Hedge funds have a role as investors that require them to move around in order to secure the best returns for their beneficiaries.[66] As a result, fund managers are normally rewarded for making high profits in a short-term. [67]

Empirical evidence shows that hedge funds expect substantial quarterly earnings and high dividends payment which pressures directors of investee companies to focus on high profitability.[68] Since the market values short-term profit, the managers seem to have responded by driving corporate strategies in that direction. Thus, market short-termism is translated into board-short-termism owing to the pressure from fund managers who stand to lose investments if they fail to make attractive gains for their investors.[69]

---

[65] Fiona Stewart, Proving Incentives for Long-Term Investment by Pension Funds -The Use of Outcome-Based Benchmarks. World Bank Policy Research Working Paper No. 6885 (2014) 11; Claudio Raddatz and Sergio Schmukler, Institutional Investors and Long-Term Investment: Evidence from Chile (2014) World Bank Policy Research Working Paper No. 6922, 38.

[66] Helen Short and Kevin Keasey, Institutional Shareholders and Corporate Governance in the United Kingdom, in Kevin Keasey, Steve Thompson and Mike Wright, *Corporate Governance: Economic, Management and Financial Issues*, (New York: Oxford University Press,1997) 22.

[67] Andrew Keay, The Kay Review of UK equity markets and long-term decision making, (July 2012) 80.

[68] Marcel Kahan and Edward Rock, Hedge Funds in Corporate Governance and Corporate Control, (2007)155 (5) University of Pennsylvania Law Review 1021, 1083.

[69] Andrew Keay, The Kay Review of UK equity markets and long-term decision making, (July 2012) 80.

The impact of investor short-termism on managerial decision making has been documented in a number of studies. A study by Baums found that short-termism led to reduced long-term expenditure on research and development (R&D).[70] A similar study carried out in the US found that the threat of takeovers caused by short-termism during the 1980s and 90s led to a shift from retention of labour and re-investing corporate earnings to profit maximisation in order to deter hostile bidders.[71] The researchers concluded that companies were becoming less innovative due to cutbacks in R&D and employees were less motivated due to a lack of job security. Another study on corporate governance reforms within the UK companies during the 1980s and 90s found that profit distributions to shareholders (dividends) grew by a ratio of nearly 3:1.[72] The researcher concluded that this was due to investor and managerial short-termism.

One study found a negative impact on the UK economy caused by investor short-termism. During the 1970s and 80s, there was an increased perception that the US and UK was losing ground on Germany and Japan.[73] In many sectors, Germany and Japanese companies were outperforming their counterparts. [74] Their companies took a more long-term approach towards capital investment and had a better employer and employee relationship in which long-term commitment was rewarded. The culture of short-term investment for profit was one of the factors blamed for the perceived decline in UK and US. Finding a solution to the decline meant learning from the more inclusive and stakeholder friendly models in Japan and Germany.[75]

Since 2000, the UK government commissioned a review into the UK equity market and in particular, the issue of short-termism. Lord Myners published his Review of Institutional Investment in the United Kingdom (the Myners Review) in 2001. It recommended that private equity requires a sustained long-term approach rather than the quick entry and exit strategies driven by short-term profit performance expectations.[76] Short-termism was

---

[70] Theodor Baums, Takeovers versus Institutions in Corporate Governance in Germany, in Daniel D Prentice & Peter Holland, *Contemporary Issues in Corporate Governance* (Clarendon Press, Oxford, 1993) 181. However, the evidence is not on UK which creates challenges in translation of evidence.

[71] William Lazonick and Mary O'Sullivan, Maximizing Shareholder Value: A New Ideology for Corporate Governance, (2000) 29 (1) Economy and Society 13, 15.

[72] Janet Williamson, A Trade Union Congress Perspective on the Company Law Review and Corporate Governance Reform Since 1997 (2003) 41(3) British Journal of Industrial Relations 5311, 512.

[73] Joan Cox and Herbert Kriegbaum, *Innovation and Industrial Strength: A study in the UK, West Germany, the United States and Japan* (Policy Studies Institutive, London, 1989) 54.

[74] Andrew Gamble and Gavin Kelly, Shareholder value and the stakeholder debate in the UK (2001) 9 (2) Corporate Governance: An International Review 110, 115.

[75] *Ibid* 115-117.

[76] Lord Myners, Myners Review of institutional investment: Final Report, (March 2001) 4.

again subject to a government commissioned review in 2012 resulting in the Keay report. In his report, he warned that short-termism was hurting the British economy. He criticised policies that focus on quick gains especially the remuneration of fund managers.[77]

Recent legal developments have also fallen short of fostering a long-term approach among institutional shareholders. For example, a Stewardship Code was issued by the Financial Reporting Council (FRC) in 2010 to foster a long-term approach among institutional shareholders.[78] However, it works on a 'comply or explain' basis. Thus institutional investors such as hedge funds that fail to comply to any of the provisions would merely provide an explanation.[79] It is also governed by reputational sanctions which are far less threatening to fund managers than failure to maximise wealth for their beneficiaries.

While respecting that shareholders are the residual company owners, these examples show that the government has a stake in ensuring that companies not only maximise shareholder value, but also limit the impact on non-shareholding stakeholders' interests and society at large. The arguments in support of shareholder primacy are critically examined below.

The primary-risk argument

Since company laws were passed in the nineteenth century, the legal position has been that shareholders own the company and directors fiduciary duties are owed to the company for the benefit of its shareholders.[80] This is the dominant view of the Anglo-American corporate governance model which is premised on the view that shareholders are the primary risk bearers for setting up the company and thus they are the ultimate owners. [81]

---

[77] Andrew Keay, The Kay Review of UK equity markets and long-term decision making, (July 2012) 13-29.
[78] Conduct of Business Sourcebook (Stewardship Code) Instrument 2010.
[79] See Iris Chiu, Stewardship as a Force for Governance: Critically Assessing the Aspirations and Weaknesses of the UK Stewardship Code, (2012) 9 (1)European Company Law 5, 7; Iris Chiu, Turning Institutional Investors into Stewards: Exploring the Meaning and Objectives of Stewardship, (2013) 66 (1) Current Legal Problems 443, 479.
[80] In a study on corporate governance in the nineteenth and twentieth centuries, Talbot found that: "[t]he historical evidence presented on the development of the market economy and company law in the United Kingdom... shows that the dispersed ownership model did not originate in economic efficiencies. Instead it was prompted by the desire to engineer the economy in the interests of the largest investors..." Lorraine Talbot, *Progressive corporate governance for the 21ˢᵗcentury* (Oxford: Routledge, 2013) 13.
[81] Michael Jensen and Clifford Smith, Stockholder, Manager and Creditor Interests: Applications of Agency Theory, in Edward Altman and Marti Subrahmanyam, (Eds), *Recent Advances in Corporate Finance*, (Irwin Professional Publishing: Homewood, USA, 1985) 93-131.

Supporters of shareholder primacy argue that other stakeholders such as creditors can hedge their risk by agreeing favourable terms in their contracts. In regards to contractual safeguards, for example, creditors can use covenants to minimise the risk of default.[82] Covenants can be distinguished between positive and negative covenants. The latter preclude debtors from diluting the interests of creditors through activities such as disposition of assets. Positive covenants require the debtor to maintain their position on matters such as the legal status of the company or keeping certain executives on the company's board. Both covenants can constrain the debtor company through the potential exit of the creditor upon default. Exit can be in the form of reduced or non-renewal of the financing contract or enforcement of security instruments.

However, the costs incurred in negotiating favourable contractual terms and monitoring debtors reduces the effectiveness of covenants.[83] Nonetheless, the premium charged by creditors can to some extent mitigate those concerns. A study conducted in the 1990s examined the relationship between bank loans and the size of premium incorporated in the loan's interest rate.[84] The study found a positive relationship between the value of the covenants and the risk premium incorporated.[85] The study also found that debtors are able to buy out financial covenants thus limiting their effectiveness.

Unlike creditors, employees are unable to individually foresee dangers such as a risky takeover in the future, unless supported by their respective trade unions.[86] Similarly, even if the risk is foreseen, they are unable to insert or bargain on corresponding terms to protect their interests. On that basis, employees take on risk by contracting to work for the company. But to the advantage of employees, the demise of a company still leaves them with their labour and skill which they can sell or utilise elsewhere.

The risk bearing argument has received little support in research literature. It has been argued that the "link between risk-taking and the right to control…is a fragile foundation on which to base shareholder

---

[82] George Triantis and Ronald Daniels, The Role of Debt in Interactive Corporate Governance (1995), 83 (4) California Law Review, 1073, 1085.
[83] Philipe Aghion and Patrick Bolton, An Incomplete Contracts Approach to Financial Contracting, (1992) 59 (3) Review of Economic Studies 473, 491.
[84] Judy Day and Peter Taylor, Evidence on the Practices of UK Bankers in Contracting for Medium-term Debt, (1995) 10 (9) Journal of International Banking Law 394, 398.
[85] *Ibid* 398.
[86] Maryalice Citera and Joan Rentsch, Is There Justice in Organizational Acquisitions? The Role of Distributive and Procedural Fairness in Corporate Acquisitions, in Russell Cropanzano (ed), *Justice in the Workplace: Approaching Fairness in Human Resources Management*, (Lawrence Erlbaum Associates: Hillsdale, NJ, 1993) 211-130.

(primacy)."[87] In other words, both shareholders and other company stakeholders take on risk by supplying the company or investing in the company thus giving shareholders primacy over other stakeholders is unjustified. Even some researchers argue that the risk assumed by shareholders when investing in the company is similar to the risk assumed by creditors when contracting with the company.[88]

Similarly, shareholders have the ability to diversify their investments by holding many portfolios.[89] This allows them to spread the risk around and thus reduce the impact of a fall in the company's share value or liquidation. In particular, institutional shareholders often hold "literally a thousand or more stocks."[90] As a result, active management of the company is offset by the low expected return from individual portfolios. Fund managers, who are remunerated according to the performance of the fund, manage institutional investment. As a result, they often pursue a diversified investment policy to reduce the risk of the whole portfolio. This offers support to the case for giving primacy to stakeholders such as employees who are unable to spread their risk in the same manner as shareholders.

Another challenge to the risk bearing argument is that shareholders have advance knowledge of the company's financial state as compared to other stakeholders such as employees.[91] Knowledge of the company's financial standing allows shareholders to walk away at any time whereas non-shareholding stakeholders cannot. A stakeholder such as an employees' risk is unforeseen and unknown whereas shareholders know in advance that the company is struggling through company reports and independent audits. This separates shareholders from non-shareholding stakeholders such as banks with unfulfilled contracts and employees who have exchanged their labour for remuneration.

Directors' duties owed to shareholders

Pro-capitalist scholars such as Milton Friedman argued that directors' duties are owed to shareholders. He observed that "few trends could so thoroughly undermine the very foundations our free society as the acceptance of by corporate officials of a social responsibility other than to

---

[87] Michel Aglietta and Antoine Reberioux, *Corporate Governance Adrift: A Critique of Shareholder Value*, (Cheltenham: Edward Elgar, 2005) 34.
[88] Eugene Fama and Michael Jensen, Separation of Ownership & Control, (1983) 26 (2) Journal of Law & Economics 301, 308.
[89] John Coffee, Institutional Investors as Corporate Monitors: Are Takeovers Obsolete?, in John Farrar, (ed), *Takeovers Institutional Investors and the Modernization of Corporate Laws*, (Oxford University Press: Oxford,1993) 12.
[90] *Ibid* 82.
[91] George Goyder, *The Future of Private Enterprise* (Oxford: Blackwell, 1951) 17.

make as much money for their stockholders as possible."[92] He was critical of the position directors were taking on by balancing the interests of many company constituents in their decision making process.

Friedman believed that placing social responsibilities on managers changes the very nature of their role in the company. He argued that "if businessmen are taken as civil servants rather than employees of the shareholders then it is fair to say that directors will soon or later be chosen by the public in the form of elections or appointment."[93] Thus, if directors' private decisions turn into public matters, then this undermines the importance of having directors in the first place.

Essentially, balancing many interests creates inefficiency as it destructs the company from its goal of profit maximisation.[94] The single objective argument received support from a study which examined company law cases and legislation in the UK and found that directors' decision-making powers were expressed in terms of benefiting the company and not its shareholders.[95] Based on these findings, the researcher argued that it is irrational to have duties that benefit an artificial entity, but rather the duties serve a human interest or objective of which the company is merely a vehicle. The researcher concluded that the human interest to which directors' duties are formulated is that of shareholders.

Subsequent company law reforms reaffirmed shareholder primacy despite recognising the need to consider other stakeholders' interests. This trade-off is the basis of the enlightened shareholder value approach under the Companies Act 2006. Policy makers in the UK took the view that long-term corporate success requires some trade-off with shareholders but maintained that shareholders' interests have primacy over other stakeholders. Under section 172(1) of the Companies Act 2006, directors must 'have regard to' the interests of stakeholders when formulating the objectives of the company for the benefit of its members. The enlightened shareholder value approach marks a small step towards stakeholder value but in law it remains that shareholders have primacy above other stakeholders. This means that after the board of directors reaches a conclusion that a particular objective would advance the interests of shareholders then they could consider how it may also advance other stakeholders' interests.

---

[92] Milton Friedman, *Capitalism and Freedom* (University of Chicago Press: Chicago 1962) 133.
[93] *Ibid* 134.
[94] Jeswald Salacuse, Corporate Governance in the New Century (2004) 25 (3) Company Lawyer 69, 77.
[95] James Wallace, Value Maximisation and Stakeholder Theory: Compatible or Not? (2003)15 (3) Journal of Applied Corporate Finance I20, 121.

A similar position is found under General Principle 3 of the Takeover Code 2016 which requires directors to take into consideration the interests of non-shareholding stakeholders when recommending a bid to shareholders. Rule 21 of the Takeover Code 2016 does not permit shareholders to frustrate a takeover unless the shareholders accept or have had a chance to determine the merits of a takeover bid. This automatically makes shareholders the decision makers in the event of a takeover.

This is supported by a study on corporate governance practices in the UK which found very few similarities between shareholders' interests and those of other stakeholders.[96] Based on these findings, the researcher argued that shareholders are mainly interested in short-term wealth maximisation, which is markedly different from employees who want long-term job security and a good salary. The researchers concluded that only the company has similar objectives as every stakeholder, thus directors' duties should be owed to all stakeholders rather than giving primacy to shareholders.

Theoretically, the argument that a company has many objectives and directors' duties should be owed to all the company stakeholders has been advanced under Blair and Stout's team production theory.[97] They argued that the modern public company is made up of many stakeholders who have brought their resources together in order to form a team known as a company. This model suggests that a public company is nothing more than a nexus of firm specific investments made by many stakeholders. These stakeholders voluntarily give up control over the investments or resources to the board in the hope of sharing in the profits from the team production.

Furthermore, the ultimate decision making body within the company, the board is not subject to the direct control or supervision by any stakeholder including shareholders. Although it is shareholders who elect directors, they cannot tell them what to do. Company directors are not agents in a strict legal sense because agency law requires the principal to control the agent yet control is limited both in policy and practice.

Summary

The twentieth century witnessed ground-breaking works challenging, engaging and holding companies accountable to responsible capitalism. In the latter half of the century, these works supported the development

---

[96] Michael Mumford, Strategic Directions for Corporate Governance (2000) Lancaster University Management School Working Paper 024, 6.
[97] Margaret Blair and Lynn Stout, A team production theory of corporate law, (1999) 85 (2) Virginia Law Review 247, 326.

of a role for companies in society that challenged the traditional capitalist model in which the company and society exist as distinct and separate constructs. This accompanied the emergence of a theory of the modern corporation, ESV, that recognised accountability and responsibility to society beyond profit-making.

It has also shown that while companies in the past centuries took on a more long-term vision, twenty-first century shareholders and company managers are doing the opposite. A focus on profit maximisation over and above other interests has promoted short-termism; a factor blamed for the declining levels of investment in the UK and the failure of companies such Cadbury to fend off unwanted takeovers.

As a solution, greater consideration of other stakeholders' interests and legal safeguards to that effect are necessary. This is the fundamental basis of this book. However, drastic reforms such as giving primacy to all stakeholders are not recommended because they override capitalism and interfere with property rights.[98] Overall, a modern capitalist economy needs socially responsible companies more than it did in the forgone centuries and if not voluntarily achieved then regulatory intervention may be necessary.

---

[98] See chapter 6.2 proposal on the disenfranchisement of short-term shareholders' voting rights.

CHAPTER 4: CASE STUDIES ON TAKEOVERS

Introduction

Following the takeover of Cadbury Plc in 2010, there was public outcry at the loss of an 186 year old British company to an American foods company Kraft Inc.[99] The takeover was accompanied by increased academic attention over UK takeover rules and questions were raised on whether it has become easy to takeover UK companies.[100] The board neutrality rule came under increased academic criticism for handing substantial decision making powers to shareholders while disenfranchising directors from their company management responsibilities.[101]

However, no empirical studies were carried out to determine whether shareholder primacy was the main reason behind the increased takeover of UK companies. Existing research evidence also showed a strong relationship between takeovers and target company shareholders' gains.[102] Thus, a study into shareholders earning would help to determine whether takeovers are a source of premium for shareholders. It will also test existing evidence which shows that the acquiring company's shareholders experience loss of value post-takeover.[103]

Furthermore, following takeover of Cadbury, employee unions expressed concern over employee jobs,[104] but again no empirical research was carried out to determine whether the concerns had actually materialised. Thus, a study into the takeover of Cadbury Plc would help to determine whether concerns over employee jobs were justified but also the actions of short-term shareholders during the offer period.

The research evidence in Chapter 2.5 showed that the impact on employee jobs differs from that of senior managers.[105] Employees are those

---

[99]   The Telegraph, Kraft agrees to buy Cadbury for 11.9bn (19/01/2010).
[100]   Carsten Gerner-Beuerle, David Kershaw *and* Matteols Solinas, The Board Neutrality Rule Trivial? Amnesia about Corporate Law in European Takeover Regulation (2011) 22 (5) European Business Law Review 559, 564; Rhys Pippard, A Takeover Too Far Can the UK prohibition on board defensive action be justified any longer? (2011) SSRN Working Paper, 4.
[101]   David Kershaw, The Illusion of Importance: Reconsidering the UK's Takeover Defence Prohibition" (2007), 56 (2) International and Comparative Law Quarterly, 267, 280.
[102]   Marc Goergen and Luc Renneboog, Shareholder Wealth Effects of European Domestic and Cross-Border Takeover Bids (2004) 10 (1) European Financial Management 1, 10-13.
[103]   Tim Koller, Marc Goedhart and David Wessels, *Valuation, Measuring and managing the value of companies* (6th edn, Wiley John & Sons: New Jersey, 2015) 565-592.
[104]   Select Committee on Transport, Fourth Report: The takeover of BAA. Available at (http://www.publications.parliament.uk/pa/cm200708/cmselect/cmtran/119/11902.htm) Accessed 19/04/2016.
[105]   See Frank Lichtenberg and Donald Siegel, The Effect of Takeovers on the Employment

involved in the manufacturing and production plants whereas senior managers sit on the board of directors or are in charge of business units such as logistics and marketing. Thus, this study separates employees from senior managers and studies the impact on their interests separately.

Given that suppliers have an implicit contract, just like employees, which can be renegotiated or subject to non-renewal following a takeover, they also feature in this study. The research evidence remains largely inconclusive on whether takeovers have an adverse impact on the interests of suppliers. Empirical studies have found a positive relationship between the turnover of senior management and termination of supplier contracts, but there is no direct evidence linking takeovers with destruction of supplier contracts.[106] Thus, this chapter also explores the impact of the Cadbury takeover on supplier contracts.

The purpose of this chapter is to test the existing research evidence in Chapter 2.5. The chapter reviewed existing literature on takeovers and their impact on the target company's stakeholders. There was mixed evidence on the impact of takeovers on employees, suppliers and senior management post-takeover. Furthermore, the research evidence was mainly based on American takeover cases and was carried out using takeover samples in the twentieth century. This left a gap in research on twenty-first century takeover cases of UK companies. Thus, the evidence gathered under this chapter aims to fill this gap.

Two takeover cases are relied on for this study. First, the takeover of Cadbury by Kraft in 2010 will be examined to determine the impact the takeover had on the interests of employees, suppliers and senior management. Second, the takeover of Corus Steel by Tata Steel in 2007 features in this study,

There are several reasons for selecting Cadbury and Corus.

First, both Corus and Cadbury were taken over by foreign companies. Cadbury Plc was taken over by Kraft, an American foods company and Corus was taken over by an Indian steel maker, Tata Steel. Furthermore, both Corus and Cadbury were acquired during the first decade of this century. Thus, the findings made from both cases contribute to research

---

and Wages of Central Office and Other Personnel (1989) 33 Journal of Law and Economics 383, 388; Sanjai Bhagat, Andrei Shleifer and Robert Vishny, Hostile Takeovers in the 1980s: The Return to Corporate Specialization, in Neil Baily, Peter C. Reiss and Clifford Winston, *Brookings Papers on Economic Activity: Microeconomics* (Washington, DC: Brookings Institution, 1990) 1-7.
[106] Vincent J Intintoli, Mathew Serfling and Sarah Shaikh, The Negative Spillover Effects of CEO Turnovers: Evidence from Firm-Supplier Relations (2012), SSRN Working Paper Series, 17-20.

literature because existing research is based on twentieth century takeover cases.

Second, in both takeover cases, employee unions expressed concern over employee jobs. They feared that the foreign acquirers would close down manufacturing plants and move them abroad in order to reduce costs. Both Corus and Cadbury employed thousands of people in the UK prior to the takeovers. Thus, by studying both companies, the aim is to see whether the concerns over job losses materialised. This will contribute to existing research which suggests that takeovers have a negative impact on employee jobs, senior management turnover and supplier contracts.[107]

Third, both companies were chosen because of the large price paid to acquire them. Tata Steel paid £6.2bn to acquire Corus making it the eight largest takeover of a UK company between 2000- 2012 (see Chapter 1.3, Table 4). Similarly, Kraft paid £11.9bn to acquire Cadbury, making it the second largest takeover within that period. The aim is to see whether the takeovers created value for the acquirers given the high price they had to pay to acquire the companies. The high price also makes Corus and Cadbury good cases for studying the behaviours of shareholders during the takeover process to determine their motivations for accepting the takeover offer.

This chapter is divided into two parts. The first part looks at the takeover of Cadbury Plc by a US foods company Kraft Inc in 2010. The second part looks at the takeover of British steel maker Corus Plc by a Indian company Tata Steel in 2007. The aim is to show how the takeovers impacted on the interests of employees, suppliers and senior management and to understand the motivations and actions of shareholders during the offer period.

Case study 1: The takeover of Cadbury Plc

Company background

John Cadbury opened a shop in Birmingham, England selling hot chocolate, tea and coffee as an alternative to alcohol in 1824.[108] Three decades later, he established Bourneville plant in Birmingham as Cadbury's first production plant. Throughout its history, the company was committed to worker participation and trade union recognition. As a result, an organisational

---

[107] On job losses following a takeover, see Martin Conyon, Sourafel Girma, Steve Thompson and Peter Wright, The impact of mergers and acquisitions on company employment in the United Kingdom, (2002) 46 (1) European Economic Review 31, 33; see Chapter 2.5.1.
[108] Deborah Cadbury, Chocolate Wars: from Cadbury to Kraft—200 Years of sweet success and bitter rivalry (London: Harper Press, 2010) 3-6.

culture of labour management consultation was built up. This acted as a benchmark on which to judge changes to work organisation, industrial relations and company finances. Thus, Cadbury was built on values of employee commitment.

Throughout the twentieth century, the company grew immensely, mainly through mergers with confectioners J.S. Fry & Sons in 1919 and Schweppes in 1969. Despite their public listing in 1962, Cadbury continued its culture of worker participation and support to employees. At the turn of the twenty first century, Cadbury had established itself as one of the leading confectionery companies in the world. In 2009, Cadbury was the second largest confectionery company in the world behind Mars-Wrigley. Cadbury had strong growth in emerging markets (Latin America and India) which accounted to 40 per cent of all its revenue. The company employed over 45,000 people in 60 countries with around 1,500 people in the UK.

The British confectionery company became a target of an American foods company Kraft in 2009. Kraft was heavily dependent on the American and European markets and wanted to increase their global geographical reach.[109] Thus, the acquisition of Cadbury was seen as an opportunity for Kraft to take up a leading position in the global confectionery market (with 14.9 per cent global market share ahead of Mars Wrigley with 14.5 per cent) and expand their geographic coverage since Cadbury was well established and performing well in developing countries.

The battle to acquire Cadbury

On September 7, 2009, Kraft announced its intention to purchase the entire issued share capital of Cadbury, the second largest confectionery company in the world. The offer was 745 pence per share in cash and stock, totalling £10.2bn. The offer price represented a premium of 31 per cent on the Cadbury's share price of a couple of days earlier.

Cadbury's board actively resisted the takeover. The Chairman of Cadbury, Roger Carr, branded the offer as unattractive and one which "fundamentally undervalued the company", and urged shareholders not to let Kraft 'steal (their) company."[110] The Cadbury board advised shareholders to reject the offer because the company would be "absorbed into Kraft's low growth conglomerate business model, an unappealing prospect that

---

[109] Dominic Cadbury, The Kraft Takeover of Cadbury. Public Lecture, Birmingham Business School, (The University of Birmingham, UK. November 18, 2010).
[110] Cadbury Plc Takeover defence document No. 2. Available at:

(http://www.sec.gov/Archives/edgar/data/744473/000095012310001987/u08163 exv99wxayx13y.htm) Accessed 17/08/2016.

sharply contrasts with the Cadbury strategy of a pure play confectionery company".[111] In a letter to the Kraft's Chairman Irene Rosenfeld, Roger Carr emphasised that "the delivery of value to our shareholders remains at the top of our agenda".[112] Thus, protecting shareholders' interests was top of the board's priorities.

However, when the first offer from Kraft was announced in November 2009, it was worth only 717 pence per share due to movements in Kraft's share price (see Figure 3). On December 7, 2009, when the offer was posted to Cadbury shareholders, it was worth 713 pence per share. But Cadbury was trading above the value of Kraft's first bid and their share price continued to rise as high as 819.5 pence per share. Thus, as illustrated by Figure 3, increased buying of Cadbury shares pushed the price of Cadbury shares above Kraft's offer price.

Figure 3: Cadbury share price movement after the first bid

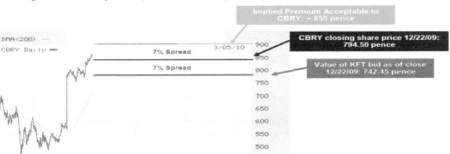

A number of factors contributed to the drop in Kraft's share value; mainly negative response to the anticipated impact of the bid on Kraft's stock valuation. Kraft trading down was also caused by arbitrageurs who were heavily buying Cadbury shares in anticipation of a raised Kraft bid while shorting or buying Kraft's shares. Thus, in case the deal was terminated, the arbitrageurs expected Kraft shares to react in an opposite fashion thus enabling them to marginally profit or reduce their losses from the rising Kraft share price.

In the second defence document, the Cadbury board recommended that shareholders reject the offer and emphasised that maximising shareholder value was best achieved through "the strong continuing performance of

---

[111] Financial Times, Case study: Kraft's takeover of Cadbury, 9 January 2012.
[112] Press Release 12 September 2009. Available at: (http://www.cadburyinvestors.com/cadbury_ir/press_releases/2009press/2009-09-12/) Accessed 18/08/2016; The Telegraph, Cadbury chairman Roger Carr writes to Kraft Food chief Irene Rosenfeld: the letter in full, 14 September 2009.

an independent Cadbury."[113] As a result, the Cadbury board put together a strong advisory team to fend off the takeover. However, this came at high cost, with the company paying roughly £2m a day in advising fees.[114] In addition, millions were paid to accountants and bankers in order to complete the takeover deal. Clearly, the longer the battle went on, the more financial value Cadbury was losing. Given that the board was focused solely on getting a higher premium, they did not put in place any takeover defences.

On January 5, 2010, eleven days before Kraft's final bid for Cadbury, one of Kraft's largest shareholders Warren Buffet voted no on a proposal to issue £370m shares to facilitate the acquisition of Cadbury.[115] Warren Buffet was worried about the dilution of Kraft's shares. Instead, the Kraft board sold their pizza business to Nestle, causing Kraft's share price to rise above 100 per cent (see Figure 4).[116] The proceeds from the sale were used to increase the cash portion in the offer for Cadbury. As a result, the board was able to bypass the need for shareholder approval to issue new shares and by selling to Nestle, they took out a potential bidder for Cadbury.

Figure 4: Major events and share price movement during the takeover negotiation period

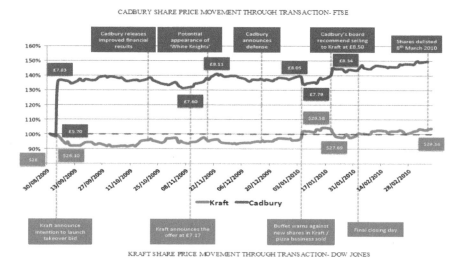

[113]   Cadbury Plc, Further reasons to reject Kraft's offer, (12 January 2010).
[114]   Zoe Wood and Jill Treanor, 2m a day cost of Cadbury deal- plus 12m for bosses, The Guardian (19 January 2010).
[115]   Justin Baer, Buffet cautions against share issue, The Financial Times (January 6, 2010).
[116]   Jonathan Birchall and Justin Baer, Buffet wades into battle for Cadbury, Financial Times (January 6 2010).

On January 19, 2010, after further discussions between the Cadbury board and Kraft, an agreement was reached.[117] The Cadbury board agreed to recommend the revised offer representing 840 pence per share plus a 10 pence special dividend. The total payout for each shareholder was 850 pence, valuing Cadbury at £11.9bn. The revised offer represented a 50 per cent or £4bn premium on the value of Cadbury before the initial offer and a 10 per cent improvement from the first offer.

The agreement was approved by the Cadbury board based on the strength of Kraft's offer.

Figure 5: Cash to equity ratio in Kraft's offer

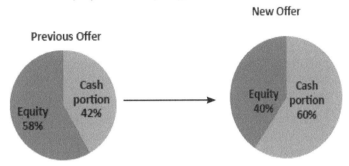

As illustrated by Figure 5, Kraft used 60 per cent cash into the acquisition and the remaining 40 per cent was offered to shareholders in form of Kraft's stock. The willingness to put so much cash into the acquisition helped to overcome the board's hostility. The equity element was also appealing to shareholders because attempts to acquire Cadbury had driven down Kraft's share price (see Figure 4) and Kraft paid an attractive 4.25 per cent yearly dividend.

Cadbury shares rose by 3.5 per cent when the 840 pence per share deal was announced. However, the board's recommendation was not binding; Cadbury still needed 50 percent of shareholders votes for the deal to succeed. Cadbury shareholders had until February 2, 2010 to approve the sale. To persuade Cadbury shareholders to agree to the offer, Rosenfeld publicly reaffirmed Kraft's commitment to "preserve Cadbury's proud heritage and traditions" and retain a strong presence in the UK.[118]

---

[117] Based on the takeover timetable which is administered by the Takeover Panel, Kraft had until January 19 2010 to revise its first offer
[118] Conference Call Transcript, Kraft Foods To Host Investor Conference Call To Discuss Recommended Final Offer for Cadbury Plc, January 19, 2010.

The takeover timetable gave rival bidders until 23 January 2010 to table competing offers. During that period, Kraft was allowed to change the terms of the proposal if it so wished. Much expected rival bids by Nestle or the American confectionery maker Hershey did not materialise.[119] However, the threat of a rival offer, even with no competing bids, pressured Kraft to increase its offer.

After the board had recommended the offer to shareholders, the Chairman of Cadbury Roger Carr softened his language: "We believe the offer represents good value for Cadbury shareholders and are pleased with the commitment that Kraft Foods has made to our heritage, values and people throughout the world. We will now work with the Kraft Foods management to ensure the continued success and growth of the business for the benefit of our customers, consumers and employees."[120] Thus, within a period of three months, the Chairman had moved from criticising Kraft to praising it. Such a radical turnaround and acceptance of defeat was influenced by the share ownership in Cadbury at the time of the final bid (see 4.1.3).

Although the Cadbury board's recommendation was not binding, it was unlikely that the company would resist a takeover when the board had surrendered. Two weeks later, 71.7 per cent of Cadbury shareholders accepted Kraft's final offer. The takeover created a company with global sales of £30bn spurning 160 countries.

However, a major Kraft shareholder, Warren Buffett raised concern over the high purchase price and warned of the risks to the company for overpaying for Cadbury.[121] He believed that it was a very bad deal for Kraft's shareholders but a great deal for Cadbury's shareholders. After the takeover, Kraft was left with debts in the region of £16bn. Fearing for the long-term health of the Kraft, on completion of the deal, Warren Buffet sold a £31.5m stake in Kraft.[122]

The role of arbitrageurs during the Cadbury takeover

Arbitrageurs are renowned for buying into companies to make a quick gain.[123] Thus, when a premium for Cadbury shares was tabled, it was unlikely that shareholders would resist the offer. The manner in which

---

[119] John Jannarone and Mathew Curtin, Hershey's Chocolate Dreams. Wall Street Journal (January 16 2010).
[120] Reported in Kraft's Press Release on January 19, 2010 and in the Revised Offer Document.
[121] Washington Post, Warren Buffet Opposed Kraft-Cadbury Merger, (January 6, 2010).
[122] George Farell, Buffet reduces Kraft holding, The Financial Times (May 19, 2010).
[123] Marcel Kahan and Edward Rock, Hedge Funds in Corporate Governance and Corporate Control, (2007)155 (5) University of Pennsylvania Law Review 1021, 1083.

share ownership changed during the bidding process raised doubts over the commitment of Cadbury's shareholders to the interests of stakeholders such as employees and suppliers. However, for the board, acting in the interest of shareholders meant recommending the offer.

In September 2009, UK based institutions owned 28 per cent of Cadbury's stock and American institutions owned 29 per cent. Roger Carr explained that American based shareholders were less worried about Cadbury falling into the hands of an American rival than their British counterparts. He explained that: "The seeds of destruction for this company lay in its [shareholder] register...If you've only got 28 per cent long domestic funds owning this company, then you know that in a bid the rest are likely to sell."[124]

The first bid sparked a 40 per cent rise in Cadbury share price.

Figure 6: Kraft's offers and level of premium

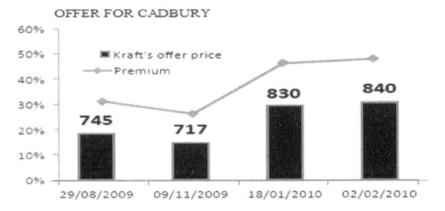

As illustrated under Figure 6, throughout the takeover process, Kraft was continuously improving the premium price in order to entice shareholders to accept their bid. Many Cadbury shareholders sought to take advantage of this premium price by selling their shares. A large proportion of these shares were bought by short-term investors, mainly arbitrageurs in anticipation of a deal. This left few long term traditional owners of Cadbury stock.

By December 2009, arbitrageurs were buying Cadbury shares at 800 pence (see Figure 3). The high probability of receiving more than invested

---

[124] Roger Carr, Cadbury: Hostile bids and takeovers (Saiid Business School, February 15, 2010).

and in a short period of time was the main reason for buying at such high levels. However, spreading the risk by buying Kraft shares was important because if the deal failed to materialise, Cadbury shares could drop to as low as 600 pence thus resulting in a 25 per cent loss.

At the time of the final Kraft bid, American ownership in Cadbury had decreased from 51 per cent to 28 per cent. UK shareholders knew the value of Cadbury and did not sell their shares. Thus, the fact that nearly half of the shareholders in Cadbury did not share Cadbury's British identity had a bearing on the outcome of the bid.

Figure 7: Share ownership in Cadbury during the takeover process

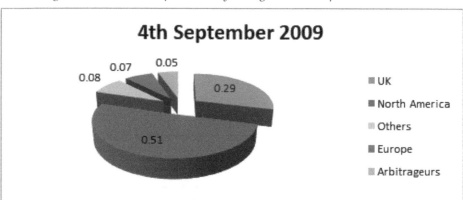

Just 136 days later

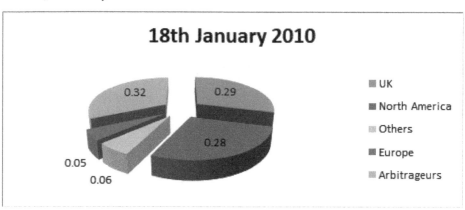

After the first failed bid, many American shareholders in Cadbury sold their shares to arbitrageurs who bought them in anticipation of a takeover deal.[125] As illustrated by Figure 7, from five per cent in September 2009, just 136 days later, arbitrageurs owned 32 per cent of Cadbury stock. When tabling its final bid in January 2010, Kraft knew that 32 per cent of the shareholders were willing to sell their shares even for a small profit margin. The only remaining hurdle was to convince another 18 per cent to sell in order to reach the 50 per cent victory threshold.

Furthermore, the Cadbury board was forced to accept the final takeover bid after Franklin Templeton, a US mutual fund that held a 7.6 per cent stake in Cadbury, declared that it would accept any offer above 830 pence per share. At the time of the second bid, Roger Carr explained that "Independence as an option had gone". Directors were unable to base their recommendations on any other criteria (such as commitment to protecting employee jobs) other than price because there was no competing bidder and the arbitrageurs were mainly interested in the premium price. Roger Carr explained that: "The cause was lost ... the decision then was to negotiate for what I and the board felt was the recommendable price."[126] Thus, the board ended up solely focusing on getting the price increased to 850 pence rather than the long-term interests of the company and its non-shareholding stakeholders.

However, not all Cadbury's shareholders were pleased with the focus on price. UK based institutional investors Standard Life indicated during the takeover negotiation period that Kraft would need to make an offer of 900 pence per share to get its support.[127] Similarly, Legal & General, Cadbury's second largest shareholder, said that it was disappointed that the board had recommended the 840 pence offer because it did not "fully reflect the long-term value of the company."[128] In the end, Franklin Templeton, a US Mutual fund that held a 7.6 per cent stake in Cadbury, walked away with an estimated profit of over £30m.

Public criticism of arbitrageurs following the takeover of Cadbury

The role of arbitrageurs in the Cadbury takeover received public criticism. The Business Secretary, Lord Mandelson complained that "...it is hard to ignore the fact that the fate of a company with a long history and many tens of thousands of employees was decided by people who had not owned the

---

[125] Jenny Wiggins and Lina Saigol, Hedge fund interest in Cadbury increases. Financial Times (November 10, 2009).
[126] Roger Carr, Cadbury: Hostile bids and takeovers (Saiid Business School, February 15, 2010).
[127] The Guardian, Reaction: Cadbury falls to leveraged bid, (January 19, 2010).
[128] Jill Treanor, Cadbury management criticised for caving in to Kraft takeover, The Guardian, (January 19, 2010).

company a few weeks earlier, and probably had no intention of owning it a few weeks later."[129] Similarly, the takeover regulatory body, the Takeover Panel, concluded in their response to a consultation on takeovers in October 2010 that "the outcome of offers, and particularly hostile offers, may be influenced unduly by the actions of so-called 'short-term' investors".[130]

Furthermore, the Deputy Secretary General of trade union Unite which represents the majority of Cadbury's employees, Jack Dromey, told the Business, Innovation and Skills Committee that: "it simply cannot be right that in the way the market works good companies can be subject to predatory bids that put at risk the real economy and the public interest with no regard for workers, local communities and suppliers."[131] Thus, concerns were raised by politicians and employee representatives over the role of short-term investors during takeovers and the risk posed to the interests of company post-takeover.

Valuation of Cadbury

In order to finance the takeover deal, £7bn (58 per cent of the purchase price) was secured by a loan from the Royal Bank of Scotland (RBS) private equity. In effect, Cadbury became a Kraft/RBS portfolio firm with Cadbury's assets becoming collateralised on RBS' accounts. Given that Cadbury was already a successful company before the takeover, it was unclear whether Kraft could make operational improvements in Cadbury in order to raise cash flow and therefore service its huge debts.

Value creation depends on added value of the combined entity and the time it takes to deliver the value.

Formula for measuring value creation

$$V(KFT+CBRY) > V(KFT) + V(CBRY) + P + E + IC$$

Value (Kraft + Cadbury) > Value (Kraft) + Value (Cadbury) + Premium + Expenses + Integration Cost

---

[129] Peter Mandelson, Secretary of State for Business, Innovation and Skills, Speech at the Trade and Industry dinner, Guildhall, the Mansion House, London (March 1, 2010).

[130] The Takeover Panel, Response Statement to the Consultation Paper on Review of Certain Aspects of the Regulation of Takeover Bids (October 2010).

[131] House of Commons, Business, Innovation and Skills Committee, Mergers Acquisitions and Takeovers: the Takeover of Cadbury by Kraft, Ninth Report of Session 2009-2010 (HC 234) 22.

Figure 8: Value creation measurements for Cadbury/Kraft

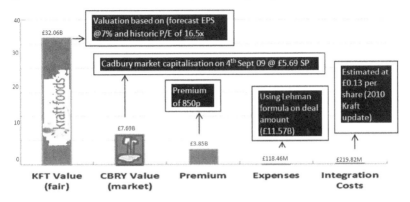

Total valuation £43,98bn.

The valuation under Figure 8 shows that Kraft/Cadbury combined value would need to exceed £43.98bn for the deal to be value creating. However, there is no specified timeline over which Kraft would assess value added.

Table 6: Kraft/Cadbury value measurements based on offer price

Valuation	850p (final offer)		830p	745p (1st offer)
Kraft Value	£31,75bn		£31,75bn	£31,75bn
Cadbury Value	£7,33bn		£7,33bn	£7,33bn
Premium	£3,66bn		£3,05bn	£1,83bn
Expenses	£118,46m		£116,01m	£104,41m
Integration costs	£219,82m		£219,82m	£219,82m
Value	£43,96bn		£43,30bn	£42,13bn
Value Kraft/Cadbury	£40,91bn	£43,35bn	£43,35bn	£43,35bn
Difference	-£2,44	-£79,49	£209	£1,222
	(Based on Kraft's market cap 22 months (9/12/2011) after acquisition (SP £22,44)	(Based on Kraft's market cap 12 months (9/12/2011) Consensus analyst estimate (SP £24)	Forward looking Kraft market Cap of CBRY offer was 830p	Forward looking Kraft market Cap of CBRY offer was 745p

Based on the market capitalisation of Kraft 22 months after the takeover, the deal did not create value rather it resulted in a £2,44bn loss in value. Furthermore, the forward looking 12 month estimates show that the deal was marginally value destroying. Based on the measurements, the right price for Cadbury should have been 830p and below. The price would have been value creating for Kraft and likely to be realised within a 12 month period.

In August 2011, almost two year after the acquisition, Kraft started restructuring and split into two companies in 2012. One is a grocery business (55 per cent of the company), which focuses on the North American food market and the other is a global snacks business named Mondelez (45 per cent of the company). Cadbury is one of the businesses placed under Mondelez. By splitting into two, Kraft was able to eliminate its conglomerate nature. However, the split has made the assessment of Cadbury/Kraft value more difficult.

The impact on Cadbury's stakeholders post-takeover

Cadbury stakeholders had a number of legitimate concerns but they could only be addressed once the deal had been completed.

EMPLOYEES

Before the takeover, Cadbury employed 5700 people at eight manufacturing plants across Britain and Ireland. The majority of its employees were based at the Bourneville plant in Birmingham, the Somerdale plant at Keysham in Bristol and the Marlbrook centre at Leominster in Herefordshire. On October 3, 2007, Cadbury announced a strategic plan to close Somerdale plant, with production being transferred to Bourneville plant and a new purposely-built plant in Poland.[132] This announcement put 400 manufacturing jobs on the line.

Two years later, on September 7, 2009, Kraft announced its plans to take over Cadbury. The announcement concluded with an explanation of Kraft's rationale for acquiring Cadbury. The Chairman and CEO of Kraft Irene Rosenfeld stated that Kraft would be able to continue operations at Somerdale plant and thus preserve the 400 manufacturing jobs. The statement read as follows: "Our current plans contemplate that the UK would be a net beneficiary in terms of jobs. For example, we believe we would be in a position to continue to operate the Somerdale facility, which is currently planned to be closed, and to invest in Bournville plant, thereby preserving the UK manufacturing jobs."[133]

---

[132] BBC News, Cadbury factories shed 700 jobs, (3 October 2007).
[133] Kraft's Takeover Proposal document, 7 September 2009; This statement was repeated

Cadbury's trade union warned shareholders that if the offer is accepted up to 30,000 jobs mainly due to the debt Kraft would be taking on. The National Officer of Unite, the representative body of Cadbury's workforce, said that: "the sad truth is that when they have to pay down that debt, the soft option is jobs and conditions".[134] In response, Kraft stated that it expected to make "meaningful cost savings" after the takeover.[135]

The offer was declared unconditional on February 2, 2010. A week later, on February 9, Kraft announced that following talks with the Cadbury board, it had come to a conclusion that plans in regards to Somerdale plant were too advanced to reverse.[136] Contrary to the assurances given before the takeover, Kraft announced that it was withdrawing plans to keep the Somerdale plant open and thus wanted to approve the decision initially made by Cadbury management to close down the plant. In a clear breach of trust, Somerdale plant was closed in January 2011 with 600 workers losing their jobs.

Kraft's defence for closing down Somerdale plant

Kraft's Chairman Irene Rosenfield responded to public criticism over the closure of Somerdale pant by stating that they were not aware of the condition, machinery and internal structure of the plant before making the statement.[137] Cadbury had already spent £100m on new manufacturing facilities in Poland, thus scraping the decision to move operations from Somerdale would have been very costly for Kraft.[138] Furthermore, on each occasion the statement about Somerdale was made, it was based on the information already available in the public domain, except on the 18 and 19 of January when senior management sat down to discuss the fate of Somerdale plant.

Kraft explained that as part of its strategic plans for purchasing Cadbury, it needed additional manufacturing capacity particularly in the growing Continental European market. Upon the successful completion of the purchase, Kraft believed it would be able to use Cadbury's new facilities in Poland to serve the need for additional manufacturing

---

on November 9, 2009 in Kraft's firm offer announcement and cited in its offer documents on December 4, 2009. On January 19, 2010, the statement was incorporated by reference in the revised offer document. Notably, this was the date the Cadbury board recommended the final offer to its shareholders.

[134] Nick Waton, Cadbury, Kraft and the politics of making chocolate. BBC News, (19 January, 2010).

[135] BBC News, Cadbury agrees Kraft takeover bid, (19 January 2010).

[136] BBC News, Cadbury's Bristol plant to close, (9 February 2010).

[137] BBC News, Dismay at Cadbury's closure plans, (10 February 2010).

[138] Panel Statement, Kraft Foods Inc. Offer for Cadbury Plc 2010/14.

capacity in Continental Europe and continue to use Somerdale's facilities to manufacture products to serve the UK market. However, Kraft made all these assumptions without full detail of Cadbury's strategic plans for Somerdale plant.

Thus, due to a lack of information over the phased closure of Somerdale plant, Kraft was unable to make a firm commitment to its statement. When Cadbury sat down with Cadbury's management after the takeover, it became clear that the plans to transfer production to Poland were more advanced than previously believed. Thus, Kraft's decision to announce the closure of Somerdale on February 9, 2010 was largely down to the new information gained during the meeting with Cadbury senior management.

Breach of Rule 19.1 of the Takeover Code 2016

Rule 19.1 of the Takeover Code 2016 requires that: "Each document, announcement or other information published, or statement made, during the course of an offer must be prepared with the highest standards of care and accuracy. The language used must clearly and concisely reflect the position being described and the information given must be adequately and fairly presented. These requirements apply whether the document, announcement or other information is published, or the statement is made, by the party concerned or by an adviser on its behalf." The rule is fundamental to the orderly functioning of the takeover process by ensuring that statements made regarding the strategic plans of the target company and any repercussions on its stakeholders are properly informed before being published.[139]

Subject to Rule 19.1, the statement of belief made by Kraft must pass both a subjective and objective test. It requires the author of the statement to honestly and genuinely believe the statement but also to have a reasonable basis for having that belief. Given the significance of the statement to Cadbury and Kraft employees and the fact it was repeatedly raised during the bidding process, a high standard of care was required before making the statement.

Thus, although Kraft held an honest and genuine belief that it could keep the plant open and based it on the publicly available information on the phased closure of Somerdale plant along with their own expert knowledge on plant closures, it fell below the high standard required under Rule 19.1. Kraft did not have a reasonable basis for believing that it

---

[139] And taken on board by the offeree company's board in order to fulfil its obligations under Rule 25.1(b) and General Principle 2

could continue to operate Somerdale plant thus the statement was in clear breach of Rule 19.1.[140]

During the offer period, limited information was provided on the status of Cadbury's 45,000 global workforce. The trade unions were concerned by the takeover because in the past ten years, Kraft had closed thirty factories resulting in a loss of over 60,000 jobs. More notably, Kraft had previously taken over a UK chocolate manufacturer Terry's and subsequently closed its plants in the UK and moved production to Poland.[141] The trade unions also pointed out that Kraft was more likely to cut jobs in the UK than in US. Despite all the concerns, the Cadbury board sought no guarantees from Kraft over the promises to employees. Clearly the board was only occupied with its legal duty to serve shareholders' interests. Thus, a lack of a directors' duty to protect employees' interests during takeovers played a part in the subsequent closure of Somerdale plant.

Duty on financial advisers

Lazard & Co. Ltd were the leading financial advisers to Kraft during the takeover. Paragraph 3(f) of the Introduction to the Takeover Code 2016 puts a responsibility on financial advisers to ensure that their client are aware of and comply with their responsibilities under the Takeover Code. This responsibility is reaffirmed by Note 1 on Rule 19.1 which requires financial advisers to guide their clients on any information published during the offer process. Thus, the financial advisers must ensure that statements adhere to the highest standard of care and accuracy.

Lazard explained that statements relating to Somerdale plant were discussed with Kraft and they explained to Kraft that a reasonable basis as well as honesty and care would be required for holding those beliefs about Somerdale plant.[142] To assist Kraft, Lazard conducted its own research from publicly available information. Lazard also took into consideration Kraft's own expert knowledge on phased closures of factories in the industry. However, in line with their duty under Paragraph 3(f), Lazard should have made further inquiries into the basis of Kraft's beliefs in relation to Somerdale. Failure to discharge their duty under Paragraph 3(f) contributed to the breach responsibilities under Note 1 on Rule 19.1.

---

[140] Similarly, employee representatives can only fulfil their obligations under Rule 30.2(b) to give opinions on the effect of the takeover on employment if the high standard is adhered to.

[141] BBC News, The end of era as Terry's site closes (September 30, 2005).

[142] Takeover Panel, Kraft Inc offer for Cadbury Plc (10 May 2010).

The UK Government's inquiry into Somerdale plant closure

After the takeover, in March 2010, the UK government commissioned an inquiry into the circumstances surrounding the takeover of Cadbury.[143] The inquiry looked into the decision to close Somerdale plant and Kraft's plans in relation to employment, social responsibility among others. During the inquiry, Kraft made a commitment that there would be no compulsory redundancies as well as closure of manufacturing facilities for at least two years.

Nearly two years after the takeover, Kraft announced that it was making a £50m investment in the UK with £14m going to Bournville plant. However, they also announced that 200 jobs would be cut through redeployment and voluntary redundancies at Bournville, Chirk and Marlbrook manufacturing plants. Thus, although the commitment not to cut jobs for two years from March 2010 until March 2012 was honoured, job losses were made after the two years. Clearly, the two year consultation period for redundancy was too short to protect employee jobs.

THE CADBURY BOARD OF DIRECTORS

The Cadbury board of directors played an important role in facilitating the takeover. However, the five months battle fought between the two boards brought tensions during the integration process after the takeover. This tension was noted by the head of Kraft's global chocolate business, Tim Cofer, who led the first phase of integration. He observed that "in the early days there was a mindset shift that needed to occur. Because just a few weeks earlier, they were in a defence mode and then we were all together."[144] Unsurprisingly, after the takeover, a number of senior managers left Cadbury.

Hours after Kraft announced the unconditional takeover of Cadbury, three of the most senior directors at Cadbury announced that they will be leaving the company.[145] First, Roger Carr who was made Non-Executive Chairman in July 2008, resigned after the takeover deal was announced. He played an important role in persuading Kraft to increase the offer to 840 pence per share with the inclusion of a special 10 pence dividend. Based on Cadbury's 2008 annual report, he earned £259,000 as Chairman of Cadbury which entitled him to thousands of pounds as a payoff on leaving the company. He also held £364,000 worth of shares in Cadbury which meant

---

[143] House of Commons, Business, Innovation and Skills Committee, Mergers Acquisitions and Takeovers: the Takeover of Cadbury by Kraft, Ninth Report of Session 2009-2010.
[144] Jill Rapperport, A bitter Taste, Financial Times (May 23, 2011).
[145] BBC News, Cadbury top bosses to step down, (3 February 2010).

that he benefited from the takeover premium and the 10 pence special dividend.

Second, Andrew Bonfield, the finance director who joined Cadbury in February 2009 also announced his departure immediately after the takeover. In addition to the premium he earned on his shareholding in Cadbury, he was also entitled to thousands of pounds in compensation. Third, Todd Stitzer, Cadbury chief executive left with a massive pay-off of £17m having been at the company for 27 years. He also owned a £5.5m stake in Cadbury and was entitled to a year's salary of £985,000 and a bonus of nearly £2m along with a right to convert shares worth £8.6m into cash. This was more value leaving the company at a time when employee jobs were in the balance.

In subsequent months, there were a number of high profile departures from Cadbury senior management including Tony Fernandez who was head of Cadbury's supply chain; Nick Canney who was the UK grocery sales director; Jim Chambers who was head of US snacks and confectionary; Timothy McLevish, chief financial officer; Alex Cole, corporate affairs director; Geoff Whyte, commercial director for Cadbury Africa and Middle East; Sanjay Purohi, head of Cadbury's Asian-Pacific region and Phil Rumbol, Cadbury's marketing executive all left the company.

Thus, the integration process resulted in a number of senior managers leaving the company. Since the integration began, 20 senior executives across functions such as finance, supply chain, legal and sales left the company. On the Executive Committee, only seven of the original 16 members of Cadbury remain.

RENEGOTIATION OF SUPPLIER CONTRACT

The takeover also impacted on the interests of Cadbury's suppliers. The breach of trust experienced by suppliers can be illustrated by the case of Burton's biscuits.[146] After a period of poor financial performance, in 2007, Burton received £4m financial support from the UK government to avoid going into insolvency. Burton entered a flexible collective bargaining agreement to provide flexible work and was promised guaranteed Cadbury work until May 2012.

However, when Kraft acquired Cadbury, that promise was broken when Kraft cancelled their agreement. In addition, Burton fell into the hands of private equity owners who had invested heavily in the poorly

---

[146] The Guardian, How do you Save a Biscuit Factory When it is Not Even Clear Who Owns It? (March 22, 2011).

performing biscuit maker in hope of a takeover deal. The private equity owners' extracted value from Burton's plant in the region of £13m through cost reductions. This value returned to the investors and also went towards the massively improved director remuneration packages. Due to Cadbury's breach of trust over the promise to provide work and private equity owners' decision to extract value from the company, in January 2011, Burton announced the closure of its Merseyside plant leading to the loss of 300 jobs.

Cadbury's financial performance post-takeover

After the takeover of Cadbury, Kraft became the world's leading confectionery company. The amalgamation of both companies created a portfolio of 81 brands of chocolate and confectionary products. The CEO of Kraft, Irene Rosenfeld, responded to the acquisition by stating that: "With such a powerful array of household-name products, Kraft and Cadbury make for truly a transformational combination".[147]

However, in the last three months of 2010, largely due to the cost of integrating Cadbury into Kraft's business, both companies' performances were affected. Kraft's net profit decreased by 24 per cent to £330m and Cadbury 2.2 per cent rise in sales was behind the five per cent sales growth reported in 2009 when Cadbury was still an independent company.

In 2011, Kraft's original plans of improving its geographical distributions showed signs of improvement with developing markets such as India contributing to nearly 30 per cent of sales compared to ten per cent in 2001. However, Cadbury was still not meeting Kraft's growth objectives and failing to reduce its debts. Kraft's debt increased from £16.7bn in 2010 to £17.1bn in 2011.

Despite attempts by the Cadbury board to fend off the takeover bid by Kraft, in the end, the share register and the short-term interests of arbitrageurs provided to be the deciding factor, leaving the board no choice but to seek the highest possible price for Cadbury's shareholders. The takeover highlights three major governance issues; (i) how to limit the influence of arbitrageurs during takeovers; (ii) how to ensure adherence to Rule 19.1 on the standard of information; (iii) how to promote the long-term success of the company during takeovers when shareholders are the ultimate decision makers due to Rule 21 of the Takeover Code. Case study two (below) on the takeover of Corus Steel by Tata Steel in 2007 highlights similar governance issues.

---

[147] David Lieberman and Matt Krantz, Is Kraft's $19B Cadbury Buy a Sweet Deal? Buffett has Doubts, US Today (January 20, 2010).

Case study 2: Corus Group

Tata Steel, an Indian steel manufacturer acquired the Anglo-Dutch steel maker, Corus Group Ltd, on January 30, 2007 through a takeover. After the takeover, Corus changed its name to Tata Steel Europe and is now one of the companies under the Tata Group.

The takeover was India's largest ever foreign acquisition worth £6.2bn. The deal is significant to this study because it had a major impact on Corus' stakeholders in the UK and for the high level of debt used in the deal. It is also important to understand why Corus decided to sell off to a small scale steel producer from a developing country.

Company background

Corus was born out of a merger between the Dutch steel company Koninklijke and British Steel on October 6, 1999. However, in early 2000, due to internal disputes and poor financial trading, the company's workforce was reduced to 24,000 through cutbacks and redundancies. In 2003, Corus wanted to sell Koninklijke in order to reduce its mounting debts but could not reach an agreement with the Dutch Works Council. High debts threatened the company's future but a sudden rise in demand for steel in 2004 resulted in improved financial trading.

In 2005, Corus was Europe's second largest steel producer and the ninth largest steel producer in the world, with annual revenue of £9.2bn. Corus' global presence extended to 50 countries; however its main steelmaking operations were located in Netherlands and UK. Corus was the leading steel supplier to most countries in Europe in areas such as mechanical and electronic engineering, construction and automotive.

Before the takeover negotiations, Corus and Tata Steel were interested in entering a merger deal since both companies shared similar ambitions in terms of growth. In 2005, Tata steel, the 56th largest steel manufacturer in the world, expressed an interest in merging with a company in Europe in order to expand its global presence[148]. This was the same period Corus officially expressed an interest in cheaper steel production in Brazil, China and India.

Although Tata Steel was a very profitable company, it was very small size and expanding organically would have taken it at least ten years and with a lot of execution risks. Corus had a steel production capacity of 18 million tons per annum compared to Tata Steel's 6.8 million tons per

---

[148] Rajesh B Kumar, *Mega Mergers and Acquisitions: Case Studies from Key Industries* (Hampshire: Palgrave Macmillan, Basingstoke 2012) 207.

annum. Establishing a production facility the size of Corus would have cost over 50 per cent more than a takeover. Since European markets were already very competitive, it would have been hard for Tata Steel to quickly establish itself in the market. Thus merging with Corus was seen as a less risky and fast growth option.

Corus had an operating margin of 9.2 per cent in the third quarter ending September 2006 compared to 32 per cent by Tata Steel for their third quarter ending December 2006.[149] Thus, the low operating margin provided scope for improvement for the benefit of both companies' shareholders. It also meant that in the long-term, there was scope to restructure some of the high cost Corus plants in the UK.

The battle to acquire Corus

Speculation of an all cash offer for Corus by Tata Steel reached the media on September 26 2006. Securities markets trading activity intensified on October 17, 2006, with an offer of 455 pence per share eagerly anticipated. The offer represented an 11 per cent premium on the three month average share price of Corus. It was 25 per cent premium on the share price of Corus on September 25, 2006, the day before Corus made it public that it was engaged in talks with Tata Steel for a possible takeover.

Figure 9: Corus stock price moved upwards during the bidding process

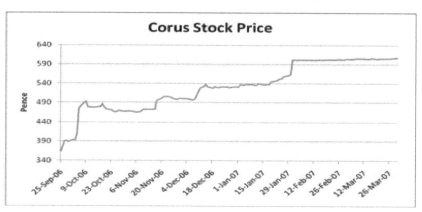

On October 17, 2006, Tata Steel announced an agreement to acquire Corus in a cash deal of 455 pence per share. Two days later, the Corus board accepted 455 pence per share offer which valued Corus at £4.3bn.

---

[149] Corus' Financial Accounts (Profit and Loss) 2006.

Tata Steel had the intention of completing the takeover in the financial year ending February 2007. This gave arbitrageurs an investment window of three months. However, as illustrated by Figure 9, since Corus had already announced on 25 September 2006 that talks of a takeover with Tata Steel were ongoing the market had already factored in the forecasted increases in share price. Consequently, on October 17, 2006 Corus shares traded around 480 pence. Thus, arbitrageurs were not in a profitable position to buy Corus shares since the bid price was lower than the stock market price of Corus shares.

However, there was a much anticipated bidding war between the Brazilian steel company Companhia Siderurgica Nacional (CSN) and Tata Steel. CSN was already a shareholder in Corus with a 3.6 per cent shareholding and had expressed an interest in a counter offer. A bidding war was likely to substantially increase Corus stock price thus placing arbitrageurs who had bought stock around 17 October in a profitable position.

As anticipated, the bidding war materialised and Corus stock price increased significantly. On November 17 2006, Brazilian company CSN approached Corus with a counter offer of 475 pence per share. The sign of a bidding war was much-welcomed by the arbitrageurs who raised the price of Corus shares to 495.5 pence, valuing it higher than the CSN bid. Tata Steel responded to CSN's bid with 500 pence per share offer which CSN outbid with 515 pence on December 11, 2006. However, the Corus board did not recommend CSN's offer to shareholders.

On December 19, 2006, the Takeover Panel announced that Tata Steel and CSN had until January 30, 2007 to come up with a revised offer unless an auction process would be triggered if an agreement is not reached by that date. Following a lack of agreement, on 31 January 2007, the auction process was triggered and conducted by the Takeover Panel in line with its powers under Rule 32.5 of the Takeover Code 2016.

After nine rounds of auctioning, on January 31, 2007, Tata Steel increased the offer price to 608 pence outbidding CSN's 603 pence per share. This was 5 pence more than the 603 pence tabled by the rival bidder CSN. It was also 34 per cent higher than Tata Steel's first offer. On the day the 608 pence per share in cash deal was announced, the stock prices closed at 607 pence and traded around that figure until the deal was completed (see Figure 9).

The following day after the auction, the Corus board recommended the 608 pence offer to shareholders. It received the approval of shareholders. The takeover was 100 per cent acquisition of all Corus stock. The total value of the takeover amounted to £6.2bn. It was an all-cash deal financed by debt and equity. However, if the takeover deal did not materialise due to a lack of shareholder approval, the stock price would have sunk to the September 2006 levels. The arbitrageurs stood to make a 67.03 per cent return (between the deal announcement on October 20, 2007 to its conclusion on January 31, 2007).[150]

As illustrated by Figure 10, from the day the deal was announced until its completion, Tata Steel stock lost 12 per cent while Corus stock gained 68 per cent.

Figure 10: Tata Steel/Corus share price reaction

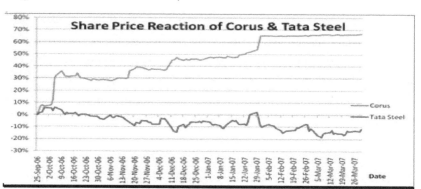

There were mixed responses to the deal. The Corus Chairman Jim Leng responded by stating that: "this combination with Tata, for Corus shareholders and employees alike, represents the right partner at the right time at the right price and on the right terms."[151] However, Denis MacShane MP for Rotherham called for more caution, especially in regards to employee jobs: "we would want to know what the deal means for our members' jobs in the manufacturing side of Corus as well as all the former workers whose pensions are also very much on our mind."[152]

Financing Corus' takeover

In September 2005, Dutch bank ABN Amro was commissioned by Tata Steel to structure a financial deal that would enable the successful acquisition of Corus. Within three months, the structure of the financing deal was internally agreed plus a further eight months of negotiations with Tata Steel before the first offer of 455 pence per share was made. The bank took

---

[150] An official declaration of the takeover was deemed effective on April 2, 2007 by the Court of Justice.

[151] Vishwanath S.R, *Cases in corporate finance* (Tata McGraw-Hill Education, 2009) 201.

[152] BBC News, Corus accepts £4.3bn Tata offer, 20 October 2006.

the view that Corus stock was undervalued and trading at a fraction of the final bid of 608 pence per share. Maarten Terlouw, ABN Amro's head of structural financial solutions observed that: "We knew there was a steel recovery coming, driven by demand from emerging markets, so we looked at Corus and felt the company was substantially undervalued."[153]

The financial structure of the deal was in the form of a leveraged buyout (LBO). Through an LBO, Tata Steel was able to limit its risk to the equity invested and increase its debt. The debt was to be repaid by a Special Purpose Vehicle (SPV) called Tata Steel UK through future cash flows. The subsidiary was set up to raise debt capital for the deal rather than having Tata Steel raising it by itself. Maarten Terlouw summed up the financial structure as follows: "We came up with a structure that was essentially taken from the venture capital industry, and we applied it to a corporate entity".[154]

Tata Steel financed £1.85bn of the purchase price from internal resources meaning that more than two-thirds of the purchase price came from loans from major banks. The final price paid represented a 49 per cent premium on the closing price of Corus on October 4, 2006 and a 68 per cent premium on the average closing share price over the 12 months period leading up to the takeover. Tata Steel's £4bn total debts were expected to generate 8 per cent annual interest rate amounting to £320m combined with Corus' existing £200m debt interest charges.

As illustrated by Figure 11, a day after the takeover was announced, the Bombay Stock Exchange reacted to the increase in debt with a 10.7 per cent drop in Tata Steel's share price.

Figure 11: Tata Steel's stock price moved downwards

[153] Commodity Risk, Tata Steel's acquisition of Corus brokered by ABN Amro, Available at http://www.incisivemedia.com/energyrisk/Commodity_Risk/PDFs/Summer2008/DoY_ABNAmro.pdf (Accessed 16/08/2016).
[154] *Ibid*1.

Tata Steel's stock price declined significantly resulting in Standard & Poor's downgrading it and placing it on Credit Watch.[155] However, the share price soon recovered from 459 to 471 Rupees on April 16, 2007 and it reached 935 Rupees on January 2, 2008.

Shareholder value

The shareholders of Tata Steel were left unhappy about the high purchase price and were immediately penalised by the stock market with a drop in Tata Steel's share price. The Chairman of Tata Steel, Ratan Tata responded by assuring shareholders that despite the drop in share price, the takeover would create shareholder value in the long-term. He observed that: "Quite frankly I do feel [the stock market] is taking a short-term and harsh view. In the future somebody will look back and say we did the right thing."[156]

However, for Tata Steel's shareholders, the company overpaid with a price of 9 times Corus' Earnings Before Interest Tax Depreciation and Amortization (EBITDA). The takeover price of 608 pence represented a 68 per cent premium on Corus' share value before Tata Steel's approach for the company. Thus, Tata Steel paid a premium of £2.2bn to Corus' outgoing shareholder leaving the company £1bn in extra debt.

Figure 12: Tata Steel's debt to equity ratio following the takeover

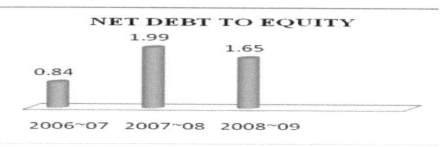

As illustrated by Figure 12, the debt to equity ratio increased from 0.84 before the takeover to a massive 1.99 after the takeover. This left Tata Steel's shareholder worried about the long-term financial health of the company and its ability to repay the debt. However, Tata Steel's executives were confident that Corus' cash flow would be sufficient to meet the debt

---

[155] Brian Bremmer and Nandini Lakshman, Tata Steel bags Corus- but at what price?, Global economics, (January 31, 2007).
[156] Anil K Gupta, Toshiro Wakayama, Srinivasa Rangan, *Global Strategies for Emerging Asia* (Wiley, John & Sons: USA, 2012) 143.

demands and the costs would be significantly reduced by expected saving of over £200m though synergies.

Tata Steel also saw value in improving the efficiency of Corus, who had a profit margin of 7 per cent in 2005, a quarter of that of Tata steel (30 per cent). However, the £1bn extra debt left shareholders and other stakeholders deeply concerned about the future of the company.

Employee jobs

Throughout the negotiation process, Tata Steel made it clear that the takeover would not affect jobs in the UK. Tata Steel promised to fund the pension funds of 47,000 Corus employees and to safeguard jobs in Corus' manufacturing plants.

However, trade unions feared that due to the high debt burden, the job cuts Tata Steel were ruling out would become a reality when the company begins to implement cost reduction measures. They also feared that UK manufacturing plants would be closed down and production transferred to India. Tata Steel assured them that there were "no short-term plans for any relocation of plants" but no assurances were given over employee jobs and the Corus board did not seek such assurances.[157] Employees were worried that the high purchase price for Corus could cost them their jobs.

After the acquisition, Tata Steel made a £74m investment at the Port Talbot plant as a sign of its commitment to protect employee jobs. Tata Steel also assured unions that it will make contributions to the fund from 10 per cent to 12 per cent by 2009 plus £126m in the under-funded Corus Engineering Steels Pension Scheme. Corus' pension fund had 16000 members in the UK including former British steel workers. The company delivered the financial commitments to Corus' pension funds after the takeover.

However, since 2008, Corus has cut over 5000 jobs, mostly from UK manufacturing plants. In 2008, 500 jobs were lost within the packaging unit of Corus in a bid to reduce its capacity and cut down on costs. In 2011, 1500 jobs were cut in Scunthorpe, Teesside, Lackenby Beam Mill and Skinningrove production site. In 2012, 900 jobs were cut at the Port Talbot site in South Wales. In October 2013, Tata Steel announced that a further 500 jobs would be cut at three manufacturing plants, Scunthorpe, Teesside and Worthington in the UK. In 2005, Corus had a workforce of 24000 in the UK but by 2013, the workforce had been reduced to 18500. The union

---

[157] Reuters, Tata Steel won't rule out Corus job cuts (October 20, 2006).

Community's general secretary Michael Leahy described it as the "worst period for Corus for industrial relations" in 45 years.[158]

In response to the job losses planned by the company, the chief executive of Tata Steel's European operations, Karl Köhler, explained that: "these restructuring proposals will help make our business more successful and sustainable, but the job losses are regrettable and I know this will be a difficult and unsettling time for the employees and their families affected."[159] This is a clear breach of trust since Tata Steel promised prior to the takeover that manufacturing jobs would be protected.

Board of directors

From their past experiences of mergers and acquisitions, both Corus and Tata Steel's board were aware of the challenges of post-takeover integration. They relied on this experience to draw up a 'light touch' integration plan, facilitated by a Strategic Integration Committee (SIC), in a bid to minimise job losses and maintain all strategic advantages.

Tata Steel paid particular attention to cross-cultural issues between India and Europe. They were aware of the possibility of British employees resenting managers from India and the concern that Tata Steel would move production to the low cost Indian market. Tata Steel addressed these concerns by not changing Corus' senior management. Senior managers were assigned the task of integrating and building trust between employees and the new owners. As a result, 80 per cent of Corus top management was retained.

During the July 18, 2007 Annual General Meeting (AGM), Tata Steel passed a resolution to appoint four directors of Corus onto its board. Jim Leng, Jacobus Schraven, Philippe Varin and Anthony Hayward were all appointed. Jim Leng became deputy chairman. Ratan Tata became Chairman. Malcolm McOmish, the managing director of Corus packaging was also retained. However, less than two year after the takeover, Philippe Varin's was replaced as CEO by Kirby Adams in 2009 and Jim Leng left the company in the same year. Three other Corus executives lost their jobs; Marjan Oudeman head of strip products, Scott MacDonald head of distributions and Phil Dryden.

---

[158] Peter Marsh, Tata confident Corus will regain its lustre, Financial Times (4 May, 2010).
[159] BBC News, Tata Steel: 600 Welsh jobs cut mainly at Port Talbot, (23 November, 2012).

Corus' financial performance after the takeover

Whether a takeover creates or destroys value is not always clear from the beginning. However, the financial performances afterwards provide a good indication.

Due to the global economic downturn between 2007- 2009, most of the anticipated gains from the deal were not realised. Tata steel's stock price fell to 168.05 Rupees by February 2009 on the Bombay Stock Exchange. Corus made EBIDTA losses of over £500m in the first nine months of 2009 but made positive EBIDTA earnings of £71m in the final three months. Despite the poor financial performance, Tata Steel's Vice-Chairman, B. Muthuraman disputed any concerns and firmly believes that the deal would create value: "We are extremely confident that with the economy and markets gradually improving, Corus will create value for Tata over the long term."[160]

However, in May 2013, Tata Steel Europe (formerly Corus) undertook a massive £1bn write-down of goodwill assets. Tata's management largely blamed it on the economic downturn and fall in demand for steel. However, this could be a sign that the value of Corus was less than Tata originally thought meaning that extra billions in the purchase price must have been spent on making outgoing shareholder wealthy while reducing the value of the company.

In the end, Tata Steel acquired a British steel company that has been a symbol of British industrial power for nearly a century. For employees, suppliers and the senior management, the deal left them unsure of their long-term future. For Corus' outgoing shareholders, a 68 per cent premium above Corus' average price left them fully satisfied. For Tata Steel's remaining shareholders, a massive drop in share price and mounting debt left them deeply worried about the future.

---

[160] Peter Marsh, Tata confident Corus will regain its lustre (Financial Times, 4 May 2010).

CHAPTER 5: ANALYSIS OF FINDINGS

Introduction

Since the turn of the twenty-first century, the takeover activity in the UK has seen household brands including Cadbury and Corus fall in the hands of foreign companies. However, it was the takeover of Cadbury in 2010 that brought increased media and academic attention on takeover regulation in the UK and the lack of protection to non-shareholding stakeholders' interests during a takeover. This study contributes to a growing body of research on shareholder primacy and the impact on the interests of non- shareholding stakeholders during takeovers. Other commentators include Professor Clarke who called for stronger decision making powers for directors during takeovers[1] and Professor Kershaw who found weak justification for the continued imposition of the board neutrality rule (Rule 21 of the Takeover Code 2016), which is the source of shareholder primacy under UK takeover law.[2]

This chapter tests whether concerns over shareholder primacy and the impact on other target company stakeholders following a takeover are justified using the findings from Cadbury and Corus takeover cases. Before analysing the findings from both cases, an overview of the opinions of the business community on reducing shareholder primacy is provided. It finds that while policy makers and academics believe that shareholder primacy allows companies to fall easily in the hands of foreigners and it pushes the board to ignore the interests of non-shareholding stakeholders, the business community does not support reform to shareholder primacy.

The findings in this chapter will provide the foundation for the reform proposals in Chapter 6. This chapter starts by providing an overview of the opinions of the business community derived from the Takeover Panel's consultations on reforming the Takeover Code 2016. Secondly, it examines shareholder primacy and the influence it had on the outcome of both the Cadbury and Corus takeovers, in particular the role played by short-term investors such as hedge funds. Thirdly, it analyses the impact on the target company's senior management positions, employee jobs and supplier contracts. The impact will be discussed alongside existing research literature to determine its implication and contribution to literature. Finally, it brings together the various strands of argument throughout the chapter.

---

[1] Blanaid Clarke, Directors' Duties during an Offer Period, Lessons from the Cadbury PLC Takeover (2011), University College Dublin, Working Papers in Law, Criminology & Socio-Legal Studies Research Paper No 44, 5.
[2] David Kershaw, The Illusion of Importance: Reconsidering the UK's Takeover Defence Prohibition (2007) 56 (2), International and Comparative Law Quarterly 267, 280.

Reforming shareholder primacy: A contrast in opinion

The Takeover Panel carried out public consultations on reforming the Takeover Code in 2010 and 2011 and this provided a platform for the business community to express its views on shareholder primacy and its influence on takeovers.[3] The Takeover Panel carried out public consultations because "a number of commentators had expressed concern that it [has become] too easy for offerors to obtain control of more than 50 per cent of the voting rights of an offeree company and that the outcomes of takeover bids, particularly hostile offers, are unduly influenced by the actions of short-term investors."[4] However, the Takeover Panel Committee stated from the beginning that selling shares during takeovers, regardless of the impact on other stakeholders, "is a legitimate commercial activity".[5]

Prior to the consultations, the former Chairman of Cadbury Plc, Roger Carr had expressed concern over the actions of short-term shareholders during the takeover process and blamed them for the takeover of Cadbury by Kraft Plc. He observed that: "The seeds of destruction for this company are laid in its [share] register...If you've only got 28 per cent long-term domestic funds owning this company, then you know that in a bid the rest are likely to sell."[6] The same concern was expressed by the then UK Secretary of State for Business Lord Mandelson who called for long-term investment to overcome risky 'perverse incentives' of excessive short-termism.[7]

Although politicians and academics are critical of the role of shareholder primacy during takeovers, the business community is opposed to reforming the Takeover Code. Respondents to the consultation were overwhelmingly against proposals to reduce shareholder decision making powers during takeovers. The Association of British Insurers (ABI) which is the voice of the insurance and investment industry rejected the proposals to reduce the voting rights of short-term shareholders by stating that they "see no

---

[3] The Takeover Panel, Response Statement to the Consultation Paper on Review of Certain Aspects of the Regulation of Takeover Bids (October 2010). The Takeover Panel, Consultation Paper Issued by the Code Committee of the Panel: Review of Certain Aspects of the Regulation of Takeover Bids (21 October 2010). The Takeover Panel, Reviews of Certain Aspects of the Regulation of Takeovers Bids: proposed amendments to the Takeover Code, London (May 2011).
[4] The Takeover Panel, Consultation Paper Issued by the Code Committee of the Panel: Review of Certain Aspects of the Regulation of Takeover Bids (21 October 2010), p 4, paragraph 1.11.
[5] *Ibid* 4, Paragraph 1.12.
[6] Roger Carr, Cadbury: Hostile bids and takeovers (Saiid Business School, February 15, 2010).
[7] Peter Mandelson, Britain needs investors for the long-term, The Financial Times (January 13, 2010).

principled basis on which to distinguish good from bad shareholders."[8] Similarly, the Investment Management Association which represents the asset management industry in the UK with members including fund managers believed that such changes were 'unnecessary'.[9]

The Association for Financial Markets in Europe argued that reducing shareholder primacy would be contrary to shareholder democracy and property rights. They stated that: "we do not consider that disenfranchisement of shares purchased in an offer period would be appropriate. The ability of a shareholder to vote its shares is a fundamental shareholder right."[10] A similar position was taken by the Quoted Companies Alliance, stating that: "such proposals [to reduce shareholder primacy] would be contrary to the basis upon which UK company law has developed to date, particularly the fundamental principle of "one-share-one-vote".[11]

Thus, the business community was overwhelmingly against reform to reduce shareholder primacy despite the concerns raised over the actions of short-term investors. However, the question is whether the concerns were justified. The next step is to analyse the findings from the case studies in order to determine whether there is a case for reducing shareholder primacy during takeovers. The empirical case for takeover reform is determined by the existence of a strong relationship between shareholder primacy during takeovers and evading of non-shareholding stakeholders' interests. A positive relationship will strengthen justification for reducing shareholder primacy whereas a negative or weak relationship will provide empirical challenge to any reform proposals.

Takeover defences during the offer period

During the offer period, the boards of Corus and Cadbury did not make any attempts to frustrate the takeover bids. This is due to the restrictions imposed by General Principle 4 of the Takeover Code 2016 which states that: "the board…must not deny the holders of securities the opportunity to decide on the merits of the bid."[12] It is supplemented by Rule 21.1 which

[8] The ABI's Response to Takeover Panel consultation paper PCP 2010/2. Available at: https://www.abi.org.uk/~/media/Files/Documents/Consultation%20papers/2010/07/POTAM%20pcp%202010%202.ashx (Accessed 18/07/2016), 4-5.

[9] The IMA's Response to Takeover Panel consultation paper PCP 2011/1. Web link: http://www.thetakeoverpanel.org.uk/wp-content/uploads/2008/11/PCP201101response22.pdf (Accessed 18/07/2013).

[10] The AFME's Response to Takeover Panel consultation paper PCP 2010/2. Available at: http://www.afme.eu/WorkArea/DownloadAsset.aspx?id=5163 (Accessed 18/07/2016).

[11] The QCA's Response to Takeover Panel consultation paper PCP 2010/2. Available at: http://www.theqca.com/article_assets/articledir_43/21831/QCAResponse_TakeoverPanel_ReviewTakeoverBids_Jul10.pdf (Accessed 10/07/2016).

[12] Takeover Code 2016, General Principle 3.

states that: "the board must not, without approval of the shareholders… take any action which may result in any offer…being frustrated." Thus, both the Cadbury and Corus boards adhered-to the requirements under the Takeover Code by recommending a bid adjudged to be in the interest of shareholders.

The boards were also deterred from frustrating the takeover bid by provisions in the Companies Act 2006. The target company board cannot put in place poison pills (which are found in Delaware Corporation Law, see Chapter 6.1.5) because the Companies Act requires them to obtain shareholder approval to issue new shares.[13] A poison pill can be created when, before the takeover bid, directors allot additional shares to themselves and the shareholders who support them in order to guarantee a majority vote over the takeover. A share allotment can be used to frustrate a takeover bid by having the majority reject the bid.[14] However, even if directors are allowed to issue shares in order to frustrate a takeover bid, existing shareholders have rights of pre-emption on any issuance of ordinary shares for cash.[15] The board cannot also sell valuable assets to deter the bidder because the UK Listing Rules require them to obtain the approval of shareholders.[16]

Although the takeover defence prohibition is absolute, the boards of Corus and Cadbury had three legally accepted methods to dampen the takeover bid. First, both boards used the defence documents to voice their informed views to shareholders over the bid and bidder. In the case of Corus, the board did not criticise Tata Steel's bid rather it recommended the first offer to the shareholders while simultaneously rejecting and criticising the offers made by the rival bidder Companhia Siderurgica Nacional (CSN). This was largely due to the fact that Tata Steel and Corus had been negotiating a potential merger a few years earlier. Thus, the Corus board was on the side of Tata Steel and had already thrown in the towel and accepted its fate. The Cadbury board, on the other hand, used the defence documents to reject two Kraft bids with words such as 'derisory' and 'unattractive' used to criticise the offers. Thus, the Corus board welcomed the bid whereas the Cadbury did not approve the bidder from the beginning.

---

[13]   Companies Act 2006, Section 551.
[14]   The two leading cases on allotment of shares to defeat a takeover are *Hogg v. Craphorn* [1967] Ch. 254 at 265; [1966] 3 W.L.R. 995; *Howard Smith v. Ampol Petroleum Ltd* [1974] A.C. 821 PC (Australia)
[15]   Companies Act 2006, Section 561.
[16]   Chapter 10 of the UK Listing Rules.

However, the Cadbury board's efforts to persuade shareholders to reject the bid were to no avail, largely due to actions of arbitrageurs who were willing to sell at any profitable price (see 5.3). Thus, the board's powers of persuasion were unlikely to succeed given shareholders interest in short-term gains rather than long-term financial value.[17] Despite that, defensive documents provide a legitimate takeover frustration measure, by criticising the bidder, although with immense difficulty in convincing shareholders to agree, especially when arbitrageurs have joined the target company.

Secondly, the boards had the option of persuading competition authorities that the bid should not be accepted on public interest grounds.[18] However, this was difficult to achieve given that shareholders of Corus and Cadbury were willing to sell at the right price and the bidders had made it public that they would be preserving jobs and the heritage of the companies. As a result, both board did not considered this option.

Third, the boards had the option of finding a White Knight or friendly rival bidder in order to create a bidding war. This would have enabled them to force the bidder to improve the terms of the offer. A White Knight was considered by the board in both takeover cases. In the Cadbury case, the board was unable to find a rival bidder to challenge Kraft as much anticipated bids from Nestle and Hershey failed to materialise. However, in the Corus case, CSN rivalled Tata Steel's offer. However, the rival bidder was a more of challenger to Tata Steel's bid than a White Knight for the board.

The rival bidder and the takeover premium

The presence of a rival bidder in the Corus takeover played a part in determining the level of premium offered to target shareholders. A rival bidder increases the wealth of shareholders by prompting other bidders to increase their bid. As shown in Table 7, Corus' shareholders made a 68 per cent premium as compared to Cadbury's 50 per cent. The importance of a rival bidder is better illustrated by the improvement made from the first offer. Due to a lack of competing bids, Cadbury's shareholders could only get a 10 per cent improvement from the first offer as compared to

---

[17] Paul Davies, *Gower and Davies' Principles of Modern Company law* (Sweet & Maxwell: London, 2012) 987.

[18] The Enterprise Act 2002, section 58 permits the Secretary of State to intervene in mergers and acquisitions on public interest grounds such as financial stability and national security; See Table of frequency in Daniel D Prentice & Peter Holland, *Contemporary Issues in Corporate Governance* (Clarendon Press, Oxford, 1993) 141.

34 per cent for Corus' shareholders. Thus, the findings show a positive relationship between rival bidding and the premium price.

Table 7: Summary of Cadbury and Corus shareholder premium

	Cadbury	Corus
Value of first offer	745 pence (£10.2bn)	455 pence (£4.5bn)
Value of final offer	850 pence (£11.9bn)	608 pence (£6.2bn)
Premium (on the share value before announcement of a takeover approach)	£4bn (50 per cent premium)	£2.2bn (68 per cent premium)
Improvement from first offer	10 per cent.	34 per cent
Rival bids	No rival bidders	CSN
Period until completion of the deal	Three months	Six months

Furthermore, Table 7 shows that the long timetable between the first offer and its acceptance by the shareholders plays a part in securing a high premium for the target company's shareholders. The takeover of Corus lasted twice as long as the Cadbury takeover. This window fosters competitive bids by giving directors time to search for competing bidders and for short-term investors to buy the rising shares of the target company.

The shares of the target company are in fact put through an auction process in a bid to secure the best possible price for the target company's shareholders. This is facilitated by Rule 31.1 of the Takeover Code 2016 which allows the offer to be open for a maximum of 21 days. Thus, the long timetable encourages the auctioning of target companies and arbitrageurs behaviour to the benefit of the target company shareholders.

Having found that a prohibition on takeover defences can operate to the benefit of shareholders, the next line of inquiry is the degree of influence short-term investors or arbitrageurs have on the outcome of a takeover bid.

Short-termism and its influence on takeovers

The findings in Table 7 have shown that the period between the first offer and the final offer is very profitable and provides a window for short-term investors who are looking to profit on the rising shares of the target company before the final bid. The original shareholders (holders of stock before the takeover announcement) may be willing to sell to short-term investors due to the risk that the anticipated takeover may fall through and therefore result in shares falling back to their pre-takeover announcement value. For the remaining shareholders, this would mean a missed opportunity to profit from the rising shares of the company. With that in mind, many long-term shareholders would be willing to sell to short-term investors who are prepared to bear the risk in the hope of marginally benefiting from premium price tabled in the final offer.

Short-termism and its influence on the outcome of takeovers is illustrated under Table 8. It shows that Corus' share value rose from 360 to 560 pence within a period of three months. Before the opening bid of 455 pence was tabled by Tata Steel, arbitrageurs were already buying Corus shares in anticipation of a takeover. As a result, by the time the bid was announced, the price was lower than the stock market price of Corus shares. Thus, arbitrageurs were in a losing position.

Table 8: Short-termism in Cadbury and Corus during the offer period

	Corus	Cadbury
Announcement of takeover interest	September 25, 2006 with Corus shares trading at 360 pence	August 30, 2009 with Cadbury shares trading at 570 pence
First offer	October 20, 2006 (455 pence per share)	November 10, 2009 (745 pence per share)
The value of the first bid	Bid price was lower than the stock market price of Corus shares	Cadbury was trading above the value of the first bid
Rival bid	Brazilian steel company Companhia Siderurgica Nacional (CSN)	None
Reaction to rival bid	Arbitrageurs raised the price of Corus shares to 495.5 pence, valuing it higher than the CSN's rival bid	Even with no competing bids, much anticipated rival bids by Nestle and Hershey pressured Kraft to increase its offer

Risk on arbitrageurs in case the deal collapsed	The stock value would have sunk to the September 2006 levels of 360 pence per share (45 per cent loss)	The stock value would have dropped to as low as 600 pence per share (25 per cent loss)
Final offer	608 pence per share	850 pence per share
Gains made by arbitrageurs between the deal announcement and its finalisation	68 per cent	50 per cent
Improvement from first offer	34 per cent	10 per cent.

The bidding war between Tata Steel and CSN helped to drive up the offer price and arbitrageurs continued to buy the shares of Corus in anticipation of an even higher premium from the two rivals. In the end, the shareholders who held on to their shares from the announcement date walked away with a 68 per cent premium on their shares. The arbitrageurs who bought Corus shares after the first bid received on average 34 per cent premium.

Thus, despite the high risk of either takeover bids falling through, the arbitrageurs were willing to take the risk by buying the shares at their inflated value. With a better price being the main motive behind the share purchase, it makes it highly unlikely that the short-term shareholders would consider non-price related factors such as employee jobs, if raised by the board.[19]

In Cadbury, the share price rose from 570 pence before the bid to 900 pence within a period of six months. Kraft's cash and equity offer in the first bid resulted in a 40 per cent rise in Cadbury shares but the falling value of Kraft's shares meant that the equity element was below its intended value. The market value of Kraft's shares had fallen largely due to the huge debts they had taken on and uncertainty surrounding the takeover.

Short-term investors were buying the highly inflated Cadbury shares in anticipation of a takeover deal. If the deal failed to materialise, the shares would have dropped to as low at 600 pence thus resulting in a 25 per cent loss. Shareholders who held on to their shares from the beginning received a 50 per cent premium. The majority of the arbitrageurs who bought Cadbury shares after the first bid walked away with a 10 per cent premium on average.

[19] Sam Jones, How the Hedge Fund Industry Influences Boardroom Battles (Financial Times 22 June, 2010).

Having analysed the actions of arbitrageurs in both takeovers, it begs the question; given the level of risk arbitrageurs are willing to take on even to earn a small profit, was there any chance of the target companies resisting a takeover once arbitrageurs had come on board?

To answer this question, take Cadbury as an example, after the first bid, few long-term owners of Cadbury stock were left. Arbitrageurs acquired five per cent of Cadbury shares in time for the first offer in September 2009, however, by January 2010 the arbitrageurs had gained 32 per cent of Cadbury shares.[20] To compound the matter further, a US mutual fund Franklin Templeton which held a 7.6 per cent stake in Cadbury, set a price of 830 pence for Cadbury shares.

At that point, the Cadbury Chairman Roger Carr conceded that "independence as an option was gone" and the emphasis was on getting a good price. Arbitrageurs made it easy for Kraft to acquire Cadbury because 32 per cent of them were willing to accept any premium price and thus leaving Kraft needing another 18 per cent to reach the 50 per cent threshold. Control of a company could become effective without acquiring 100 per cent of the issued share capital. Fifty per cent plus one vote is the minimum acceptance threshold required for an offer to succeed.[21] Shareholders who do not accept the offer would be entitled to remain in the company as minority shareholders.[22]

Evidence from Cadbury and Corus takeover cases shows that during takeovers, short-term investors buy up a large percentage of the target company shares and this enables them to vote in support of a takeover and eventually walk away with a premium on their investment. They normally pay little or no regard to the interest of non- shareholding stakeholders. Thus, in order to find a solution to the short-termism during takeovers, this book explores whether the board neutrality rule should be retained.

Short-termism during takeovers: Causes and consequences

The Department for Business, Innovation and Skills (BIS) carried out a consultation following the takeover of Cadbury by Kraft in 2010.[23] They

---

[20] It is worth noting that American ownership in Cadbury decreased from 51 per cent in September 2010 to 28 per cent by January 2010. Yet, UK ownership was 29 per cent in 2009 and remained largely unchanged by January 2010. Thus, the American shareholders sold out to arbitrageurs.

[21] Rule 9 of the Takeover Code 2016.

[22] This is because, under section 979 of the Companies Act 2006, an offeror which satisfies these 90% tests will then be able to serve compulsory acquisition notices on any dissenting shareholders.

[23] Department for Business Innovation and Skills, A Long-term Focus for Corporate Britain, Summary of Responses (March 2011).

found that it is often difficult for the board not to recommend an offer to shareholders where the price was high. Short-term investors often want to make quick gains and to serve their interests, as a result the board is forced to ignore long-term interests such as employee jobs in order to serve the interests of shareholders.

Academics point to a combination of shareholder primacy and the constant threat of hostile takeovers as drivers of short-termism.[24] In a hostile takeover bid, one where the board has refused to recommend a bid to shareholders, the bidder can approach shareholders directly for their shares. Faced with a possibility of earning substantially more on their investment, short-term shareholders would be willing to accept a hostile takeover. Even in a friendly takeover, one where the board is willing to recommend the takeover bid, shareholders are likely to vote in support of a takeover given the chance of short-term profit. Since shareholders have the power to make the final takeover decision, the fate of the other stakeholders depends on their decision.

As a result, hostile takeovers have become a common method of taking over companies because shareholders are inclined to accept the premium price regardless of the opposition of the board and the impact on other stakeholders. This constant threat has pushed directors to maintain high share price in order to deter bidders. It has also created a situation where short-term financial goals are given priority over the long-term stability of the company.[25]

Furthermore, there is empirical research which shows that companies that put in place takeover defences are able to engage in profitable long-term investments such as research and development (R&D).[26] Management would be less fearful of a takeover thus enabling them to pursue long-term objectives rather than short-term financial objectives. However, due to the prohibition on takeover defences under UK takeover law, managers are not permitted to fashion takeover defences. This has left management vulnerable to market forces such as takeovers to the benefit of short-term investors that target companies subject to takeover bids for quick gain. This is supported by a study into managerial short-termism in the UK

---

[24] Stewart Robinson, A change in the legal wind- how a new direction for corporate governance could affect takeover regulation (2012) 23 (9) International Company and Commercial Law Review 292, 294-297.
[25] Sarah Kiarie, At Crossroads: shareholder value, stakeholder value and enlightened shareholder value: Which road should the United Kingdom take? (2006)17 (11), International Company and Commercial Law Review, 329, 334.
[26] Theodor Baums, Takeovers versus Institutions in Corporate Governance in Germany, in Daniel D Prentice & Peter Holland, *Contemporary Issues in Corporate Governance* (Clarendon Press, Oxford, 1993) 181.

which found that a quarter of Times100 companies would forego long-term investments such as R&D for short-term profits because shareholders would not agree to an increase in expenditure on future investments that is likely to lower their earnings potential.[27]

Research evidence also shows that companies that successfully fend off takeover bids tend to decrease their R&D spending afterwards. This is because management moves away from long-term investments and turns its focus on maintaining a high share price in order to deter other potential bidders.[28] The aim of maintaining a high share price is to please shareholders and deter potential bidders. However, this is at the expense of long-term investment which is important for the company's long-term success.

Given the evidence showing that directors are pressured by shareholders to act and think short-term, the next line of inquiry is whether there is economic value in short-termism.

The economics of short-termism

Empirical evidence shows that shareholders who seek short-term gains benefit more than those who stay in the company for long-term gains after a takeover. First, studies have found that target shareholders who sell their stake during a takeover make substantial earnings but those who hold on to their stock find its value diminishing over time.[29] The fall in share value following a takeover is caused by uncertainty over the company's continuing financial health.

Second, empirical studies have shown that high debt levels after a takeover have a negative impact on the company in the long-run. A study on successful takeovers in the UK between 1984- 1992 with a value of over £10 million found that the post-takeover share performance of the companies was overwhelmingly negative.[30] The findings were backed up by two other studies published in 2001 and 2005.[31] Both studies found a

---

[27] John Grinyer, Alex Russell and David Collison, Evidence of Managerial Short-termism in the UK (1998) 9 (1), British Journal of Management 13, 19.

[28] Federico Munari and Mourizio Sobrero, Corporate Governance and Innovation, in Mario Calderini, Paolo Garrone and Mourizio Sobrero, (eds) *Corporate Governance, Market Structure and Innovation* (Cheltenham: Edward Elgar, 2003) 6.

[29] Tim Loughran and Anand Vijh, Do Long-Term Shareholders Benefit from Corporate Acquisitions? (1997) 52 (5), Journal of Finance *1765*, 1782; Kenneth Martin and John McConnell, Corporate Performance, Corporate Takeovers and Management Turnover (1991) 46 (2), Journal of Finance *671*, 686.

[30] Alan Gregory, An Examination of the Long Run Performance of UK Acquiring Firms (1997) 24 (7), Journal of Business Finance and Accounting 971,100.

[31] Roy D Baker and Robin Limmack, UK takeovers and acquiring company wealth

relationship between takeovers and negative returns in the long-run. The studies provide empirical support that debt levels amassed during takeovers have a long-term effect on the financial stability of the both the bidding and target company.

Third, findings from the takeovers of Corus and Cadbury have shown that short-termism was justified. As illustrated under Table 9, both companies struggled to maintain high stock value as the market reacted to the high premium the outgoing shareholders had received. The debt levels of the companies also went up and this affected the value of their stock.

Table 9: Tata Steel and Kraft's share price performance post-takeover

	Tata	Kraft
Borrowing to finance takeover	£4.7bn	£7bn
Total debt after takeover	£5.7bn	£16.7
Loss/gain in stock value from announcement to completion of takeover	12 per cent loss in stock in value	4 per cent loss in stock value
Share value before takeover	495 Rupees	$31
Share value after takeover	440 Rupees (at 26 march 2007) and 168.05 Rupees by February 2009	$29.34

In the case of Kraft, the takeover had a lot of long-term value by allowing Kraft to take up a leading position in the global confectionery market as well as expansion of geographical coverage in developing countries. Thus, shareholders who elected to retain their shares in Cadbury and Kraft were promised long-term gains. However, Kraft's debts in excess of £16bn pushed down the value of their stock following the takeover and Cadbury's financial performance also suffered in the first year thus reducing their stock value further. The fear of further deterioration in stock value led Warren Buffet, one of Kraft's largest shareholders, to sell a £31.5m stake in the company after the takeover. [32]

changes: The impact of survivorship and other potential selection biases on post-outcome performance (2001), Working Paper, University of Stirling, 27-28.; Sara B Moeller, Frederik P Schlingemann and Rene M Stulz, Wealth destruction on a massive scale, a study of acquiring firm returns in the recent merger wave (2005) 60(2) Journal of Finance 757, 775-777.

[32]   George Farell, Buffet reduces Kraft holding, The Financial Times (May 19, 2010).

The same effect can be found in the case of Corus where the world's 56th largest steel maker was able to take over a company ranked 9th in the world. For Tata Steel, the takeover meant greater global presence and higher stock value in the long-term. However, after the takeover, Tata steel's stock price fell from 495 Rupees before the takeover to 168.05 Rupees by February 2009 on the Bombay Stock Exchange. Thus, shareholders who held on to Tata Steel's stock experienced massive losses immediately following the takeover. Corus also made losses of over £500m in 2009. In May 2013, Tata Steel Europe (formerly Corus) undertook a massive £1bn write-down of goodwill assets to correspond with falling value of Corus stock. Thus, the findings show that short-termism is often pursued due to the risk of a major fall in stock value and poor financial performance after the takeover.

However, short-termism is not only driven by the risk of losing stock value; institutional shareholders such as hedge funds have a role as investors that requires them to move around in order to secure the best return for the beneficiaries of their funds.[33] Empirical evidence shows that fund managers seek substantial quarterly earnings and high dividend payments which pushes directors of investee companies to focus on high profitability and increasing market share.[34] Thus, given the value and focus on short-term gain, it is unlikely that the hedge funds that bought Cadbury and Corus shares after the first bid would have resisted the premium offer or held on to their stock for long-term gain.

Despite the availability of evidence that supports short-term investment over long-term investment after a takeover, there are empirical studies that support long-term investment as a greater source of shareholder value. A study on German and Japanese companies found that they were more successful at sustaining long-term investment programmes and utilising their human capital though measures that reward long-term performance and commitment.[35] Through a long-term approach, the companies were able to maximise shareholder value and increase human capital investment.

However, there are no studies that measure the earnings made during the takeover period as compared to those of shareholder who stay in the company for long-term gain. Since takeovers are completed on substantial

[33] Helen Short and Kevin Keasey, Institutional Shareholders and Corporate Governance in the United Kingdom, in Kevin Keasey, Steve Thompson and Mike Wright, *Corporate Governance: Economic, Management and Financial Issues*, (New York: Oxford University Press,1997) 22.
[34] Marcel Kahan and Edward Rock, Hedge Funds in Corporate Governance and Corporate Control, (2007)155 (5) University of Pennsylvania Law Review 1021, 1083.
[35] Jun-Koo Kang and Anil Shivdasani, Does the Japanese Governance System Enhance Shareholder Wealth? Evidence from the Stock-price Effects of Top Management Turnover (1996) 9 (4), Review of Financial Studies 1061, 1093.

premiums, it is unlikely that after the takeover, the company would ever afford to hand out such premiums to its remaining shareholders. Thus, takeovers provide a rare opportunity for shareholders to make substantial profit and this may explain why many UK companies such as Cadbury and Corus have easily fallen in the hands of foreign bidders.

In light of the influence of short-term investors on the outcome of takeovers, the next step is to determine whether the board has a legal duty to prioritise short-term interests during takeovers.

Short-termism and the role of directors during takeovers

The target board plays an important role during the takeover process by acting as gatekeepers, although in an ineffective manner in light of the conditions imposed by Rule 21, to the target company. A negative response or rejection of the offer by the target board could incentivise the bidder company to make an improved offer. For example, based on the Annual Report of the Takeover Panel for the year ending 31 March 2010, of the 88 takeovers where formal documents were sent to shareholders, only 11 out of 15 hostile takeovers succeeded.[36] This can be contrasted with the 2 out of 73 friendly or recommended bids that eventually failed. This shows that bidder companies want the cooperation of the target board in order to ensure that the bid succeeds.

Furthermore, a unwanted bid could strengthen the resolve of shareholders to demand an improved offer and this means more financial demands on the bidder company. For example, when the Cadbury board branded the first official bid by Kraft 'derisory', a majority of shareholders agreed and demanded that Kraft tables a higher price for their shares. Similarly, when the Corus board rejected the CSN bid, the shareholders agreed and called on both Tata and CSN to table increased offers. Thus, the board of the target company facilitates short-term gains by pushing for a high premium price for its shareholders.

Getting the approval of the board is also very important because the bidder may fail to obtain the necessary financing if the bid is hostile because of the need to table a much higher premium. For example, the bid for Manchester United in 2005 was structured by way of a scheme of arrangement or special purpose vehicle controlled by the Glazer family. Due to the hostile nature of the bid, the banks were unwilling to finance the

---

[36] The Takeover Panel, Report and accounts for the year ended 31 March 2010. Available at: http://www.thetakeoverpanel.org.uk/wp-content/uploads/2008/11/report2010.pdf   (Accessed 13/09/2016) 23.

bid until the later stages due to uncertainty over the success of the takeover and the high premium demanded by the shareholders.[37]

Similarly, the takeover of Corus by Tata Steel was through a special purpose vehicle which was recommended by the Corus board. However, the long takeover timetable allowed rivals CSN to enter the fold which transformed a friendly takeover into a contested battle for Corus. Tata Steel was able to obtain the funding it needed from the bank for the first offer but struggled to convince the bank to provide more funding as the bidding war went on. Thus, getting the approval of the board from the beginning is important for the bidder.

Despite the important role played by the target board during takeovers, they are sometimes pressured by shareholders to prioritise short-term financial interests with no regard to the interests of other stakeholders such as employees. Since shareholders are the main decision makers, directors have no option but to ignore the interests of other stakeholders during takeovers. The former Chairman of Cadbury, Roger Carr pointed out that during the takeover negotiation process, the board was left with only the option of negotiating a higher bid since shareholders had already indicated that they would be accepting any premium price. This short-term approach raises three major issues.

First, taking a short-term approach is contrary to the policy justification behind enlightened shareholder value which is premised on protecting the long-term interests of all company constituents. Enlightened shareholder value is found under section 172 of the Companies Act 2006 and it requires directors to take into account a list of non-exhaustive factors in their duty to promote the success of the company. This list includes shareholders and other stakeholders who are impacted on or contribute to the company's success.[38]

Thus, it is contrary to policy that directors prioritise shareholders' interests during takeovers and ignore the long-term interests of other stakeholders such as employees. This is evident both in Corus and Cadbury takeover cases where employees, senior management and suppliers had their interests negatively impacted on following the takeover (see 5.4) and the acquiring companies' took on huge debts which affected their long-term financial performance.

---

[37] Husnara Begum, Analysis: Theatre of schemes, (The Lawyer, May 30 2005) 18.
[38] Company Law Review Steering Committee, Modern Company law for a Competitive Economy: Developing the Framework, URN 00/656, (London: Department of Trade and Industry, 2010) paragraphs 3.12 to 3.85.

Second, the short-term approach serves the interests of shareholders but has a negative effect on other stakeholders such as employees and creditors (see 5.2.2). Employees often have implicit long-term contract that include rewards for performing well. These contracts are not legally binding because the expectations under them are undefined to be guaranteed legal protection but they secure benefits to employees. Following a takeover, the new management would have no moral obligation to honour such implicit contracts. The new management team may breach these contracts by reducing employee wages or cutting any other benefits. As a result, employees may become reluctant to invest firm specific human capital, such as specialised skills because of the consequences of takeovers.

Third and lastly, the Takeover Code creates uncertainty by stating under General Principle 3 that directors must act in the "interest of the company as a whole" yet at the same time Rule 21 hands decision making powers to shareholders. It begs the question; do the interests of the company equate to those of shareholders or rather the company means all the stakeholders including shareholders and employees?

The courts have been unable to distinguish the interests of shareholders from those of the company.[39] In *Greenhalgh v. Arderne*, the court held that the interests of the company are the same as the interests of the members (shareholders) of the company.[40] However, in cases where there is only one bidder, as it was in Cadbury, case law shows that directors are not obliged to recommend the bid if they believe it is not in the long-term interest of the company.[41] Directors have been given freedom to take action which they believe is in the best interest of the company even though it may affect shareholders' interests such as a frustration of a bidder's offer which is deemed not in the long-term interest of the company.

However, in cases where there are competing bids and the target board has elected to sell, case law supports the view that the only duty left for directors is to obtain the best price.[42] The board would only recommend a

---

[39] See *Fulham Football Club v. Cabra Estates Plc* [1994] 1 B.C.L.C. 363; *Dawson International v. Coats Paton* [1989] B.C.L.C. 233; *BCE v. 1976 Debenture Holders* [2008] 3 S.C.R. 560.

[40] *Greenhalgh v. Arderne* [1951] Ch. 286 CA at 291; See also *Peter's American Delicacy Co. v. Heath* (1939) 61 C.L.R. 457 (holding that the company as a whole is a corporate entity consisting all of the shareholders).

[41] See *Darvall v. North Sydney Brick and Tile Co Ltd* (1987) 12 A.C.L.R. 537; affirmed (1989) 15 A.C.L.R. 230 (selling off substantial properties was considered to be in the interest of the company as a whole, even though it defeated another bid).

[42] See *Re Mincom* [2007] QSC 3 Fryberg J. (the directors have a duty to secure for shareholders the best price possible for their shares); See *Cayne and Munro Bank v. Global Natural Resources Plc* Unreported August 12, 1982; affirmed [1984] 1 All E.R. 225, per Sir Robert Megarry V.C. (it is within the powers of directors to take steps to produce a better price for the shareholders even if it means defeating an existing bid).

lower offer if the high price is not in the interest of shareholders in cases where there is uncertainty on whether the bidder would be able to pay the amounts demanded.[43] There is no positive duty on directors to obtain or recommend the highest price to shareholders.[44] Thus, in cases where directors consider the company to be a healthy revenue generating entity, they can recommend a bid on a criterion other than price.

In practice, however, there are documented examples where the board takes the view that the interests of the company are not the same as those of shareholders. In the takeover of Manchester United by the Glazer family in 2005, the board took the view that the takeover was not in the interest of the company because the financing structure would result in a "financial strain on the business" even though it was deemed by the board to be a fair price for the company's shares.[45] As a result, the Manchester United board declined to recommend the offer because it went against the interests of the company rather than the shareholders' interests.

On that background, there is no settled position on whether the board should act in the interest of shareholders or the company as a whole including non-shareholding entities. Despite the lack of clarity, takeover law has taken the view that the interests of the company are the same as the shareholders thus giving shareholders primacy over the entire takeover process.[46] Although the position taken under takeover law is not supported by case law or company law principles, in practice, unless there is little prospect of a higher bid succeeding, directors will face difficulty in recommending a lower bid based on a criteria other than price. As shown in 5.3.2, arbitrageurs buy shares of target companies in hope of a premium and they would be expecting directors to serve their interests by recommending the highest bid. Recommending a lower price would not serve the interests of shareholders as required under takeover law. Thus, once the board had come to realise that the company would not remain independent, they must take steps to facilitate the highest price while

---

[43] *Heron International* [1983] 1 B.C.L.C. 244 at 265, Per Lawton L.J. (the directors took the view that the conditions of the higher bid could not be satisfied).

[44] *Re a Company* [1986] B.C.L.C. 382 at 389, per Hoffmann J

[45] The board of Manchester United took the view that the proposed offer from the Glazer family of 300p (valuing Manchester United at £790.3 million) was fair, but would not support the proposal, on the grounds that it was not in the best interest of the company, see Manchester United Plc, Club Responds to Glazer (February 11, 2005).

[46] This is supported by legal scholars such as Professor Parkinson who argued that a company is merely an 'artificial person' whose interests cannot be separate from those of its stakeholders such as shareholders and employees, John Parkinson, *Corporate Power and Responsibility: Issues in the Theory of Company Law* (Oxford: Oxford University Press, 1993) 76-77.

simultaneously rejecting the lower bids regardless of their non-price merits such as a preservation of employee jobs.

The analysis in this part has shown that directors have no duty to maximise the short-term gains of shareholders. While section 172 of the Companies Act 2006 requires directors to promote the success of "the company as whole" including shareholders and other stakeholders, it places the decision making powers in the hands of those who are responsible for serving these interests. Takeover law, however, has created confusion by promoting enlightened shareholder value but at the same time handing decision making powers not to the board of directors but to shareholders. As a result, during takeovers, directors are left with little option but to serve the often short-term interests of shareholders. Thus, promoting the success of the company as whole is in practice difficult if shareholders who are increasingly driven by the high premium during takeovers are in charge of their own fate.

Short-termism: the new research evidence

Studies have shown that more than half of all takeovers in the UK are likely to succeed.[47] This is because institutional investors such as hedge funds prey on takeover targets because they are a source of short-term gains and they pressure directors to take a short-term approach.[48] Findings from Cadbury and Corus takeover cases have shown that arbitrageurs buy out long-term owners of stock in order to benefit from the premium price on offer. Based on the summary of shareholders earning in Table 7, Cadbury shareholders walked away with a £4bn premium and Corus shareholders earned a £2.2bn premium on their stock. Thus, both arbitrageurs and original owners of stock in the target companies made substantial gains from their holdings.

Furthermore, empirical evidence shows that having multiple bidders' results in higher returns for shareholders as compared to a single bidder.[49] This is supported by the findings from the Corus and Cadbury takeover cases. Corus' shareholders earned a 68 per cent premium because of CSN's rival bid as compared to 50 per cent for Cadbury's shareholders where there was no rival bidder. The effect is even more profound when we consider the improvement from the first offer when Cadbury's shareholders

---

[47] Saira Aga, A Review and Comparison of Takeover Defences in the US and UK (2010), SSRN Working Paper, 8.
[48] Sam Jones, How the Hedge Fund Industry Influences Boardroom Battles (Financial Times, 22 June 2010).
[49] Julian Franks and Robert Harris, Shareholder Wealth Effects of Corporate Takeovers: The UK Experience 1955-1965 (2002) 23 (2), Journal of Financial Economics 225, 228.

experienced only a 10 per cent increase while Corus' shareholders received a 34 per cent increase.

The multiple bidders for Corus helped to improve the premium available to shareholders. Empirical evidence shows that even though a bidder accurately estimates the value of the target company, they must ensure that they win the auction process by overestimating the target company's value and thus overpaying the shareholders.[50] This could explain why Corus' shareholders walked away with a much larger premium as compared to Cadbury shareholders.

Research evidence also shows that the acquiring company's stock is negatively impacted on by a takeover. Both Tata Steel and Kraft's stock lost value following the takeover. Tata Steel overpaid with a price of 9 times Corus' Earnings before Interest Tax Depreciation and Amortization (EBITDA) and the final price of 608 pence represented a 68 per cent premium on Corus' share value before Tata Steel's initial approach for the company. As a result, Tata Steel made £2.2bn losses in value and it went to outgoing shareholders in the form of a premium. Tata Steel had to make operational improvements in an already efficiently run company to recoup the £2.2bn premium paid to shareholders. Given that six years after the takeover, the combined company undertook a massive £1bn write-down of goodwill assets to correspond with falling value of its stock, shows that the deal was value destroying.

In the case of Kraft, the combined value of both Kraft and Cadbury had to exceed £43.93bn for it to create value (see Chapter 4.1.5, Table 6). However, it was not clear whether Kraft could make operational improvements that would generate that value since Cadbury was already a successful company. Based on the market capitalisation of Kraft 22 months after the takeover, the deal did not create value rather it resulted in £2.44bn losses in value. However, if Kraft had stopped on the first or second offer, the deal would have created value after two years of operation.

Furthermore, Tata Steel's stock lost 12 per cent of its value after the takeover while Kraft's stock lost 4 per cent value. The markets were reacting to the huge debts the two companies had taken on and handed to outgoing shareholders in form of premiums. The negative impact on Tata Steel and Kraft's stock following the takeover is supported by existing research evidence. Studies carried out in America and UK measured the performance of the bidder's share price six months before and after the

---

[50] Bernard S Black, Bidder Overpayment in Takeovers (1989) 41 (3), Stanford Law Review 625, 626.

announcement and completion of the takeover.[51] The studies found that bidder companies' shareholders experience a reduction in share value whereas the target company's shareholders receive a large premium on their shareholding. Furthermore, the acquiring company's shareholders did not only suffer loss of value due to the takeover, they were also locked into the company until the share price recovered. Thus, following a takeover, the acquiring company's shareholders would be unwilling to sell their shares because the price would reflect a loss on their investment.

Overall, the analysis above has shown that short-term investors prey on target companies in a bid to make a quick gain from the anticipated takeover premium. It has also shown that although there is no duty on directors to prioritise short-term shareholders' interests, directors are pressured by the takeover market and demands of their shareholders to think and act short-term. Furthermore, directors are unable to give greater consideration to non-shareholding stakeholders' interests because shareholders make the final takeover decision and would choose a position that serves their interests.

Takeovers and the impact on non-shareholding stakeholders

Based on the above analysis and discussion, takeover law prioritises the target company's shareholders' interests above the long-term interests of the company as a legal entity. This can be contrasted with company law which requires directors to act in the interest of the company rather than shareholders alone. This principle is enshrined under the concept of enlightened shareholder value under section 172 of the companies Act 2006.

However, directors can only take into account stakeholders' interests if they would enable them to promote the success of the company for the benefit of the shareholders. Thus, directors may pursue a policy that minimises job losses or enhances supplier relations if the ultimate objective is to advance the interests of shareholders. The emphasis on long-term objectives under section 172(1)(a) places the interests of stakeholders such as employees at the centre of managerial decision making.

Enlightened shareholder value also forms part of takeover law, although it has been largely watered-down by shareholder primacy under Rule 21 of the Takeover Code 2016. General Principle 3 of the Takeover Code requires shareholder to serve the interests of the company as a whole. However, the interests of stakeholders only feature in the defence document in which the

---

[51] Anthanasios Kouloridas, *The Law and Economics of Takeovers* (Hart Publishing: Oregon, 2008) 2-5.

board would use to persuade shareholders to reject the takeover on non-price related reasons such as employee jobs.

Guided by section 172 and General Principle 3, when making recommendations to shareholders in the course of a takeover bid, the board has to consider the interests of stakeholders such as employees and suppliers when assessing the impact of a takeover on the company. However, section 172 prioritises shareholders' interests above those of other stakeholders. The board is required to have ' regards to' other stakeholders interests after deciding on shareholders' interests It is thus left to directors to determine what is in the interest of the shareholders as a whole, which could be short-term or long-term increase in share value.

In light of the requirements under section 172 and General Principle 3, the findings from the Corus and Cadbury takeover cases show that directors face immense difficulty in discharging this duty and often than not end up ignoring the interests of non-shareholding stakeholders.[52]

In the case of Cadbury, after Kraft made the first offer, the board had to make a choice on whether the company should remain independent or be sold for a substantial premium. The Cadbury board concluded that remaining independent would result in greater long-term wealth creation for current shareholders than accepting Kraft's offer. However, since Kraft offered a 50 per cent premium on the value of Cadbury shares, directors were placed in a difficult position to persuade shareholders that remaining independent would create more value. It is also worth mentioning that arbitrageurs had already bought the inflated Cadbury stock in hope of a higher bid that would put them in a profitable position. It was unlikely that they would forego the premium price for non–price related considerations.

Thus, when it came to discharging their duties under section 172 and General Principle 3, the Cadbury board knew that the majority of shareholders were interested in short-term financial gains than the long-term value sought by non-shareholding stakeholders. And since takeover law require directors to prioritise shareholders' interests, the Cadbury board had to pursue the short-term financial goals of shareholders in order to discharge their duties.

In the case of Corus, the board had decided that the target company would be sold and was faced with competing bids. Given that takeover law does not regard a company as having an interest that is separate from

---

[52]   Blanaid Clarke, Directors' Duties during an Offer Period, Lessons from the Cadbury PLC Takeover, University College Dublin, Working Papers in Law, Criminology & Socio-Legal Studies Research Paper (2011), No 44, 5.

shareholders (see 5.3.3), it becomes difficult for directors to recommend a lower bid, despite it being in the interest of the company as a whole. Such a recommendation would be contrary to General Principle 3 because it will not be serving the interests of shareholders.

For example, Tata Steel's bid for Corus had over 70 per cent debt (borrowing) which was likely to affect the long-term financial health of the company and the interests of its stakeholders such as employees. The rival bidder CSN tabled a marginally lower offer but with less debt and more cash component, and thus the impact on the long-term health of Corus would have been minimal and also it would have been more in the interest of non-shareholding stakeholders than the Tata Steel bid. However, the board decided to recommend the Tata bid because it served the short-term interests of shareholders and they rejected the CSN bid which was more in the long-term interest of the company and its non-shareholding stakeholders.

Thus, it is submitted that takeover law promotes the view that shareholders are company owners by placing their interests ahead of those of the company and its other stakeholders. Evidence from the Cadbury and Corus takeover cases shows that once the board had reached a conclusion that the company would not remain independent, other stakeholders interests would be set aside in order to facilitate a high price for shareholders.

Furthermore, non-shareholding stakeholders do not have standing to enforce the legal duties under section 172 and General Principle 3 on directors. If stakeholders such as employees want to complain that their interests were ignored, they would be unable to complain in court, only the board and shareholders can enforce the duties. Even after a change in control, the new board is unlikely to bring an action against the directors for recommending their own offer.[53]

Alternatively, before a takeover is finalised, they may solicit the help of sympathetic shareholders to bring a derivative action on behalf of the company to stop directors from acting without regard to the interests of non-shareholding stakeholders.[54] Yet again, they would need leave from court and prove that the derivative action is justifiable. However, such action may be regarded by the Takeover Panel as an attempt by some shareholders to use litigation to frustrate a takeover and would only approve it if the majority of the shareholders approve the legal action to

---

[53] *Regal Hastings v. Gulliver* [1942] 1 All E.R. 378 HL (the new board brought an action, on behalf of the company, against the former directors) However, it was not a takeover situation.
[54] Part 11, Companies Act 2006 sections 260-264 (injunctive relief).

proceed. Even though after gaining leave the court accepts the shareholders argument that directors should not ignore non-shareholding stakeholders interests, the court will not grant any relief until the takeover is complete.[55] This will defeat the very purpose of seeking injunctive relief in the first place.

In light of the above analysis, directors cannot downgrade shareholders' interests even when non-shareholding stakeholders' interests are threatened. During a takeover, directors are pushed to serve shareholders' interests while giving secondary or sometimes no consideration to other stakeholders' interests. Without legal standing to enforce the duties on directors, the fate of non-shareholding stakeholders is left in the hands of shareholders and at the mercy of the acquiring company. Thus, non-shareholding stakeholders have weak safeguards during takeovers.

Employees' interests and takeovers

The analysis above has shown that the target company's shareholders use the primacy given to them by takeover law to secure a high premium during takeovers. However, for the target company's non-shareholding stakeholders such as employees, shareholder primacy means that their interests become secondary and sometimes not given consideration.

In both Corus and Cadbury takeover cases, there were signs prior to the takeover that employee jobs could be adversely affected. Leading up to the takeover of Cadbury, Kraft's record on protecting jobs was very poor having closed down factories of a UK chocolate manufacturer Terry's and moved them to Poland.[56] Ten years prior to the takeover of Cadbury, Kraft had closed 30 factories with the loss of 60,000 jobs. This was known to the Cadbury board and the trade unions were voicing these concerns throughout the negotiation period. Similarly, the high debt component of Tata Steel's bid for Corus and the likely effect on the company's employees was known by the board. Thus, the Cadbury and Corus boards were aware of the likely effect on the employment after the takeover. Despite the early signs that employment could be adversely affected, the takeovers were eventually recommended by the boards and shareholders accepted.

As illustrated in Table 10, before the takeover of Cadbury, the company had 5700 employees in England and Ireland and three years after the takeover, this number had been reduced to 4500. On average, 14 per cent of employees lost their jobs within the three year period. Similarly, Corus

---

[55] See *R. v. Panel on Takeovers and Mergers Ex p. Datafin* [1987] 1 Q.B. 815 CA (Civ Div) and *R. v Panel of Takeovers and Mergers, Ex p. Guinness* [1990] 1 Q.B. 146.
[56] BBC News, The end of era as Terry's site closes (September 30, 2005).

had 24000 employees in the UK before the takeover and three years after the takeover; this number had been reduced to 18500. On average, 22 per cent of Corus employees lost their jobs.

Table 10: Summary of impact on employees following the takeover

	Cadbury	Corus
Total workforce in the UK before takeover	5700 people at eight manufacturing plants across Britain and Ireland.	A workforce of 24000 in the UK
Promises made by the bidder during the takeover negotiation process	Kraft promised to continue operations at Somerdale plant and preserve 400 manufacturing jobs.	Tata Steel promised to ensure that the pension funds of 47,000 Corus employees were fully funded and to safeguard jobs
Investments made after the takeover	A £50m investment in the UK with £14m going to Bournville plant	A £74m investment at the Port Talbot plant. £126m in the under-funded Corus Engineering Steels Pension Scheme.
Number employees in the UK after takeover	By 2013, the workforce had been reduced to 4500 (12.6 per cent decline)	By 2013, the workforce had been reduced to 18500 (13 per cent decline)

The level of job loss in Cadbury and Corus is higher than that found in other empirical studies. Prior to 2000, two large empirical studies tested the effect of takeovers on employment in the UK. First, a study of 240 takeovers between 1983- 1996 found a 7.5 per cent decline in employment within the acquired companies.[57] In a follow up study on takeovers between 1967- 1996, a 9 per cent decline in employment was found.[58] Thus, the 14 per cent average

---

[57] Martin Conyon, Sourafel Girma, Steve Thompson and Peter Wright, Do hostile mergers destroy jobs? (2001) 45 (4), Journal of Economic Behaviour and Organization 427, 438.

[58] Martin Conyon, Sourafel Girma, Steve Thompson and Peter Wright, The impact of mergers and acquisitions on company employment in the United Kingdom (2002) 46 (1), European Economic Review 31, 38.

loss of jobs in both Cadbury and Corus following the takeovers supports the findings made in prior studies but also shows that takeovers are more destructive to employee jobs than previously documented.

On comparison, shareholders walked away with an average of 30 per cent premium on their shares whereas the employees experienced on average 14 per cent job decline. These findings offer support to the breach of trust hypobook advanced by Shleifer and Summers that a wealth transfer occurs between employees and the target company's shareholders after a takeover.[59] Following the takeover of Cadbury, the Kraft Chairman stated that they expected to make "meaningful cost savings."[60] Based on the evidence from the Cadbury and Corus takeover cases, it can be argued that the massive loss of jobs was a response to the huge debts the companies had taken on to facilitate a premium for the outgoing shareholders.

PROTECTION OF EMPLOYMENT UNDER THE TAKEOVER CODE AND TAKEOVER DIRECTIVE

In light of the loss of jobs in Cadbury and Corus, it is important to critically examine the protection afforded to employees under takeover law. It is stated under General Principle 3 of the Takeover Code that the board of the target company will have to act in the interest of the company as a whole as well as not denying the securities holders a right to decide the merits of the bid. General Principle 2 of the Takeover Code 2016 also makes reference to the impact on the interests of employees when giving their 'views' to shareholders regarding the takeover. Thus, there is no direct duty towards employees during takeovers.

The same reading can be found under Article 3(1)(c) of the Takeover Directive.[61] Although shareholder protection was one of the motivations behind the Takeover Directive, the preliminary stages of the debates included protection of employee interests. In fact, at one stage during the drafting process, a duty was imposed on the board to act in the interest of the company including the safeguarding of employee jobs.[62]

If the reference to employment remained in the Directive, it would have offered a strong safeguard to employee jobs but at the same time created conflict with shareholders' interests. Evidence from the Cadbury and

---

[59] Andrei Shleifer and Lawrence H Summers, Breach of Trust in Hostile Takeovers in Alan J Auerbach, *Corporate Takeovers: Causes and Consequences* (University of Chicago Press: Chicago 1988) 50-51.

[60] BBC News, Cadbury agrees Kraft takeover bid (19 January 2010).

[61] Council Directive 2004/25/EC on Takeover Bids.

[62] Official Journal C 222 , 21/07/1997 P. 0020. It was then amended to refer to the interests of the company including employment COM/97/0565 final C 378 13.12.1997, p. 0010

Corus takeover cases show that shareholders stand to earn large premiums on their investments during takeovers and directors pay little attention to non-price factors such as employee jobs. Putting employee jobs in the same bracket as shareholders wealth would have completely changed the paradigm of directors' duties during takeovers. Directors would have been required to balance employee jobs and the offer price before recommending the bid. However, recommending a lower bid because of the better protection it affords to employment as opposed to a higher bid was still unlikely to be accepted by shareholders since they make the final decision over a takeover.

In the final reading of the Directive, reference to employment was removed on the basis that the obligation on the bidder, under Article 6(3)(i) of the Directive, to provide information on their intentions with regard to the future business and how it will safeguard jobs including material changes in employment, was deemed to be serving that purpose. As a result, General Principle 3 has no reference to employment and the only reference can be found under Rule 24.2 which implemented Article 6(3)(i) and General Principle 2. However, downgrading employment from the main constituents that should be considered by the board to a position where the bidding company has to offer information on their intentions towards them, without any firm guarantees, places them in a less secure position.

On that background, the only plausible protection for employees under takeover law is the information provided by the bidder and the board of the target company in the defence documents. The requirements in relation to the quality of information that should be provided by the bidder company can be found under Rule 19.1 of the Takeover Code. The failure of this safeguard during takeovers is discussed below.

EMPLOYMENT PROTECTION AND STANDARD OF INFORMATION

In compliance with Rule 24.2 of the Takeover Code, both Kraft and Tata Steel made promises in their offer documents to shareholders in relation to employee jobs. It is supplemented by Rule 19.1 which requires information provided in the offer and response documents to have a reasonable basis and a highest standard of accuracy.

Tata Steel assured Corus' shareholders that there would be no job cuts or factory closures that would result in a transfer of jobs to India. In addition to safeguarding of jobs, Tata Steel promised to fund Corus' pension funds. As summarised in Table 10, Tata Steel was able to fund Corus' pensions as promised prior to the takeover. However, there was a 13 per cent decline in jobs following the takeover. Thus, it can be argued that Corus' statement in regards to safeguarding jobs was not subject to the highest standard of accuracy. Thus, there was a failure of Rule 24.2 and 19.1 to properly safeguard the interests of employees in Corus.

The failure of Rule 24.2 was more pronounced in the case of Cadbury. Kraft's offer document published December 2009 stated that due to the complimentary fit between the two companies, there would be opportunities for talented employees as a result of the takeover. The section on employment also contained a provision that: "Kraft Foods has given assurances to the Cadbury directors that, on the offer becoming or being declared wholly unconditional, the existing contractual employment rights, including pension rights, of all employees of Cadbury and its subsidiaries will be fully safeguarded".[63] This information was of little value to employee representatives let alone shareholders or the board of directors.

Most significantly, Kraft reiterated a belief that it would be able to keep Somerdale plant open and thus save 400 manufacturing jobs. The same section on employment was referred to in the revised offer document published on 19 January 2010. The board's response document was equally less informative as on the position of employees. The board stated that they could only base their views in regards to employees on the information provided by Kraft in the offer document. The board also recognised that there was "insufficient information in the offer documents about Kraft's plans in relation to Cadbury to comment further".[64] Thus there was failure on behalf of Kraft to produce relevant information.

However, there was not only a failure to provide information as required under Rule 24.2, there was also a failure to provide meaningful and relevant information as required under Rule 19.1. The information provided by Cadbury was not sufficient for Kraft to base their judgement on regarding the continuation of Somerdale plant and Kraft also seemed unwilling or uninterested in seeking further information pertaining to employment. During the takeover negotiation process, Cadbury gave little information to Kraft regarding the phased closure of Somerdale plant. As a result, Kraft relied on the information available in the public domain that the transfer of jobs from UK to Poland was scheduled for late 2010.

---

[63] Offer document, December 2009. Available at: http://www.sec.gov/Archives/edgar/data/1103982/000119312509228547/dex991.htm (Accessed 16/08/2014).
[64] Defence document "reject Kraft's offer". Available at: http://online.wsj.com/public/resources/documents/CadburyDefenceDocument2009part2.pdf (Accessed 19/08/2016).

Thus, Kraft based their belief that they could continue operations at Somerdale plant on publicly available information. Representatives from both Cadbury and Corus only touched on the closure of Somerdale plant after the Cadbury board had recommended the offer on 18 January 2010.[65] This shows that Cadbury and Kraft did not fully adhere-to the requirements under Rule 24.2 to provide relevant information relating to employment.

Given that Rule 19.1 requires all the documents to be prepared with the highest standard of accuracy and care, Kraft cannot argue that the statement regarding the continuation of Somerdale plant was an opinion based on public information. They were required to honestly and genuinely hold the belief and also have a reasonable basis for holding that belief that operations at the plant would be continued.

Following the takeover of Cadbury, the Takeover Panel criticised Kraft by stating that the importance and prominence of the statement, and the fact it was repeatedly stated meant that it was vitally important to ensure that it was genuine and based on a reasonable basis.[66] Kraft had no reasonable basis for stating that it can continue Somerdale plant.

However, it is questionable whether the information provided by both the target and bidder companies would have safeguarded employee jobs. In the Cadbury case, information regarding the phased closure of Somerdale plant is unlikely to have had a major influence on shareholders' decision and even Cadbury had previously agreed to close the plant. Shareholders seemed to be more inclined on securing a high premium for their shares rather than the long-term value of the company. For directors, even with the information on the adverse impact on employment, they are unlikely to effectively use this information in terms of their section 172 duty because shareholders make the final decision.

Thus, in both takeover case studies, there was a failure on the boards of the target and bidder companies to provide accurate information in relation to employment. As aforementioned, the Takeover Directive removed the duty on directors to safeguard the interests of employees because Article 6(3)(i) already placed an obligation on the bidder to provide information on their intentions in relation to employee jobs. The failure of Rule 24.2, which implemented Article 6(3)(i), leaves employees with no plausible safeguard. This failure is compounded by the fact that companies that fail to adhere-to the requirements under 19.1 and 24.2 only face reputational costs.[67]

---

[65] Panel Statement, Kraft Foods Inc. Offer for Cadbury Plc 2010/14.
[66] *Ibid*
[67] James Wallace, Value Maximisation and Stakeholder Theory: Compatible or Not? (2003) 15 (3),Journal of Applied Corporate Finance 120, 125. (He argued that focusing on

The 2011 Amendments to the Takeover Code and employee protection

Following the takeover of Cadbury by Kraft, the Takeover Panel Committee (Code Committee hereafter) made a number of changes to the Takeover Code in 2011. The changes were in response to the public outcry at the loss of an iconic British brand and the lack of protection for employee jobs.[68] On the issue of employee jobs, the failure of Kraft to honour its promise to safeguard jobs at Summerdale plant led to an amendment of the information requirements under Rule 24.2 of the Takeover Code in 2011.

The Code Committee wanted to improve the quality of disclosure in relation to the bidder's intentions regarding the target company and its employees. A new Note 3 on Rule 19.1 provides that if a bidder or target company makes a statement in relation to any particular course of action, they would be regarded as being committed to that course of action for a period of 12 months after the takeover or for the period specified in the statement.

Furthermore, rule changes for the purpose of improving communication between employee representatives and the target board were made. The Code Committee wanted employee representatives to be more effective in offering their opinion on the effect of the takeover on employment. Amendments were made to Rule 2.12 requiring the target company to make announcements of an offer to its employee representatives and to be informed of their right to have an opinion on the impact of the takeover bid on employment. The target board is also required to pay employee representatives for the costs reasonably incurred in obtaining advice required for the verification of information expressed in their opinion. The purpose of this requirement is to improve the standard and accuracy of information as required under Rule 19.1.

A review on the performance of the Takeover Code amendments found that there has been an improvement in the quality and detail of disclosure of information made by the bidding company.[69] However, in most cases,

---

shareholder value can lead the firm neglecting other stakeholders' interests and damaging the company's reputation); John Armour and David A Skeel, Who Writes the Rules for Hostile Takeovers, and Why?-The Peculiar Divergence of US and UK Takeover Regulation (2007) 95 Georgetown Law Journal 1727; ("In London, City professionals—in particular, institutional investors— avoided the need for ex post litigation by developing a body of norms, which eventually gave rise to the Takeover Code. These norms were, and still are, enforced by reputational sanctions...") at 1731.

[68] See Peetz Matthew, Protecting shareholders from themselves: How the United Kingdom's 2011 Takeover Code Amendments hit their mark (2013) 2 (2), Pennsylvania State Journal of Law& International Affairs 409, 411.

[69] The Takeover Panel, A review of the 2011 Amendments to the Takeover Code (26, November2012).

the disclosure was general and not specific. Bidding companies were able to satisfy the requirements under 24.2 by stating that they intend to undertake a review of the target company's business after the completion of the takeover at which point they will be in a position to state their intentions for the company and its stakeholders.[70] This allowed them to escape the high standard of disclosure required under Rule 19.1. It is also difficult to hold them to a promise to act in good faith if reputational sanctions are the only recourse.

Thus, the 2011 reforms have added more layers of information requirement for the bidder and target boards without tackling the main issue of having guarantees over the intentions of the bidders. The main issue identified in the Cadbury and Corus takeover cases is that companies are willing to provide information but the information normally does not meet the standard required under Rule 19.1. Thus, without any legal sanctions for not adhering to the standard under Rule 19.1, rules requiring both the bidder and target boards to publish information are unlikely to achieve the intended purpose of protecting employee jobs. It is not surprising, therefore, that the review found that bidder companies' boards are sometimes providing general information without any guarantees over their intentions for the target company's business and employee jobs.

The failure of takeover law to protect employee jobs leads us back to the question of whether shareholder primacy is justified while employees' interests are left in a balance (see discussion on property rights and shareholder primacy under Chapter 3.1 and 3.2).

The economic case for withholding information during takeovers

It can be argued that the nature of market competition makes it difficult for both the target and bidder to provide sufficient and accurate information on their position regarding employees and other stakeholders. Since there is no prohibition on distribution of information given to shareholders during a takeover, there are plausible commercial reasons why accurate information may not be handed out, especially when the bidder companies are in the same sector as the target company. In case the takeover is not successful, the public would have sensitive information about the target company and its future strategic plans. The same applies to the bidding company, it may not want to give out sensitive information regarding its intentions for the business to the general public because potential bidders

---

[70] *Ibid* Paragraph 7.

and competitors in the market may rely on this information to obtain a strategic advantage.[71]

Senior management and agency costs

The introduction to the Takeover Code 2016 states that the Code is: "designed principally to ensure that shareholders are treated fairly and are not denied an opportunity to decide on the merits of a takeover."[72] Furthermore, General Principle 3 and Rule 21 provide safeguards against any takeover defensive measures that may act contrary to the interests of shareholders. Thus, takeover law is designed to shield shareholders from any attempts by the management board to deny them a final say on a takeover bid.

Further protection is provided under Rules 3.1 and 37.3. First, Rule 3.1 requires the target board to provide competent advice to all the shareholders on the offers. The board is not required to direct shareholders on accepting a particular bid regardless of its merits but can comment on the adequacy of its value. Second, Rule 37.3 supplemented by Rule 21 provides a list of non-exhaustive frustration actions the board is prohibited from implementing. The Takeover Code does not prohibit corporate actions that may frustrate a bid but requires the decision to deploy them be made by shareholders rather than directors.

The rationale behind such enhanced protection of shareholders' interests during takeovers is the threat of agency costs. The agency costs arise when another management team competes for the right to manage the resources of another company. Put in such a position, shareholders' interests lie in the price offered for control over the company. Target management, however, are at risk of losing their jobs and therefore may act to protect themselves by seeking to frustrate the takeover.[73]

The seminal work of Berle and Means identified that companies would be operated for the sole interest of the management board if legal or economic safeguards are not put in place to overcome the division between ownership and control.[74] The fear was that senior management

---

[71] New rival bidders are a supposed to be given all the necessary information available to the initial bidder (Rule 20.2, Takeover Code 2016); Simon Wong, Long-Term versus Short-Term Distinction in the UK Takeover Review Misses the Point, The Financial Times, (August 23 2010) 2 (He argued that insider trading rules affect disclosure of sensitive information during takeovers).

[72] Takeover Code, Section A.1.

[73] Henry G Manne, Mergers and the Market for Corporate Control (1965) 73 (2) Journal of Political Economy 110, 112-114.

[74] Adolf Berle and Gardner Means, *The Modern Corporation and Private Property* (Commerce Clearing House, New York 1932) 34.

would be able to impose agency costs on shareholders by making decisions that operate contrary to their interest and damaging to the value of the company.

Fundamental to the argument that directors should not be allowed to frustrate a takeover is the idea that when a company's share price underperforms, this makes it a takeover target. In 1965, Henry Manne famously put forward this explanation for takeovers through his theory on the market for corporate control.[75] The market for corporate control is created by the interrelation between managerial performance and share prices. Thus, managerial inefficiency would lead to a decrease in the company's share price. Consequently, this would lead to another company's management bidding to take over the company in order to replace the inefficient management and run the company in an efficient manner for profit. Thus, allowing directors to frustrate takeovers destroys the efficient workings of the market for corporate control.

Furthermore, a prominent Harvard economist Professor Bebchuk argued that decisions regarding takeovers are more value maximising if placed in the hands of shareholders.[76] The scholar advanced the argument that without any powers to stop a takeover bid, this gives management a stronger incentive to serve the interests of shareholders. However, if senior management are given the discretion to defend takeovers, this may lead them to assume that even if they perform badly, they would be able to fend off a unwanted bidder and maintain their positions or extract favourable deals in exchange for allowing the bidders to take over the company. As a result, the disciplinary element of the takeover threat would be lost.

The disciplinary effect of takeovers in Cadbury and Corus is illustrated under Table 11 below.

Senior management turnover in Cadbury post-takeover

During the integration process, board members and senior managers lost their jobs in Cadbury and Corus. It should be emphasised again that board members (especially executive and non-executive directors) are often also senior managers and employees of the company. Despite the overlap, the board of directors and senior management are treated as separate groups for ease of collecting and analysing data. However, the emphasis here is on senior management rather than the board of directors.

---

[75] Henry G Manne, Mergers and the Market for Corporate Control (1965) 73 (2) Journal of Political Economy 110,112.
[76] Lucian Bebchuk, The Case Against Board Veto in Corporate Takeovers (2002) 69 (3), The University of Chicago Law Review 973, 991–993.

Table 11: Summary of senior management turnover in Cadbury and Corus post-takeover

	Cadbury	Corus
The board of directors	7/out of the original 20 remained (35 per cent)	5/ out of the original 15 remained (33 per cent)
Senior management	65 per cent retention	80 per cent retention

In the case of Cadbury, 20 senior managers across functions such as finance, supply chain, legal and sales left the organisation in the first three years with 65 per cent of senior managers retaining their jobs. On the board of directors, 35 per cent left. The high turnover of senior management and board members was expected "because just a few weeks earlier, they were in a defence mode and then we were all together."[77] In the case of Corus, 80 per cent of senior managers retained their positions and on the board of directors, 33 per cent left.

The findings show that takeovers result in over 60 per cent of board members losing their positions. The impact on senior managers is rather modest although Cadbury experienced higher senior management turnover as compared to Corus. There are two reasons that could explain this.

First, Tata steel, an Indian company, was worried about cross-cultural problems that could arise if senior managers in Corus were replaced by those in Tata steel and as a result, they put in place a 'light touch' integration plan. Cadbury, on the other hand, was taken over by an American foods company Kraft. The company did not see any major cross-cultural issues given the common language and similarity in cultural and commercial practices employed in both UK and US. This contributed to the high retention of senior management in Corus as compared to Cadbury.

Second, Tata Steel was involved in merger negotiations prior to the takeover thus the board was already open to the idea of a potential takeover. Kraft on the other hand launched a unsolicited takeover for Cadbury and the board was not open to the idea of a takeover. Thus, the fact that the Tata Steel takeover was recommended by the board from the beginning and the Corus board did not recommend the bid could explain difference in the retention of senior management across functions.

Furthermore, Shleifer and Summers argued that if a target company management is not replaced after a takeover, implicit contracts are unlikely

---

[77] Jill Rapperport, A bitter Taste, Financial Times (May 23, 2011).

to be breached for fear that the company's reputation may be damaged.[78] In contrast, a new management team would aim to realize short-term gains in order to recoup the costs of the takeover through asset disposal and downsizing of labour force.

However, the change in management had little influence on the level of job losses in both companies. Cadbury experienced a 20 per cent reduction in its workforce and Corus experienced a 22 per cent reduction despite a 15 per cent difference in the number of senior management retained. The findings in the Cadbury and Corus takeover cases do not support those by Shleifer and Summers that lower senior management turnover results in lower loss of employee jobs.[79]

Given the prohibition on frustration action under Rule 21, the target board is left with one main option to deter a unsolicited bidder that threatens their positions. The board is allowed to persuade shareholders to continue to trust the management board and thus to reject the bidder. To achieve this, the board must issue convincing defence documents to shareholders.

The media can also play a major part especially when a company has a strong national identity or significant job losses are on the line.[80] However, media criticism is unlikely to deter short-term shareholders from selling their shares and the nature of dispersed ownership means that most of the shareholders in the target company may not share the national identity. For example, 51 per cent of Cadburys shareholders were American and it is not surprising that by the time the final bid was tabled, American ownership had gone down to 28 per cent having sold to short-term arbitrageurs. The argument that jobs could be affected is also unlikely to convince shareholders not to sell. For example, in the both Cadbury and Corus takeover cases, trade unions warned of major jobs cuts yet it did not influence the outcome of the bid. Thus, shareholder primacy makes it extremely difficult for directors to succeed in convincing shareholders to reject the offer.

However, takeovers are indiscriminative and loom over not only the poor performers but also the best performing companies.[81] This is

78

79   Andrei Shleifer and Lawrence H Summers, Breach of Trust in Hostile Takeovers in Alan J Auerbach, *Corporate Takeovers: Causes and Consequences* (University of Chicago Press: Chicago 1988) 50-51.

80   Andrew Ward, Pfizer admits defeat in AstraZeneca Bid, The Financial Times, (May 26 2014) (Public and political criticism of Pfizer's bid for the British Pharmaceutical company AstraZeneca forced them to withdraw their offer and even rule out a potential hostile bid).

81   Julian Franks and Colin Mayer, Hostile takeovers and the Correction of Managerial

supported by the findings from the Corus and Cadbury takeover cases. In 2005, Corus was Europe's second largest steel producer and the ninth largest steel producer in the world whereas Tata steel was the world's 56th largest steel maker. Tata steel acquired Corus in order to enter the European market, thus it was a quick option and not necessarily because Corus management was underperforming. Similarly, Cadbury was the second largest confectionery company in the world with strong growth in emerging markets. Kraft took over Cadbury as a growth option rather than for its inefficiency. Thus, the findings show that takeovers are indiscriminative in disciplining management since both companies were efficiently run yet fell prey to companies that were willing to pay above and beyond to acquire them.

Since Corus and Cadbury were not acquired due to underperformance, it can be argued that inability to bring about further efficiency gains from already efficient companies contributed to the major cost reductions in areas such as employee jobs post-takeover. In the case of Corus, inability to restructure an already efficiently run company led to £500m losses in 2009 and in 2013, Tata Steel Europe (formerly Corus) undertook a massive £1bn write-down of goodwill. Cadbury also failed to meet Kraft's growth objectives and was unable to reduce debts which increased from £16.7bn in 2010 to £17.1bn in 2011 and £14.4bn by 2013.

Thus, the findings from the case studies of Corus and Cadbury have shown that shareholders were able to earn large premiums on their investments yet employees and senior managers ended up losing their jobs in the aftermath. The analysis in 5.2.1 has shown that shareholder primacy plays a part in the breach experienced by constituents such as employees and senior managers. Emphasis now turns to company suppliers in order to determine the impact the takeovers had on their interests. Similar to employees and senior managers, suppliers have interests that they would need protection against during a takeover.

Renegotiation of supplier contracts post-takeover

As discussed in Chapter 1, suppliers have contracts with the company for continued supply of resources such raw material. Suppliers have two

---

Failure (1996) 40 (1) Journal of Financial Economics 163,171-174; See Blanaid Clarke, Articles 9 and 11 of the Takeover Directive (2004/25) and the Market for Corporate Control (2006) 26 (2) Journal of Business Law,355, 358. (He questioned the assumption that takeovers provide a solution to managerial inefficiency).

main interests during a takeover; continued contractual relations with the company and payment of the amounts due to them.

Suppliers face uncertainty over their interests during a takeover despite the protection given under section 172 of the Companies Act 2006 and General Principle 3 of the Takeover Code. The analysis in 5.1 has shown that long-term target company shareholders are bought out by arbitrageurs who are motivated by the premium price rather than the long-term financial value of the company. The fact that both company law and takeover law place shareholders at the centre of directors' decision making makes it difficult for directors to serve the interests of other company constituents ahead of shareholders' interests during a takeover.

In order to protect the interests of creditors such as suppliers, the board of directors has to take into consideration the risk of transferring production from UK into other countries when advising shareholders. In the case of Cadbury, Kraft's previous conduct of transferring manufacturing jobs to Poland warranted guarantees that they will not be moving production to Poland after the takeover to the detriment of local suppliers. Similarly, in the case of Corus, the massive borrowing the company had taken on to finance the takeover deal was a sign that they would need to engage in cost reduction measures to repay the debts. Thus, to serve the interests of suppliers, the boards needed to get guarantees from the bidders. However, guarantees were not sought and suppliers' interests were left at the mercy of the acquiring company.

After the takeover of Cadbury, one of their major suppliers, Burton Biscuits, had their contract terminated by Kraft. Burtons Biscuits was already facing financial problems prior to agreeing with Cadbury's management to supply them for two years and they were in talks of extending this contract. After the takeover, the new Cadbury board did not share the same relations with Burtons Biscuits and the fact that they wanted to engage in cost reduction measures led them to renegotiate the agreement. This not only drove Burtons Biscuits to near insolvency, it led to the loss of 300 jobs after the closure of their Mereton (UK) plant. Thus the renegotiation of the supply contract, which Burtons Biscuits depended on for their immediate financial stability, was severe enough to put them into financial difficulty. This was a difficult position for Burtons Biscuits to take especially since the shareholders of Cadbury were walking away with on average 30 per cent premium on their shares.

There was no known termination or renegotiation of supplier contract in Corus following their takeover by Tata Steel. This could be explained by the empirical evidence showing that companies which replace their senior management are more likely to terminate supplier contracts. A US based study on the effect of CEO turnover on suppliers found that on average, suppliers lost 20 per cent in sales due to a firm replacing its CEO.[82] Cadbury retained 65 per cent of their senior managers as compared to 80 per cent by Corus. Thus, it can be argued that senior management turnover is one of the factors behind termination or renegotiation of supplier contracts.

However, the board of directors makes the main decisions such as long-term supply contracts thus the replacement of senior management in other business units is unlikely to have influenced the decision to terminate Burtons Biscuits' contract. Given that both Corus and Cadbury had over 50 per cent of their board members replaced, the findings do not provide conclusive evidence that replacement of board members increases the risk on suppliers following a takeover.

Thus, evidence from the Cadbury takeover shows that suppliers' interests can be negatively impacted on by takeovers. However, Corus' suppliers did not experience the same effect. As a result, there is a weak relationship between takeovers and renegotiation or termination of supplier contracts. Future research that examines the impact of takeovers on supplier contracts over a longer period of time should be able to provide more conclusive results.

Summary

The main finding from the case study analysis is that shareholder short-termism during takeovers allows target companies to easily fall prey to bidders and this may threaten the long-term interests of the company and its non-shareholding stakeholders. Despite that, neither company law nor takeover law require directors to prioritise short-term interests over the long-term interests of the shareholders. However, shareholder primacy during takeovers puts pressure on the board to ignore non-price related factors such as employee jobs and recommend a bid deemed to be in the interest of the shareholders even though it threatens the long-term interests of the company and its stakeholders.

Although section 172 of the Companies Act 2006 requires directors to take into account the long-term interests of stakeholders, these interests cannot override shareholders' interests. As a result, research evidence has shown that the target company's stakeholders' interests may be adversely impacted on following a takeover. Employees stand to lose jobs, senior

---

[82] Vincent J Intintoli, Mathew Serfling and Sarah Shaikh, The Negative Spillover Effects of CEO Turnovers: Evidence from Firm-Supplier Relations(2012), SSRN Working Paper Series, 17-22.

management stand to be replaced and a supplier (in the case of Cadbury) had their contract renegotiated. This is compounded by the fact that non-shareholding stakeholders have no effective enforcement remedy in case directors choose to overlook their interests and serve the short-term interests of shareholders.

In light of these findings, an important question is whether there should be a fundamental change in takeover regulation in order to facilitate more protection to non-shareholding stakeholders and place limits on the influence of short-term shareholders. It should be emphasised that although the findings from Cadbury and Corus takeovers show an adverse effect on the interests of employees, senior management and one large supplier, and although policy makers and academics are critical of the actions of short-term shareholders during takeovers, the business community is opposed to reforming the takeover system. Despite that, the positive relationship between takeovers, shareholder primacy and the destruction of non-shareholding stakeholders' interests means that calls by politicians and academics to reform rules on shareholder primacy in order to minimise the risk on non-shareholding stakeholders are justified.

CHAPTER 6: REGULATORY REFORM PROPOSALS

Introduction

The findings in Chapter 5 have provided a platform for a discussion on takeover law reform in the UK. The research evidence has shown that many takeovers start off as hostile and become recommended after the target board succumbs to pressure from short-term investors and enters into negotiations with the bidders for the best price. Short-term investors such as hedge funds buy up a large stake in the target company during the offer period and influence the outcome of the bid. This operates to the detriment of non-shareholding stakeholders, who are placed in a vulnerable position following a takeover.

Although buying and selling shares during a takeover is legitimate commercial practice, Chapter 3 showed that a modern company has a social responsibility and the government has a stake in regulating its activities to minimise the negative impact on society. Companies have immense social-economic power which makes their operations and activities crucial to the welfare of society and the economy. Although takeovers have a net economic benefit, the subsequent job losses go against the interests of society, even though they are legitimate business decisions.

Thus, policy makers have a responsibility to intervene and safeguard society from the negative externalities of takeovers. For example, the financial crisis that occurred between 2007- 2009 caused wide-scale damage to the global economy and society at large. It was blamed on failures in corporate governance practices in companies, especially in the banking sector.[1] The government responded through regulatory reform to deter risk taking and promote greater transparency and accountability.[2] The same way the UK government was concerned by the challenges posed by the financial crisis, is the same way they ought to be concerned by the challenges posed by the takeover activity in the UK because of the impact on the welfare of society.

The evidence in Chapter 5 indicates the significance of the challenge posed by takeovers in the UK. The most significant impact was on employee jobs which fell by 14 per cent on average in both Cadbury and Corus while shareholders walked away with a up to 50 per cent premium on their

---

[1]   OECD, Corporate Governance and the Financial Crisis: Key findings and main message (OECD Corporate Governance Committee. 2; See Hector Sants, The crisis: The role of investors, Speech at the NAFT Investment Conference, (March 112009) (UK Financial Services Authority).

[2]   Tomothy Edmonds, Dominic Webb and Rob Long, The economic crisis: policy responses, House of Commons Library, SN/BT/4968(2011) 3.

shares. The manner in which arbitrageurs or short-term investors preyed on the target companies makes it unlikely that they would turn down a takeover offer regardless of the risk posed to the long-term interests of the company. Public concern and dismay at the loss of Cadbury to Kraft was captured in the words of the then Business Secretary, Lord Mandelson: "... it is hard to ignore the fact that the fate of a company with a long history and many tens of thousands of employees was decided by people who had not owned the company a few weeks earlier, and probably had no intention of owning it a few weeks later."[3] Thus, there is empirical evidence which shows that takeovers have an adverse impact on employee jobs and that short-term shareholders conduct themselves in a manner that leads to companies being takeover over easily.

In light of these findings, an important question is whether there should be a fundamental change in takeover regulation in order to facilitate more protection to non-shareholding stakeholders. This chapter considers reform proposals in response to the challenges posed by takeovers in the UK. The proposals are premised on finding ways of providing greater protection to non-stakeholders' interests during takeovers and reducing the influence of short-term investors on the outcome of takeover bids.

However, the reform proposals to reduce shareholder primacy during takeovers suffer from three major problems. First, the business community was overwhelmingly against a Takeover Panel consultation in 2010 on reforming the Takeover Code to reduce the voting rights of short-term investors.[4] Without the support of the business community, it is unlikely that reform proposals to reduce shareholder control over the takeover process and bring greater protection to the interests of non-shareholding stakeholders would be considered again by the Takeover Panel and eventually implemented. As a solution, variations to some of the reform proposals in the 2010 public consultation are proposed and less drastic solutions from areas such as corporate governance are put forward.

Second, there is insufficient empirical evidence to support a radical change to takeover law. This study found major job losses but the impact on suppliers was limited as only one supplier had their contract renegotiated. This is insufficient evidence to support a reduction in shareholders' powers during takeovers. Thus, there is a need for a larger study to test and expand on the findings in this study before consideration can be given to reform proposals to reduce shareholder primacy.

---

[3] Peter Mandelson, Secretary of State for Business, Innovation and Skills, Speech at the Trade and Industry dinner, Guildhall, the Mansion House, London (March 1, 2010).
[4] The Takeover Panel, Response Statement to the Consultation Paper on Review of Certain Aspects of the Regulation of Takeover Bids (October 2010).

Third, a takeover is essentially a question of transferability of private property to the acquirer at a given price rather than a strategic growth decision to which directors' orthodox management powers would be necessary. Only shareholders can make the final decision over the transferability of their property during takeovers rather than directors or other stakeholders. Any reform proposal must respect private property rights.

In light of the adverse impact on non-shareholding stakeholders and predatory actions of short-term investors during takeovers, two regulatory reform proposals are considered in this chapter. This chapter is divided into two main parts. The first part examines the Delaware board-centric model of takeover regulation in order to determine whether, if implemented in the UK, it would provide more protection to non-shareholding stakeholders while preserving shareholder value. This would mean that shareholders would retain their decision making powers but the board would have the power to frustrate takeovers that threaten the long-term success of the company. The board would be expected to discharge their section 172 duty by taking into consideration the interests of all stakeholders when faced with a takeover bid. It would also mean abolishing the board neutrality rule (Rule 21 of the Takeover Code) in order to enable directors to fend off unwanted bidders. However, the main challenge to this reform proposal is whether in the absence of the Rule 21, the board would be in a position to frustrate non-value maximising takeovers.

The second part considers a proposal to disenfranchise the voting rights of short-term shareholders during takeovers. The rationale is to deny shareholders who acquire the target company's stock immediately after the announcement of a bid, the right to vote on the takeover. The aim is to ensure that only the long-term shareholders (those who hold the target company's stock prior to the takeover announcement) are in a position to vote. However, due to many challenges facing the implementation of this proposal, two variations of the proposal are considered. These variations could provide a better solution to shareholder short-termism.

Finally, after critically examining the two reform proposals, lighter regulatory solutions are considered as the way forward. The three major limitations to reducing shareholder primacy identified above played a key part in this decision; (1) insufficient empirical evidence to justify fundamental takeover law reform; (2) the business community remains hostile to reform; and (3) private property rights must be respected. Consideration is given to approaches that may encourage long-term shareholding such increased responsibilities under the Stewardship Code 2012.

A divergence in takeover regulation between UK and US

In the field of corporate governance, the UK and US are often studied along the "Anglo-American" model. Empirical studies have shown that medium and large-sized companies in the Anglo-American system are widely-held.[5] This is largely due to the open market for company shares in both jurisdictions.

Despite the existence of widely- held companies in both jurisdictions, they have each taken a different approach to takeover regulation. In the UK, the self-regulatory approach has resulted in a takeover regime largely driven by the interests of shareholders.[6] Takeovers are regulated by the Takeover Code 2016, which is written and administered by the Takeover Panel. The Panel is staffed by people from the professional community and handles takeover disputes in a flexible and fast manner as opposed to a courtroom. In contrast, US judicial lawmaking has resulted in a takeover system that gives immense control power to managers and limits shareholders' influence on rule making.

However, it is not only the mode of takeover regulation that is different but the substance of the law is also different.[7] The UK takeover system gives shareholders primacy during takeovers. The Takeover Code prohibits management from frustrating actual or anticipated takeovers. In contrast, management in US have flexibility to deploy takeover defensives, provided they are not in breach of their fiduciary duties. This makes the US a good candidate for comparison purposes in order to determine whether their system offers more protection to non-shareholding stakeholders during takeovers and at the same time creating value for shareholders.

Takeover regulation in the US

The US has a system of federalism under which, two legal systems federal and state law coexist through division of power.[8] However, states retain and can exercise all the regulatory powers except those which are deemed exclusive to the federal government. It means that laws passed by Congress and states to regulate takeovers are both applicable. While corporate law such as takeover defences are governed by individual state law,

---

[5] Rafael La Porta, Florencio Lopez-de-Silanes and Andrei Shleifer, Corporate Ownership Around the World (1999) 54 (2), Journal of Finance *471*, 583-586.
[6] John Armour and David A Skeel, Who Writes the Rules for Hostile Takeovers, and Why?- The Peculiar Divergence of US and UK Takeover Regulation (2007) 95 Georgetown Law Journal 1727, 1734.
[7] *Ibid* 1734-1738.
[8] On the American legal system, see Jay M Feinman, *Law 101: Everything You Need to Know about the American Legal System* (Oxford University Press 2006) 16.

tender offers and securities regulation fall under federal law.[9] Although takeovers in the US are regulated both by state and federal law, each has its own focus. An issue of shares to public investors in the US is primarily governed by federal law. Federal laws such as the Securities Act of 1933, which deals with primary issues, and the Securities Exchange Act of 1934, for secondary markets, require prompt and full disclosure of relevant information during mergers and takeovers. In addition to establishing a governmental body called the Securities Exchange Commission (SEC) to regulate and administer securities law,[10] the SEA 1934 allows amendments over the regulation of takeover transactions.

An amendment to the SEA was made in 1968 under the Williams Act, which regulates takeovers at federal level. The aim of the legislation is to protect the target company by preventing inappropriately coercive takeovers.[11] It contains disclosure rules requiring both the target and bidding board to disclose information about the offer but also provisions governing the process of tender offers. The Williams Act was enacted at a time when tender offers were emerging. A tender offer arises where a premium over the market price of shares is offered by the bidder directly to the target shareholders in a bid to achieve a control stake in the target company.[12] Prior to the Williams Act, tender offers were often made on a first come first serve basis thus compelling shareholders to make pressured and uninformed decisions in order to avoid being left with minority interest following the takeover, and vulnerable to a squeezed out at a lower price.[13] Furthermore, cash tender offers were totally unregulated.[14] These regulatory gaps led to practices such as Saturday Night Special where a tender offer was made on the weekend, coercing shareholders to make quick and uninformed decisions while the bidder was subject to no disclosure requirements other than identification of the location where the shares are to be tendered and the price for them.

---

[9] William C Tyson, The Proper Relationship Between Federal and State Law in the Regulation of Tender Offers

(1990) 66 Notre Dame Law Review 241, 278-79; Guido Ferrarini and Geoffrey P Miller, A Simple Theory of Takeover Regulation in the United States and Europe (2009) Cornell International Law Journal 301, 304.

[10] Security Exchange Act 1934, section 12 (j).

[11] It arrived in the same year as the first UK Takeover code.

[12] In *Wellman v Dickinson* 632 F 2d 355 (2d Cir 1982) the court set out eight factors, now called the *Wellman* factors, to identify the existence of a tender offer and therefore subject to the Williams Act.

[13] Stephen Kenyon-Slade, *Mergers and Takeovers in the US and UK* (Oxford University Press 2004) 52.

[14] Samuel L Hayes and Russell A Taussig, Tactics of Cash Takeover Bids (1967) 45 Harvard Business Review 135, 136-7.

The William Act was enacted as an amendment to SEA 1934, with the aim of curbing coercive tender offers and increasing disclosure requirements.[15] First and foremost, under section 13(d), a person who directly or indirectly acquires five per cent or more of a company's equity of any class to file a disclosure statement with SEC within ten days of reaching five per cent.[16] The required information includes identify of the bidder, future plans for the company and its business and the source of the funds. Furthermore, Rule 13d-2 requires a prompt filing with the SEC when there has been a material change; one per cent increase or decrease in ownership. Section 14(d) also requires anyone intending to make a tender offer to file "Tender Offer Statement on Schedule TO" with SEC, detailing their underlying intention and relevant information must be made available to the target company's shareholders.

Secondly, Rule 14e-1 requires the tender offer to be left open for at least twenty working days before finalising the purchase of the shares, thus giving shareholders sufficient time to make informed decisions about the share offer.[17] Similarly, Rule 14d-10 requires a tender offer to be made open to all shareholders of the class of securities subject to tender in order to avoid discriminatory treatment. Since the Williams Act does not regulate all aspects of takeovers, states have been able to exercise authority over corporate law matters by enacting a wide range of anti-takeover statues.

US corporate law is state-based law and rules vary state to state. The corporate law statutes enacted by states have gone through three generations of reform. The first were challenged in *Edgar v. MITE Corp* on the ground of being unconstitutional.[18] In that case, the Illonois Business Takeover Act 1982 was found to be indirectly inhibiting inter-state trade. Subsequent reform led to a second generation of takeover statutes.[19] They impose strict conditions which may frustrate takeovers. These include "control share cash-out statutes" which grant the right to demand the bidder to purchase the target shareholders' shares at a fair value after exceeding a certain threshold.[20] Other states, such as Delaware, have gone a step further by enacting third generation statutes, the so-called "business

[15] Barbara White, Conflicts in the Regulation of Hostile Business Takeovers in the United States and the European Union (2003) 9 IusGentium 161, 173-174.
[16] Securities Exchange Act 1934, rules 13d-3(d)(2) - (4).
[17] Rule 14e -1(g)(3) defines a business day as any day, other than Saturday, Sunday or a Federal holiday.
[18] *Edgar v. MITE Corp* U.S. 624, 630-31 (1982).
[19] They were approved in *CTS Corp. v. Dynamics Corporation of America* 481 U.S. 69, 77-78 (1987).
[20] Edwin Miller, Mergers and Acquisitions: A Step-by-Step Legal and Practical Guide, (John Wiley & Sons: Hoboken, 2008) 280-82.

combination statutes."[21] They prevent the bidder from engaging in certain transactions without the target board or shareholders' consent.

Furthermore, federal and state corporation law does not regulate the use of board controlled takeover defences. The regulation is placed in the hands of courts to decide the legitimacy of takeover defences. The courts rely on the test developed in *Unocal Corporation v. Mesa Petroleum Co.*[22] when deciding on the legitimacy and legality of takeover defences.[23]

Thus, despite their common law orientation and dispersal of share ownership, the UK and US use very different approaches to takeover regulation; the question is why? This question can only be answered after examining the various factors that influenced the development of takeover regulation in both countries.

Origins of the takeover regulatory models in the UK and US

Researchers who have studied the origins of the board-centric takeover model in the US point to regulatory competition.[24] In regulatory competition, corporation law reflects the preferences of the groups that are acquiring or bidding for it. Professor Bebchuk argues that since managers of listed companies in the US had immense influence on the choice of governing corporate law, they ended up selecting rules to favour their cause during takeovers.[25] In addition, Professors Armour and Skeel argued that the mode of regulation determined by the substance of the law. They found that the shareholder- centric model in the UK is linked to the emergence of self-regulation whereas managerial discretion in US is linked to judicial control over the takeover process.[26]

The UK self-regulatory takeover model was designed by the community of mainly institutional shareholders and investment bankers from the City of London.[27] Consequently, debating a board-centric takeover model with

---

[21]   See Lucian Bebchuk and Allen Ferrell, On Takeover law and Regulatory Competition (2002) 57 (3), Business Lawyer 1047. They argued that business combination statutes were not designed to protect shareholders' interests but merely to frustrate takeovers, at 1182.

[22]   *Unocal Corporation v. Mesa Petroleum Co.* 493 A.2d 946 (Del. 1985).

[23]   *Ibid* 955. "a) they had reasonable grounds for believing that a danger to corporate policy and effectiveness existed" and (b) the defence was "reasonable in relation to the threat posed."

[24]   Lucian Bebchuk, The Case for Increasing Shareholder Power (2005) 118 (3), Harvard Law Review *833*, 847.

[25]   See Lucian Bebchuk and Allen Ferrell, On Takeover law and Regulatory Competition (2002) 57 (3), Business Lawyer 1047, 1182- 83.

[26]   John Armour and David A Skeel, Who Writes the Rules for Hostile Takeovers, and Why?- The Peculiar Divergence of US and UK Takeover Regulation (2007) 95 Georgetown Law Journal 1727, 1765.

[27]   *Ibid* 1767- 1776.

an audience dominated by city professionals was like debating solar energy with oil executives. The audience was sided towards one particular interest, shareholder control, regardless of the merits of opposing arguments. This is because corporate managers were not organised as a constituency and thus had little influence on the formation and substance of takeover law. The outcome was the development of shareholder primacy above managerial control in the UK.

In contrast, the development of takeover rules in the US was based upon common law precedents.[28] The development of common law depends on the incentives of parties to bring cases to court rather than settling disputes out of court. Thus, if one group is better organised or funded to bring cases as compared to other groups, the substance of the law may over time develop in a manner that reflects their interests. This might explain the managerial friendly takeover laws in US.

Thus, the US judicial control over takeover matters is down to a lack of coordination between institutional shareholders in the development phases of the law. Armour and Skeel argued that because ordinary shareholders in US accounted for a much larger proportion of the stock market as opposed to institutional shareholders, coordination was seen as less worthwhile for such investors.[29] As a result, they had little influence on the development of rules which ended up favouring managers.

The factors that influenced the development of takeover law in the US are supported by evidence of takeover law in the UK before the advent of the Takeover Code. Case law was the main source of regulation and as a result, case law from the before the Takeover Code period was overwhelmingly managerial friendly.[30] The privatization of takeover law helped to transform its substance over time from managerial friendly to shareholder friendly. The change was driven by the development of a body of principles, enforced by reputational sanctions rather than court litigation.

A lack of shareholder involvement in takeover development in the US has been subject to a number of studies. Professor Mark Roe found that US federal regulation during the 1930s restricted the services of institutional shareholders, which affected their development and ability to coordinate.[31] In contrast, the UK being a safe place for pensions strengthened the

---

[28] *Ibid* 1776.
[29] *Ibid* 1765.
[30] *Ibid* 1776.
[31] See Mark Roe, *Strong Managers, Weak Owners: The Political Roots of American Corporate Finance* (Princeton: Princeton University Press, 1994) 102-118.

development of institutional shareholders such as pension and hedge funds.[32] Thus, UK's self-regulatory takeover system was developed by institutional shareholders whereas US was characterised by ordinary shareholders who lacked the ability to coordinate.

Having examined the differences in takeover regulation in the UK and US, it has been shown that institutional shareholders influenced the development of the UK shareholder-centric model whereas managers influenced the board-centric model in the US.

The state of Delaware is selected for this study because more than 50 per cent of all publicly companies in the US are incorporated in that state.[33] As a result, Delaware law is important in most of the takeovers thus making it the most influential source of takeover regulation in the US.[34] The aim of carrying out an analysis of takeover regulation in the US is to determine whether the Delaware board-centric takeover model provides more safeguards to shareholders and stakeholders as opposed to the UK shareholder-centric model.

The board-centric model and managerial accountability

Under a board-centric model, the bidder would need the consent of the target board to pursue a takeover. As a result, bidders are more likely to negotiate with the board for a friendly takeover than pursue a hostile takeover. One study found that friendly and hostile takeovers have become difficult to distinguish because the difference is now down to the negotiation tactics of the bidder.[35]

For the target company's shareholders, the economic benefits flowing from the negotiation between the bidder and the target board would depend on the incentives of the board. Having the interests of the board aligned with those of shareholders would mean that the board would be more likely to negotiate a shareholder value maximising price. The shareholders can ensure that the board negotiates in their favour by putting in place corporate governance mechanisms such as compensation packages linked to the share price and non-executive directors to keep an eye on executive

---

[32] See Bernard Black and John Coffee, Hail Britannia? Institutional investor Behavior under limited regulation (1997) 97 (7), Michigan Law Review 1997, 2004.

[33] Delaware, Why incorporate in Delaware, available at http://corp.delaware.gov/ (Accessed 18/04/2016)

[34] John Armour and David A Skeel, Who Writes the Rules for Hostile Takeovers, and Why?-The Peculiar Divergence of US and UK Takeover Regulation (2007) 95 Georgetown Law Journal 1727, 1735.

[35] William Schwert, Hostility in Takeovers: In the Eyes of the Beholder? (2000) 55 (6), Journal of Finance 2599, 2638-2639.

directors.[36] This simply means that in order to achieve outcomes that are in the shareholders' interests, they need to contract around.

However, the ability to contract around is limited on three grounds. First, board discretion during takeovers can only work to shareholders advantage if the board is incentivised to work in the shareholders interest. Thus, if the board does not have large stock options in the company or not monitored by non-executive directors, they may fend off value maximising takeovers in order to retain their jobs or accept non-value maximising bidders with a promise of better retirement packages or other benefits.

Second, since directors can fend off a takeover bid, they end up not fearing underperformance. This is supported by studies which show that anti-takeover law has a negative effect on the stock value of listed firms in that jurisdiction. One study found that the introduction of anti-takeover legislation in New York during the 1980s negatively impacted on the market value of companies registered there.[37] Similarly, managerial underperformance following the adoption of anti-takeover defences is supported by studies which found reduced returns to shareholders.[38]

Last but not least, incentivising the board with stock market based compensation does not necessarily solve the issue of director self-interest. In the 1990s, there was a rise in stock options based pay given to US executives and this was implicated in the eventual downfall of companies such as WorldCom and Enron.[39] Options based pay gave managers the incentive to push up the stock price in order to profit yet they were not punished if the share price fell because they could fend off unwanted bidders.

Thus, on that background, the UK takeover system makes managers more directly accountable to shareholders because they cannot fend off a potential takeover and the notion of contracting around is severely limited by managerial self-interest. The cost of contracting around also seems to be high especially when needing to give managers stock options. Thus, the UK takeover system guarantees more protection to shareholders and stakeholders and at less cost.

---

[36] Sara T Moeller, Let's Make a Deal! How Shareholder Control Impacts Merger Payoffs (2005) 76 (1), Journal of Financial Economics 167, 186.
[37] Lawrence Schumann, State Regulation of Takeovers and Shareholder Wealth: The Case of New York's 1985 Takeover Statutes (1988) 19 (4), Rand Journal of Economics 557, 565.
[38] Paul Gompers, Joy Ishii and Andrew Metrick, Corporate Governance and Equity Prices (2003) 118 (1), The Quarterly Journal of *Economics* 107, 138.
[39] William Bratton, Enron and the Dark Side of Shareholder Value (2002) 76 (2), Tulane Law Review *1275*, 1358.

The next line of inquiry is whether permitting the board to fashion anti-takeover defences would allow them to maintain shareholder value at the same time safeguard the interests of non-shareholding stakeholders.

Anti-takeover defences and shareholder value

Debates over the relationship between shareholder value and takeover defences have been taking place in the US since the mid-twentieth century. One study surveyed hostile takeovers between 1962-1983 and found negative stock market returns when defensive restructuring was announced.[40] However, the small size of the sample and the fact that the analysis did not extend beyond announcement date reduced the significance of the results.[41]

Similarly, a study into poison pills and staggered boards found that a staggered board increases the chances of a company remaining independent following a hostile takeover.[42] The evidence showed that 60 per cent of the 45 companies that had a staggered board and poison pill remained independent. This can be contrasted with 34 per cent of target companies without a staggered board that remained independent.[43] They also found that the companies that remained independent had 36 per cent lower short-term returns and 55 per cent lower returns in the long-run as compared to those sold. Thus their findings show that poison pills destroy shareholder value in the short-term and most significantly in the long-run.

However, there is empirical evidence which shows that a combination of poison pill and staggered board increases the returns for shareholders.[44] A study found that poison pills increase takeover premium in the region of 7.8 and 21.4 per cent.[45] This is because directors are able to bargain with the bidder for a higher premium. Comparative empirical research has shown that average premiums in US hostile and friendly takeover deals

---

[40] Larry Dann and Harry DeAngelo, Corporate Financial Policy and Corporate Control (1988) 20 (2), Journal of Financial Economics 87, 123.

[41] Another study found that operation performance improves five years following a poison pill, see Morris Danielson and Jonathan Karpoff, Do pills poison operating performance (2006) 12 (3), Journal of Corporate Finance 536, 552.

[42] Lucian Bebchuk, John Coates, and Guhan Subramanian, The Powerful Antitakeover Force of Staggered Boards: Theory, Evidence and Policy (2002) 55 (5), Stanford Law Review 887, 929.

[43] *Ibid* 930.

[44] Mark Gordon, Takeover Defences Work. Is That Such a Bad Thing? (2002) 55 (3), Stanford Law Review 819, 823; See Lucian Bebchuk, John Coates, and Guhan Subramanian, The Powerful Antitakeover Force of Staggered Boards: Theory, Evidence and Policy (2002) 55 (5), Stanford Law Review 887, 906.

[45] Guhan Subramanian, Bargaining in the Shadow of Takeover Defenses (2003) 113 (3), Yale Law Journal 621, 636..

were between 3.8 per cent and 6.4 per cent higher than in the UK.[46] This is because boards in the US have more power to negotiate takeovers as compared to those in the UK

Professor Coates, however, questioned the empirical support for takeover defences as a source of higher premiums for shareholders. He reviewed existing empirical studies and reached a conclusion that the relationship between takeover defences and shareholder value remains undetermined.[47] He concluded that the empirical studies are inconsistent and suffer from methodological shortfalls.[48] In regards to takeover defences and shareholder premium, he observed that studies consistently show that a company with a poison pill achieves higher premium. He argued that since a company can adopt a position pill any time before or during a bid, the studies end up not separating companies with and without poison pills.[49]

The theoretical support for takeover defences is also mixed. American scholars Easterbrook and Fischel proposed that managers should be prohibited from frustrating takeovers in order to allow shareholders to decide on the merits of a bid.[50] They stressed that the conflict of interest between shareholders wealth and target management's jobs would often lead to decisions not in the interest of the company if managers are allowed to frustrate takeovers.

However, Professors Black and Kraakmann argue that managers deserve the discretion to negotiate takeovers because information asymmetry makes share price a poor measure of a company's true value, which the board of directors is in a better position to understand.[51] However, Lipton argues that managers should be allowed to frustrate takeovers in order to generate the best price for company shareholders and deter value destroying bidders.[52] Although matters such as research and development (R&D) may not be reflected in the stock value and managers may have

---

[46]   George Alexandridis, Dimitris Petmezas and Nickolaos Travlos, Gains from Mergers and Acquisitions Around the World: New Evidence (2010) 39 (4), Journal of Financial Management 1671, 1691.

[47]   John Coates, The Contestability of Corporate Control: A Critique of the Scientific Evidence, Harvard John M Olin Center for Law, Economics and Business, Discussion Paper(1999), No. 265, 11.

[48]   *Ibid* 11.

[49]   *Ibid* 69.

[50]   Frank H Easterbrook and Daniel R Fischel, The Proper Role of a Target's Management in Responding to a Tender Offer (1981) 94 (6) Harvard Law Review 1161,1163.

[51]   Bernard Black and Reinier Kraakmann, Delaware's Takeover law: The Uncertain Search for Hidden Value (2002) 96 (2), Northwestern University Law Review 521, 566.

[52]   Martin Lipton, Takeover Bids in the Target's Boardroom (1979) 35 (1), Business Lawyer 101, 102.

better knowledge of the bidder's intentions, the benefits are outweighed by the high risk of conflict of interest.

Research is also mixed on the relationship between takeover activity and a prohibition on takeover defences. Armour and Skeel argued that takeover transactions in the UK are more likely to be hostile because shareholders are approached directly for their shares which increases the chances of success.[53] They found that in the UK, 85 per cent of all takeovers announced during 1990-2005 were hostile and 43 per cent of them were successful.[54] Compared to US, 57 per cent of takeovers announced during that period were hostile and only 23 per cent of them succeeded. This is supported by evidence showing that the increased use of takeover defences such as poison pills in the US during the 1980s-90s coincided within a decline in hostile takeovers.[55] Although the evidence shows that hostile takeover bids are more likely to collapse in US, the overall levels of takeover activity in the US, as compared to the size of their economy, is much higher than in the UK.[56]

The analysis above has shown that the board-centric model provides shareholders and other stakeholders less safeguards against director self-interest. It has also shown that the empirical evidence on the relationship between takeovers and shareholder value is largely mixed. The next line of inquiry is on whether in the absence of Rule 21 of the Takeover Code 2016, US-style takeover defences could be deployed in the UK.

Delaware-style takeover defences in the absence of the board neutrality rule

In order to implement the Delaware board-centric model in the UK, the board must be able to fashion takeover defences. However, Professor Kershaw argues that without the Board Neutrality Rule, the board would still have limited scope to fashion takeover defences in the UK.[57] He adds that all the takeover defences designed by US companies to defeat takeovers would either be 'unavailable' or 'practically ineffective' in the absence of Rule 21.[58]

---

[53] John Armour and David A Skeel, Who Writes the Rules for Hostile Takeovers, and Why?-The Peculiar Divergence of US and UK Takeover Regulation (2007) 95 Georgetown Law Journal 1727, 1736-1739.
[54] *Ibid* 1738.
[55] See Bengt Holmstrom and Steven Kaplan, Corporate Governance and Merger Activity in the United States: Making Sense of the 1980s and 1990s (2001) 15 (2), Journal of Economic Perspectives *121*, 127.
[56] Stefano Rossi and Paolo Volpin, Cross-Country Determinants of Mergers and Acquisitions (2004) 74 (3), Journal of Financial Economics 277, 281.
[57] David Kershaw, The Illusion of Importance: Reconsidering the UK's Takeover Defence Prohibition (2007)56 (2) International and Comparative Law Quarterly 267, 305.
[58] *Ibid* 267.

Other commentators offered support to Professor Kershaw's findings by examining the role of the board neutrality rule in three European jurisdictions: UK, Germany and Italy.[59] The aim was to determine whether company law in all three jurisdictions will make board controlled takeover defences unavailable or practically ineffective even in the absence of the board neutrality rule. They found that boards would find it difficult to create takeover defences in the absence of the board neutrality rule mainly because of company law rules that require the board to get shareholder approval. They concluded that although different fields of regulation such as company law and corporate governance play different roles in each jurisdiction, the bottom line is that in all three jurisdictions, the fields of regulation make it difficult to fashion takeover defences in the absence of the board neutrality rule.

There are five types of takeover defences that can be deployed in Delaware. A detailed examination of the takeover defences and their potential availability in the absence of the board neutrality rule is carried out below.

a)   Poison pills

First and foremost, shareholder rights plans or poison pills are used by Delaware companies to fend off bidders. The existing target shareholders are given warrants to buy equity in the target company or in the bidding company should they merge following a takeover. Rights on the warrants are contained in the shareholder rights plan. The warrants have no economic value until the triggering event. They would allow existing target shareholders the right to acquire voting shares in the company or in the bidder at a discount. Thus, any bidder who crosses an agreed upon threshold, often 10 or 30 per cent, would trigger the warrants.

The effect of the warrants is to devalue the bidder's holding in the target company or in the bidding company itself following a merger. This acts as a takeover frustration measure because, unless the board redeems the warrants, a unwanted takeover would be difficult to succeed. Rules that permit the board to put in place a pill at any time without the need for shareholder approval increase the effectiveness of poison pills.[60]

However, if the board can be replaced, then the pill could be redeemed thus allowing the bidders to make their bid. To achieve this, the bidder can commence a proxy contest which would involve a shareholders' meeting

---

[59]   Carsten Gerner-Beuerle, David Kershaw, Matteo Solinas, Is the Board Neutrality Rule Trivial? Amnesia about Corporate Law in European Takeover Regulation (2011) 22 (5), European Business Law Review 559, 619.
[60]   *Unitrin, Inc. v. American General Corp.*, 651 A.2d 1361 (Del. 1995).

where proposals are made for the removal of directors or appointment of new ones. However, this can only work if it is possible to oust out a majority of the board members. Under Delaware General Corporation Law (DGCL), the default position is that directors are subject to elections on a yearly basis and could be removed without any cause.[61]

Furthermore, companies can put in place staggered boards where three year terms are given to directors and a third have their terms expiring every year.[62] With a staggered board, the board of directors can only be removed with a just cause, unless the company constitution states otherwise.[63] Thus, in order to redeem a poison pill in a company with a staggered board, effective control over the board can only be achieved after two Annual General Meetings (AGMs). An amendment of the company constitution to include without cause removal of directors is also difficult because under DGCL, both shareholders and the board must approve the amendment.[64]

In the UK, the board neutrality rule does not prevent poison pills before a potential takeover is on the horizon. The prohibition comes in play when a takeover bid is announced or when a bidder requires the board to redeem a pill. Refusal to redeem a pill when demanded by the bidder or when a takeover is imminent could amount to a breach of Rule 21 of the Takeover Code. It would represent action to frustrate a takeover and denying shareholders the right to decide on the merits of the bid. However, a pill that requires no board redemption could be put in place before a takeover.[65] Consequently, it may deter value maximising friendly bidders if all the shareholders refuse to withdraw their warrants.[66]

If the UK removes Rule 21 from the Takeover Code, this would make poison pills theoretically available in the UK. A warrant could be given to shareholders as part of their interim dividends, in time to frustrate an impending takeover. The rights on the warrants would be contained in a shareholder rights plan. However, the board needs authorization from shareholders to allot the warrants.[67] This would make a pill only available after shareholder approval.

---

[61]   Section 141 DGCL.

[62]   Section 141(k) DGCL.

[63]   Section 141(d) and 141(k) DGCL. Shareholders may call an extraordinary general meeting if the company constitution does not contain a prohibition on it. It cannot be amended by a bylaw either (section 109 DGCL).

[64]   It is only possible if set out in a bylaw, Section 242(b) DGCL.

[65]   David Kershaw, The Illusion of Importance: Reconsidering the UK's Takeover Defence Prohibition (2007)56 (2) International and Comparative Law Quarterly 267, 273.

[66]   See *Criterion Properties Plc v. Stratford UK Properties LLC* [2002] EWCA Civ 1783.

[67]   Sections 549-51, Companies Act 2006.

However, even if a poison pill is made available in the UK, its effectiveness would be severely limited. The boards in the UK cannot protect themselves or delay removal from the board. The board can be removed by a majority vote at the general meeting.[68] This can be achieved without any cause. Within a period of two months, the board could have been removed in time for a takeover. Thus, poison pills would be largely ineffective in the absence of Rule 21.

Furthermore, the UK Listing Rules require all shareholders of the same class to be treated equally.[69] This would affect the discriminative element of the poison pill which negatively impacts only on the bidder. If the bidder is also allowed to purchase the shares at a discount, this would destroy the very purpose behind the pill. This leaves the target board only the option of putting forward a strong case to the UK Listing Authority in support of the violation of the equal treatment principle that the bidder did not comply with the conditions attached to the warrants, such as not to exceed a percentage of stock ownership, hence the discriminatory actions.

b)   Distributions

Second, distributions can be made to shareholders through share buybacks or extraordinary dividends with the effect of placing block shares in the hands of a friendly third party or increasing the leverage in the company. These are known as restructuring defences with the aim of making the company unappealing to a potential bidder. This is normally used as a response to a highly leverage bidder who wants to use the target company's cash flow to finance its own debts.[70]

However, an equitable bidder may not be deterred by an increase in the target company's debts. As a result, the board may need to restructure in order to prevent the bidder from gaining effecting control over the company. This is where shares are issued to friendly third parties or a share buyback to increase the stake of the friendly third party in the company.

In the UK, restructuring is less likely to work than in the US. In Delaware, for example, the board can exercise power to issue substantial share capital to a third party if the company has enough authorised share capital. Most importantly, the board does not need shareholder approval.[71] However, companies listed on the New York Stock Exchange (NYSE) would need shareholder approval to issue shares if the share value exceeds

---

[68]   Section 168 Companies Act 2006.
[69]   UKLA Listing Rule 9, 9.16- 9.17.
[70]   In the UK, this would depend on resolving the financial assistance prohibition under Part 18, Chapter 2, Companies Act 2006.
[71]   Section 161 DGCL.

20 per cent of all outstanding voting shares.[72] Furthermore, there are no pre-emption rights although companies may choose to offer them. This means that shareholders would not need to be offered the shares first before approaching a friendly third party. Delaware companies can also give substantial interim dividends even if the losses exceed the profits as long as the company was not insolvent before the dividend issue.[73]

Without Rule 21, UK companies cannot in practice issue shares to third parties without the approval of shareholders.[74] Shareholders have statutory pre-emption rights, thus if shares are issued for cash, they would need to first disapply this right before a third party can be approached.[75] Despite that, UK public companies often grant resolutions to allow share issues annually and they are normally for a specific type of share such as ordinary shares.[76] However, such a waiver is unlikely to be for more than 5 per cent of the share issue.[77] Furthermore, interim dividend distributions would only be available to companies that have a good balance sheet. This is because the company must have its total cumulative profits exceeding total cumulative losses for it to give dividends.[78] The company's net assets must also exceed its share capital.[79] Thus, it would be difficult to apply the restructuring defence in the absence of the board neutrality rule.

c) Sale of key business assets

Third, the sale of key business assets before a takeover bid is a form of takeover defence. The bidder may become disinterested in the company because of the sale of important assets. Under DGCL, shareholder approval is only required when all or substantially all of the assets are up for sale.[80] Thus, this defence can be easily deployed by boards in the US.

However, in the UK, Rule 21 prohibits the sale of company assets without shareholder approval or entering contractual agreements which are not in the ordinary course of business.[81] Thus, without Rule 21, directors' duties would provide the main safeguards during takeovers. Directors' duties will control any defences designed to deter or delay

---

[72] NYSE Listing Manual, paragraph 312.03(c).
[73] DGCL, Section 170(a). Delaware Fraudulent Conveyance Act (Delaware Code, Title 6, subtitle II, Chapter 13, Section 1305).
[74] Sections 549-51, Companies Act 2006.
[75] Sections 561, 570, 571 Companies 2006.
[76] Sections 549-51, Companies Act 2006.
[77] The only scope UK boards have to put in place this defensive mechanism is when the share issue is not for cash, see Section 565 Companies Act 2006.
[78] The net profit test, Section 830 Companies Act 2006.
[79] The net asset test, Section 831 Companies Act 2006.
[80] Section 271(a) DGCL.
[81] Rule 21.1(b)(iv) Takeover Code 2016

unwanted takeovers. The ability to implement a takeover defence in the UK would depend on compliance with the proper purpose rule.[82] Directors would need to determine whether the exercising company powers for the purposes of frustrating a takeover is a legitimate exercise of company powers.[83] The company constitution delegates powers to directors which they cannot misuse for purposes outside those powers. Thus, courts would need to examine the articles detailing the powers to determine their nature and limitations. Non-compliance with the proper purpose doctrine would leave the directors exposed to derivative suits to withdraw the defence and compensate the company if it had suffered losses.

However, Professor Kershaw argues that unlike a state constitution, a company constitution is not subject to minuted debate on the purposes and intentions pertaining to the powers.[84] Most companies use boilerplate company constitutions and the intentions are normally seen as giving the company the powers to run its business. This makes it difficult to specifically point to the purpose the powers were meant to serve.

Furthermore, company contracts are intentionally made incomplete because of the unpredictable nature of business future opportunities and threats. As result, the corporate contract does not contain an exhaustive list of proper purposes. Although the proper purpose doctrine is questionable as a rule of construction, the doctrine ensures that there is no abuse of power between shareholders and the board. Thus, in takeovers, it determines the extent to which the defensive measures fashioned by the board may impact on shareholders' rights.

In the absence of Rule 21, takeover defences would be routinely litigated in courts. Since the proper purposes restrictions apply to defensive actions aimed at affecting the control between directors and shareholders, without Rule 21, directors would attempt to fashion defences that have no effect on control in the company and which can be seen as genuine business decisions. Thus, defences such as poison pills would not be used but asset sales could work if they can show that the motive was not to frustrate a takeover. However, it would be difficult to convince the court that such an asset sell following the takeover bid was not for defensive purposes, if the directors do not have evidence that the defence was contemplated

---

[82]   Sections 260(4) Companies Act 2006.
[83]   *Howard Smith Ltd v. Ampol Petroleum Ltd* [1974] AC 821 at 834, *per* Lord Wilberforce: "it may be attacked on the ground that it was not exercised for the purpose for which it was granted".
[84]   David Kershaw, The Illusion of Importance: Reconsidering the UK's Takeover Defence Prohibition (2007)56 (2) International and Comparative Law Quarterly 267, 283.

before the bid. The boards would also be wary of the derivative suits before fashioning such takeover defensive measures.

Furthermore, the sale of substantial company assets is controlled by the Listing Rules. In particular, the board needs shareholder approval to sale class 1 transactions which represent a quarter of the target profit or market capitalisation, or gross assets.[85] Even though shareholder approval is given, the sale must be for a proper purpose.

d) Business combination defences

Fourth, US companies can use business combination defences to fend off unwanted bidders. The defence limits the acquirer from combining with the acquired company for a period of time after a takeover. This occurs when the bidder exceeds a specific stock ownership percentage in the target company without the approval of the target board. The economic consequences could be severe for the bidder because it would affect integration and delay any realization of expected synergies.

This defence is permitted under DGCL section 203 which bars a company from combining for three years after buying up over 15 per cent of voting stock. The prohibition can also be waived by the board or 75 per cent of disinterested shareholders.[86] Board consent is unlikely because a majority of the remaining shareholders following a takeover are likely to be shareholding directors and other senior managers, whose jobs would be on the line.[87]

The business combination defence can also be part of the company's constitutional documents, regardless of whether the applicable company law provides for such defences. This would require shareholder approval to amend the constitution to permit them.[88]

In the UK, shareholders would be able to amend the company constitution to include business combination defences. The defence would however be denying the shareholders their right to determine the merits of the bid because the bidder would be less willing to proceed with the bid. Thus, it would be caught under Rule 21. Without Rule 21, the right of shareholders to remove the board without cause or instruct the board through an ordinary or special resolution makes this defence largely ineffective.

---

[85] Rule 10.5 UK Listing Rules.
[86] Section 203(a)(3) DGCL.
[87] The defence does not work when, following a 15 per cent acquisition of stock, the bidder's stock ownership in the company is over 85 per cent, Section 203(a)(2) DGCL.
[88] Opting out does not apply when the business combination provisions have already been triggered, Section 203(b)(3) DGCL.

e) Litigation

Finally, takeovers in US can be frustrated through litigation. This could be due to the bidder company's failure to disclose as required under the Securities Exchange Act 1934.[89] Target companies can also bring antitrust lawsuits on the ground that they will suffer antitrust injury if the takeover succeeds.[90] However, case law suggests that the target company would struggle to obtain legal standing to bring such a claim.[91] Litigation also has the effect of delaying the bid thus allowing the board time to fashion takeover defences or depending on the outcome of the lawsuit, it can fend off the bidder. However, a poison pill would provide a longer delay to a takeover as compared to a preliminary injunction.

In the absence of Rule 21, litigation would play a major role in ensuring that the board serves the interests of shareholders. The Takeover Code received statutory force through Part 28 of the Companies Act 2006.[92] However, no person outside the Takeover Panel can apply for injunctive relief and it does not permit private law suits for breach of disclosure requirements.[93] Code-related litigation has more scope to succeed than non-code related litigation.[94] While litigation is standard procedure in Delaware, the Takeover Panel is less receptive to tactical litigation. In a study conducted by Amour and Skeel, they found 0.2 percent unwanted takeovers were litigated in the UK between 1990- 2005.[95] Thus, theoretically, litigation in the UK could act as a defensive mechanism but in practice the defence is largely ineffective.

Overall, although the evidence on the impact of takeover defences on shareholder value is generally mixed, an analysis of the position in the UK without Rule 21 has shown that the takeover defences would be severely limited. Staggered boards are not available in the UK and directors can be removed without cause. Without staggered boards, the pill can easily be redeemed by removing the board at a general meeting. Furthermore, most of the restructuring defences require shareholder approval which is

---

[89] Sections 13(d) and 14(d).
[90] Under The *Clayton* Antitrust Act of 1914.
[91] *Anago Inc v. Techno Medical Products Inc* 976 F.2d 248 (1992) where the Fifth Circuit Court of Appeals held that the target board did not have standing.
[92] Legal effect came from Takeovers Directive (Interim Implementation Regulations) 2006.
[93] Section 955(3), Companies Act 2006.

82 Section 956, Companies Act 2006.
[94] See *Dunford Elliot v. Johnston & Firth Brown* CA 1977 and *Marina Development Group v Local London* (Unpublished).
[95] House of Commons Business, Innovation and Skills Committee, Mergers, acquisitions and takeovers: The takeover of Cadbury by Kraft, Ninth Report of Session 2009-2010 (HC 234) 3.

difficult to achieve if the effect is to deny shareholders the right to determine the outcome of a takeover.

Furthermore, studies on the effect of takeover defences on shareholder value have used different measurements and as a result, this has led to largely mixed results on whether takeover defences destroy shareholder value. Takeover defences are also unlikely to work in the UK because of the restrictions imposed by company law rules.

For non-shareholding stakeholders, the evidence shows that the removal of the board neutrality rule would do little to improve their position. The protection given to shareholders under company law would limit any takeover defence fashioned by the board in the absence of Rule 21 even though it is aimed at protecting stakeholders' interests. This brings the continued imposition of Rule 21 into question; with or without Rule 21, non-shareholding stakeholders would find themselves in a secondary position to shareholders during takeovers. Furthermore, if the board neutrality rule is to be revised to offer more powers to directors, the main challenge would be providing sufficiently clear rules to avoid unnecessary legal uncertainty and misuse by the board.

The conclusion reached after examining the board-centric Delaware model is that there is insufficient evidence that the US system is better than the UK system. Rather, the research evidence generally shows that it provides less protection to shareholders and stakeholders as compared to the UK system. Even though the board-centric model is selected to replace the UK shareholder-centric model, it cannot work since both company law and UK Listing Rules impose a number of limitations that would make it difficult for the board to frustrate takeovers. Thus, for the board-centric model to work in the UK, an overhaul of company law rules would be necessary. However, findings in this study nor existing empirical evidence is not strong enough to justify a major change in takeover regulation.

Disenfranchisement of short-term shareholders' voting rights

As explained in Chapter 5, short-term investors such as hedge funds become interested in the company's stock following a public announcement of an offer. Due to their actions, the Takeover Panel reached a conclusion that short-termism allows unwanted bidders to get a tactical advantage over the target company.[96] This is supported by the findings from this study in

---

[96] The Takeover Panel, Consultation Paper Issued by the Code Committee of the Panel: Review of Certain Aspects of the Regulation of Takeover Bids (21 October 2010) 4, Paragraph 1.11.

which short-term investors took over both Cadbury and Corus and this had a major bearing on the outcome of the takeover bids.

Despite that, the post-Cadbury/Kraft changes made to the Takeover Code in 2011 did not include any reform to the board neutrality rule. The Takeover Code currently makes no distinction between persons who are already shareholders at the time of the offer period and persons who come to acquire shares in the offeree company during the course of the offer period. The offer period means the period from the time when an announcement of a proposed or possible offer is made until the first closing day.[97] Thus, both long-term shareholders (holders of the target company's stock prior to the takeover announcement) and short-term shareholders have the same rights during takeovers.

However, the Takeover Panel rejected proposals for more stringent regulation of short-term shareholders.[98] The Panel had originally proposed a rule that would disenfranchise all short-term investors who had bought up the target company's shares after the takeover bid announcement from voting on it.[99] However, this is not the first time such a proposal has been made. Lord Myners had proposed a two-tier voting structure in 2009, with long-term shareholders having more voting powers.[100] Similar proposals for a multiple-tier voting structure were proposed in the 1990s.[101] On all previous occasions, the Takeover Panel rejected the proposals. However, disenfranchisement of short-term shareholders voting rights, with variations to the original proposals, is considered in this study as a solution to the short-termism problem and the adverse impact on non-shareholding stakeholders.

Takeover arbitrage and the long-term economic interests of the company

Financial market practices have changed the nature of shareholder voting by moving them away from the original purpose of promoting the economic interests of the company. As a result, shareholders can vote against a decision which in the best interest of the company because it is contrary to their own economic interests.[102] For example, an investor may have a

---

[97] *Ibid* 20, Paragraph 3.2.
[98] The Takeover Panel, Response Statement to the Consultation Paper on Review of Certain Aspects of the Regulation of Takeover Bids (2010) 9, Paragraph 4.10.
[99] The Takeover Panel, Consultation Paper Issued by the Code Committee of the Panel: Review of Certain Aspects of the Regulation of Takeover Bids (21 October 2010) 20-29.
[100] Jonathan Russell, ABI Leads Attack on Myners Over Reform, The Telegraph, (August 1 2009).
[101] See Andy Cosh, Alan Hughes and Ajit Singh, Takeovers and Short-termism in the UK (London: Industry Policy Paper No.3, 1990) 42.
[102] Shaun Martin and Frank Partnoy, Encumbered Shares (2005) 30 (3), University of Illinois

negative economic interest if they can profit from the company's falling share price. This can be achieved through short selling which arises when an investor obtains shares from a broker and immediately sells them.[103] The investor buys identical shares to cover the shares obtained from the broker and afterwards gives the borrowed shares back to the broker. For the investor, he would be looking to make a profit by betting on the share price to fall between borrowing the shares and finding a replacement for them.

In takeovers, voting disparity normally arises when investors seek to engage in arbitrage. Takeover arbitrage arises when an investor acquires stock in the target company after the public announcement of an offer. The investor would hope to make substantial profit on the high premium tabled by the bidder which is above the market price at which the investor bought the shares. However, in case the bidder does not carry out the transaction, the share value would drop below what the investor paid to acquire them. Thus, arbitrage is driven by the desire to make short-term profit despite the risks.

In the takeover market, the most influential arbitrageurs are hedge and mutual funds.[104] Both funds are managed portfolios thus a manager places a group of securities into one portfolio. However, hedge funds are managed more aggressively because fund managers are able to make speculative decisions. Mutual funds are not permitted to take highly risky investment decisions and as a result they are safer for investors. Furthermore, mutual funds are easy to invest in with only minimal amounts of money needed. Hedge funds, on the other hand, are only available to groups of sophisticated investors with high net worth. Given the differences between the funds, it is not surprising therefore, that hedge funds often engage in takeover arbitrate.

Institutional investors such as hedge funds are the only investors with sufficient resources to buy voting rights in companies in a bid to influence the shareholder vote. For example, at the time the final offer for Cadbury shares was tabled, 33 per cent of voting rights had been bought up and that amounts to billions of pounds. Individual investors would not have the resources to acquire such a large percentage of voting rights in a short

---

Law Review *775, 810; TR Investors, LLC v. Genger*, Del. Ch. Lexis 153, 70-71 (Del. Ch. July 23, 2010).

[103] Marcelo Pinheiro, Short-selling restrictions, takeovers *and the* wealth of long-run shareholders (2009) 45 (5), Journal of Mathematical Economics 361, 374.

[104] Christopher Bruner, The Enduring Ambivalence of Corporate Law (2008) 59 (5), Alabama Law Review 1385, 1442.

period of time. Thus, the reform proposals would have a greater impact on institutional shareholders than individuals.

Institutional investors can use their stake in the company to play an influential role on the outcome of a takeover bid. For example, on the acquiring side, Deutsche Borce abandoned its bid for the London Stock Exchange (LSE) in 2004 because shareholding hedge funds and mutual funds were dissatisfied with the bid.[105] On the target side, institutional investors in Chiron were unhappy with Novartis' takeover bid for Chiron in 2005 which forced the bidder to increase the premium from 23 per cent to 32 per cent.[106] Thus, institutional investors such as hedge funds and mutual funds can play an active role that would influence the results of a takeover bid from both the target and acquiring side.

Apart from selling their shares to arbitrageurs, institutional shareholders such as hedge funds participate in buying the target company's shares after the announcement of a takeover. For example, in the *Air Product v. Airgas*, by the time the case was filed, arbitrageurs had already bought up half of the shares.[107] This was similar to Cadbury where 33 per cent of the shares were in the hands of arbitrageurs by the time the final offer was tabled. This illustrates the level of impact arbitrageurs have on the target company's share register during the takeover process. In *Air Product v. Airgas*, Chancellor Chandler derided the adverse impact arbitrageurs have on long-term health of the target company.[108]

The disconnection between economic interests and voting rights in a takeover arbitrage situation poses serious risks to long-term shareholders' interests and those of the company and its non-shareholding stakeholders. After all, it is the long-term shareholders who decide to sell their shares to arbitrageurs in a bid to satisfy their investment goals.

The "put up or shut up" deadline

The Takeover Panel set out to reduce short-termism by introducing the "Put Up or Shut Up" deadline (PUSU) in 2011. A mandatory 28 day deadline was set to overcome the virtual bid problem during a takeover. Before the amendments, the bidder could besiege the target company by announcing that they would make a bid and wait for many months without tabling one. This gave enough time to short-term investors to buy up the long-

---

[105] Marcel Kahan and Edward Rock, Hedge Funds in Corporate Governance and Corporate Control, (2007)155 (5) University of Pennsylvania Law Review 1021, 1083.

[106] Norvatis Media Release http://cws.huginonline.com/N/134323/PR/200604/1045686_5_2. html (Accessed 19/04/2014).

[107] See *Air Products and Chemicas Inc. v. Airgas*, Inc C.A. No. 5249-CC (Del. Ch. 2011).

[108] *Ibid* at 109 (citing *Mercier v. Inter-Tel (Delaware), Inc.*, 929 A.2d 786, 815 (Del. Ch. 2007).

term shareholders. PUSU requires the bidder to make a firm offer within 28 days otherwise they would need to come back in six months when they are ready.

Thus, the short window alleviates some pressure put on the target company by arbitrageurs to blindly accept a takeover offer. If a bidder can no longer besiege the target company, this means over the six months period, the price increase would be minimal to reflect uncertainty over the success of the takeover. As a result, this decreases the likelihood of the shareholder composition changing significantly through arbitrageurs buying out long-term shareholders. The target company would also have smaller voting blocks of arbitrageurs and more long-term shareholders would be available to vote on the merits of the offer. Unlike in Cadbury where 33 per cent were arbitrageurs after the first offer, the short window should prevent large scale arbitrate and protect the interests of long-term shareholders who may be intent on holding onto their stock despite the premium offer.

However, the new deadline is unlikely to prevent arbitrageurs because they would still be able to buy a large percentage of shares during the 28 day window, enough to determine the outcome of a takeover bid. One of the proposals made and later rejected by the takeover panel was to exempt short-term shareholders from voting on takeover transactions.[109] This reform proposal is considered as a better solution to takeover arbitrages than the 28 days window.

The disenfranchisement of short-term shareholders

Respondents to the Takeover Panel consultation were unanimously opposed to the proposal of disenfranchising short-term shareholders' voting rights. For example, Roger Barker, the Institute of Directors' Head of Corporate Governance said that "depriving certain shareholders of their voting rights would have been mistaken…It would be undesirable for takeover policy to be perceived as a pretext for protectionism, as part of an industrial strategy, or as the outcome of a political lobbying process."[110] Similarly, the Association of British Insurers (ABI) did not think disenfranchisement was a fair solution: "If existing shareholders do not value shares as highly as another party to whom they decide to sell those shares it is not obvious why the views of the former, whatever they are, should be thought to be

---

[109] The Takeover Panel, Consultation Paper Issued by the Code Committee of the Panel: Review of Certain Aspects of the Regulation of Takeover Bids (21 October 2010) 20-29.
[110] Roger Pilgrim, UK Takeover Panel Recommends Code Change, Tax News, (26 October2010).

the more worthy."[111] Eventually, the Takeover Panel rejected the proposal to disenfranchise short-term shareholders who had acquired company shares during the offer period from voting.[112]

The main argument in support of disenfranchisement of shares acquired during the offer period is that it would have the effect of reducing acquisition of the target company's shares by short-term shareholders. This is because the shares would not carry voting rights and this would reduce their demand resulting in shares within the target company trading at a lower price or a larger discount to the offer price. Existing shareholders would also be deterred from selling their shares to hedge against the possibility of the offer not going through. Thus, a high proportion of shares would stay in long-term shareholders' hands and they may be more willing to forego short-term gain for long-term value.

This argument is based on the assumption that shareholders who buy the target company's shares during the offer period are only interested in short-term gains, hence the punishment. It also assumes that the remaining pool of shareholders has a long-term interest in the company and their vote would reflect it.

It is true that most of the shareholders who bought Cadbury stock during the offer period wanted short-term gains at the same time, shareholders who sold to the short-term investors were arguably focused on their own short-term gains. However, all the assumptions may not always be justified. Some of the shareholders that bought shares after the announcement may have actually invested believing in the long-term value of the company.

However, it also creates uncertainty on whether the voting restrictions under a contractual offer would be the same for a scheme of arrangement. In a contractual offer to shareholders of the target company, there is no requirement that those who wish to accept the offer have to vote in favour for the bid to succeed. Shareholders are merely invited by the bidder to accept the offer by transferring the title in their shares. This should however be contrasted from a takeover by way of scheme of arrangement under which company law rules require approval of a resolution voted on by company shareholders. A scheme of arrangement is bindings on all shareholders regardless of whether they vote or not. An issue that would need to be resolved is whether voting rights would be disenfranchised only

---

[111] The ABI's Response to Takeover Panel consultation paper PCP 2010/2. Available at: https://www.abi.org.uk/~/media/Files/Documents/Consultation%20papers/2010/07/POTAM%20pcp%202010%202.ashx. (Accessed 18/07/2016) 4-5.
[112] The Takeover Panel, Response Statement to the Consultation Paper on Review of Certain Aspects of the Regulation of Takeover Bids (2010) 9, Paragraph 4.4.

for the purposes of voting during a contractual offer or for all purposes, including resolutions for approving a scheme of arrangement.

Another argument against the disenfranchisement of shares in the target company during the offer period is that it would be contrary to General Principle 1[113] of Takeover Code and "one share, one vote" principle under the Takeover Directive.[114] It states that "all holders of the securities of an offeree company of the same class must be afforded equivalent treatment". Clearly, arbitrageurs have to buy shares from long-term shareholders who are content to sell them for a return on their investment. To deny long-term shareholders the right to sell their stock to their short-term counterparts would be contravening the principles of the Takeover Code.[115] Thus, there is no objective justification for treating short-term shareholders less favourably than long-term shareholders of the same class.

Provisions on disenfranchisement of shares may also be easy to avoid. An investor could enter an agreement with existing shareholders for the economic interest and control over the shares to be transferred to the investor without legal title and without shares being disenfranchised. It also impacts on the defensive tactics used by the board to target a White Knight or friendly bidder because the bidder would not be able to vote on the acquired shares. Such a disenfranchisement of shares would also need amendment of company law rules on shares and voting rights to reflect the new classifications.

Furthermore, given that share sales would continue, irrespective of the effect on the voting rights, it would mean that a small pool of shareholders with voting rights would be left in the company to vote on the outcome of a takeover. This makes it even easier to acquire companies because fewer shareholders would be voting. It would also make it cheaper to acquire the company because fewer shareholders would need to be convinced to sell thus a hostile bidder may end up tabling a lower offer.

Given the limitations of the disenfranchisement proposal, two alternative variations are proposed. In the 2011 Takeover Panel consultation on reforming the Takeover Code, the Confederation of British Industry (CBI) gave some stern guidance on the direction policy should take:

> "[W]e believe that a broad mix of policy solutions could make a difference to promoting a long term view of ownership, not just

---

[113] Identical to Article 3(1)(a) of the Takeover Directive (2004/25).
[114] Council Directive 2004/25/EC on Takeover Bids [2005] Article 5; See Guildo Ferrarini, One Share- One Vote: A European Rule? (2006), *SSRN* Working Paper, 2.
[115] Takeover Code 2016, Introduction, at A1.

changes to takeover rules. These are matters for Government and other regulators, not the Takeover Panel, but include".[116]

The CBI supports corporate governance measures that would encourage a long-term approach rather than a disenfranchisement of voting rights or any proposal with a similar effect. These proposals are considered next.

Variations to the share disenfranchisement reform proposal

It is advanced in this book that the Takeover Panel should not foreclose the proposal on disenfranchising short-term shareholders' voting rights in its entirety. Instead of denying all the shareholders who purchase shares after the announcement date the right to vote, the Takeover Panel should consider halving the votes of short-term investors. More voting powers would remain in the hands of shareholders at the same time not severely undervaluing the shares purchased after the announcement of a possible takeover offer. This is because denying all shareholders who buy after the announcement date a right to vote would devalue the shares.

However, this variation also suffers from the same limitations as the main version because it is mainly based on the assumption that long-term shareholders would vote in the long-term interest of the company rather than short-term gain. Thus, it is unlikely that the Takeover Panel would consider it given the strong rejection of the main version by the business community.

Second, the proposal could be varied by reference to Rule 8.3 of the Takeover Code on disclosure requirements. The rule requires all who become interested in 1 per cent or more of the target or acquiring company's stock before the announcement or during the offer period to disclose details of their interest to the public.[117] Thus, if only those short-term investors with over 1 per cent interest were to have their voting powers halved then long-term shareholders who want to tender their shares to arbitrageurs would be able to while alleviating problems associated by bulk buying of shares by arbitrageurs. Halving the votes of arbitrageurs who acquire significant voting rights would leave the power to accept the bid mostly in the hands of long-term shareholders. This would optimise shareholder protection and at the same time maintaining the liquidity of the target company's stock.

---

[116] The CBI's Response to Takeover Panel consultation paper PCP 2011/1. Available at: http://www.thetakeoverpanel.org.uk/wp-content/uploads/2008/11/PCP201101response8. pdf (Accessed 18/07/2016) Paragraph 18.
[117] Takeover Code, Rule 8.3(a)-(b).

Limiting the voting rights of short-term shareholders is likely to result in less arbitrate activity. Long-term shareholders would have less option to sell their stock for a slight price increase caused by the potential offer. Would this improve the position of non-shareholding stakeholders? Given the evidence showing that arbitrageurs who are inherently short-termist buy shares to sell, this variation could overcome short-termism. One of the objectives of denying shareholders that buy shares after the announcement date the right to vote is to ensure that the outcome of a takeover bid is decided by the original shareholders who are generally more interested in the long-term interest of the company. Thus, non-shareholding stakeholders would still need the remaining shareholders to reject a short-term premium offer.

However, denying shareholders a vote or the right to transfer their property goes against the equal treatment and one share-one vote principles. This puts the reform proposals in jeopardy. Despite that, if the takeover Panel elects to implement any of the proposals, they would need to consult the business community to determine the feasibility of amending the Takeover Code to that effect. However, major challenges to this proposal are expected given that the evidence from the case studies and existing empirical studies is not strong enough to justify a change in takeover law to either a board-centric model or disenfranchisement of short-term shareholders' voting rights. After all the business community is expected to remain hostile to any reform that threatens shareholder primacy in the company.

The way forward

After an examination of the two main reform proposals, the board-centric model has been deemed impractical and unsuitable for implementation in the UK while the share disenfranchisement proposal is largely based on assumptions and suffers from many shortfalls. Disenfranchising short-term shareholders' voting rights is unlikely to work for the benefit of non-shareholding stakeholders because even long-term shareholders would be expected to support a takeover. However, the two variants to the disenfranchisement proposals provide lighter solution to shareholder short-termism even though they are premised on the same assumptions as the main proposal.

In regards to the adoption of a board-centric takeover model, given the evidence showing that takeovers negatively impact on jobs, this would still be the case even though takeover defences are permitted. Takeovers that succeed would result in restructurings that would inevitably lead to loss of jobs. Thus, permitting the board to erect defences would do little to alleviate the suffering of non-shareholding stakeholders such as employees. Even if takeover defences are permitted, due to section 172, the directors owe the duty to shareholders and other stakeholders come second. Thus, faced with a takeover, their duty would be profit maximisation by choosing the most profitable position for shareholders before considering other options. Thus, the US model would do little to improve the position of non-shareholding stakeholders in the UK unless an overhaul of company law rules is also carried out. On that background, the idea of implementing a board-centric takeover model in the UK should remain a theoretical one for now.

Due to the limitations of the abovementioned proposals, a possible solution could be to foster a long-term approach among shareholders. It is difficult for the board to act in the long-term manner if shareholders who make the final decision are only thinking short-term. The long-term approach of the directors would be invalidated by the short-term interests of shareholders to whom company law and takeover law gives primacy. Thus, the aim is to find a solution that would push shareholders to think and act long-term.

As a solution, the Stewardship Code 2012 can be relied on to foster a long-term approach among shareholders. The Code was first issued by the Financial Reporting Council (FRC) in 2010. It puts a number of obligations on fund managers including monitoring of investee firms. It is regulated by the Financial Services Authority (FSA) and works on a comply or explain basis.[118] Thus fund managers that fail to comply to any of the provisions need to provide an explanation.

The suggestion is to put more obligations on fund managers to work with a long-term vision. Institutional investors such as hedge funds were criticised in Chapter 5.3 for assessing the performance of fund managers on short-term variables and as a result, managers are encouraged to seek short-term benefits such as takeover arbitrage.[119] Putting more obligations on institutional shareholders to take a long-term approach when investing in companies could alleviate the short-term behaviours encountered in Cadbury and Corus.

However, it should be pointed out that this proposal is not a panacea. Since the Stewardship Code 2012 is governed by reputational sanctions and on a voluntary comply or explain basis, it is difficult to guarantee that

---

[118] See Iris Chiu, Stewardship as a Force for Governance: Critically Assessing the Aspirations and Weaknesses of the UK Stewardship Code (2012) 9 (1), European Company Law 5, 8.
[119] See Paul Myners, Institutional investment in the United Kingdom: a review, HM Treasury: London, (2001), paragraphs 5.64 to 5.69.

it would encourage institutional shareholders such as fund managers to think and act long-term when faced with a premium offer for their shares.

Furthermore, the FSA has limited powers to regulate foreign investors, which means the long-term approach being encouraged in the UK would not apply to foreign investors.[120] This is in light of evidence showing that foreign ownership in the UK listed companies has been steadily increasing. According to the office of National Statistics, holdings of foreign investors in the UK increased from 7.0 per cent in 1963, when the takeover market was still in its infancy, to 41.2 per cent in 2010.[121] With foreign investors able to buy shares in target companies during the offer period, it means that the long-term approach being encouraged is likely to become dysfunctional.

Summary

This chapter has shown that the board-centric model does not provide more protection to non-shareholding stakeholders or improve shareholder value. Even if it could improve shareholder value and offer more protection to other stakeholders, company law rules would make it ineffective in the UK. The shareholder disenfranchisement proposal offered a better solution to shareholder short-termism. However, it is largely premised on assumptions on how long-term shareholders would vote and does not guarantee that non-shareholding stakeholders' interests would be protected. The two variations to the proposal such as halving voting rights provide a less drastic and more realistic solution but suffer from the same shortfalls. Given the lack of sufficient empirical evidence to support far-reaching takeover law reform, it is advanced in this book that the solution to investor short-termism and protection of non-shareholding shareholders during takeovers lies outside takeover law but through broader stewardship responsibilities on institutional shareholders.

---

[120] The Takeover Code only applies to companies which have their registered office or admitted for trading in the UK, Channel Islands and Isle of Man, Takeover Code 2016 (Amendment of 2013), Rule 9.
[121] Source: Office for National Statistics, Share Ownership: A Report of Ownership on UK Shares as at (31 December 2010).

CHAPTER 7: SUMMARY, SIGNIFICANCE AND CLOSING REMARKS

Introduction

The purpose of this conclusion is to tie together the research covered within the body of the book and to comment on its meaning. This includes identifying and noting theoretical or policy implications resulting from this study as well as recommendations for further research. It also highlights the limitations of this study in order to foster a ground for future research.

There were three questions asked at the beginning of this study; (1) to what extent do takeovers impact on the interests of non-shareholding stakeholders; (2) what role does shareholder primacy play in the takeover decision making process; and (3) how can the board neutrality rule be reformed in order to provide more protection to non-shareholding stakeholders' interests during takeovers. These questions have been answered and the conclusion reached is that, even though this study found an adverse impact on the interests of non-shareholding stakeholders, the available evidence is not sufficient enough to support or provoke reform to the board neutrality rule.

A summary of the findings and their meaning in the context of future research and policy direction is explained in this chapter. The chapter is broken down into six main parts. First and foremost, justification for undertaking this study is provided. The aim is to explain the background to the research questions and the gaps in research literature that needed resolving. It refers to chapters that have shed light on the gaps within research literature and the changing social-economic environment that has altered the role of a modern company. Second, the empirical findings are explained and how they answered the research questions. Third, the law reform proposals are explained in light of the empirical findings. Fifth, the limitations of this study and the direction of future research is explained. Last but not least, a conclusion to bring the entire book to an end is provided.

Justification for undertaking this research

The impact of takeovers on the target company has been a widely debated issue in a range of disciplines including law, sociology, politics and economics since the mid-twentieth century. This debate was reinvigorated by the works of an American academic, Henry Manne in 1965, who saw hostile takeovers as a managerial disciplinary tool. Subsequent researchers extended Manne's work on hostile takeovers to include friendly takeovers.

However, a review of existing research highlighted gaps in literature; (1) most of the studies were carried out using American takeover samples; (2) most of the studies were carried out in the twentieth century, thus there was a general lack of research on the twenty-first century; and (3) there were mixed results in research literature on the extent to which takeovers impact on non-shareholding stakeholders.

The takeover of Cadbury Plc in 2010 made a study on takeovers very topical and relevant to current legal and political debates. Following the takeover, it came to light that Kraft had went back on its previous promise not to close down Somerdale plant leading to hundreds of Cadbury employees losing their jobs. As a result, there were calls from academics and politicians to put measures in place in order to stop UK companies from being taken over easily by foreign companies. The issue was not whether takeovers are good for the UK economy but whether takeovers are good for the target companies and non-shareholding stakeholders.

However, determining the extent to which takeovers impact on the interests of the target company's stakeholders was only part of the problem. The role takeover law plays in the outcome of takeovers came under scrutiny. Rule 21 of the Takeover Code 2016, the so-called board neutrality rule, does not permit the board of directors to frustrate takeovers. Thus only shareholders can have the final say on the outcome of a takeover. This has been termed shareholder primacy, the ability to exercise control over the company's decision making process. It was already document in some studies that shareholders, especially arbitrageurs who buy shares in the target company during the bidding process, rely on their decision making powers to earn a premium from takeovers. Thus, takeover law handed decision making powers to shareholders which they could use to serve their own interests during takeovers in the process putting the interests of non-shareholding stakeholders at risk. The risk came from permitting a takeover on a price based criteria that serves the interests of shareholders but ignores non-price related factors such as employee jobs and supplier contracts.

Four major issues were identified from an analysis of takeover law and company law; (1) a lack of sufficient legal protection to non-shareholding stakeholders; (2) shareholder primacy under takeover law allows them to serve their own interests; and (3) the board is required under section 172 of the Companies Act 2006 and General Principle 3 of the Takeover Code 2016 to give priority to shareholders' interests before considering other stakeholders. In practice, the board is pressured by shareholders to focus on price-rated factors when recommending a bid. Thus, while the impact on non-shareholding stakeholders was mainly a social-economic issue, the important role takeover law plays towards that outcome made it a social-legal study into the impact of takeovers on non-shareholding stakeholders.

In addition to determining the extent to which takeovers impact on target company stakeholders and the role takeover law plays towards that outcome, the possibility of strengthening non-shareholding stakeholders' rights needed to be considered. Chapter 3 played a major part in our understanding of the changing social demands on companies and the growing need for legal intervention. Leading philosophers and economics before the twentieth century such as Adam Smith did not place much emphasis on corporate social responsibility within a capitalist economic system because they believed that individuals themselves were controlled by community-based norms and institutions such as church, resulting in moral consciousness towards society. Thus, despite having legal personality, it was widely accepted that a company had no social duties and operated for the benefit of its shareholders. Even though the economic and social development experienced in the twentieth century gave companies increased social-economic power, they continued to be viewed as essentially shareholder value driven entities without social responsibilities.

Furthermore, it was recognised that a takeover decision is for shareholders and not directors because a share is a private property. This means that only the shareholders can make a decision over the transfer of shares in a takeover situation regardless of the impact on other stakeholders. Thus, safeguarded by property rights and operating in a western capitalist system, shareholders were the rightful decision makers during takeovers.

The discussion in Chapter 3 showed that in a globalised twenty-first century, companies can no longer be left to advance capitalism without any restraints by relying on shareholders and directors to exercise moral consciousness that would eventually lead to them making socially responsible decisions. This is because institutional shareholders such as hedge funds are now part of the mix, and unlike individual shareholders, they do not have moral consciousness.

Given the impact of takeovers on company stakeholders and the continued acceptance among scholars, policy makers that a modern company must have social responsibilities, this book set out to study the extent to which takeovers impact on the interests of non-shareholding stakeholders. The aim was to determine whether calls by academics and politicians to reduce shareholder control over the takeover process were justified. The emphasis was placed on Rule 21 of the Takeover Code 2016, which gives primacy to shareholders. It came to light that leading scholars such as Professor Kershaw questioned the continued imposition of Rule 21 and politicians such as Lord Mandelson believed it was unfairly relied on by short-term shareholders to the detriment of non-shareholding stakeholders. However, while politicians and academics strongly challenged the continued imposition of Rule 21, policy makers erred on the side of caution and the business community was overwhelmingly hostile to such reform.

Case studies were used to study the extent to which takeovers impact on stakeholders' interests. They were ideal for gathering varied information that would help to shade light on the various factors that determine the outcome a takeover. Selecting the right takeover samples was important because the aim was to fill the gaps in research literature. Cadbury and Corus were the two companies chosen. A small sample was selected in order to get a deeper understanding of the role of shareholders and the impact on other stakeholders rather than selecting many cases and providing limited analysis. The two companies were selected because the takeovers took place in the twenty-first century, overcoming the issue of having only twentieth century research, and for being UK companies. Other reasons include operating in different industries, thus making the findings applicable across industries.

In addition to selecting the right takeover samples, choosing the right stakeholders to study was important. Stakeholders with a contractual relationship with the company were selected for this study. These include employees who provide labour in exchange for remuneration and suppliers who provide supplies in exchange for payment. However, a sub-category of employees, senior management who sit in executive positions, were taken as a separate category because their interests are normally different from those of other employees (see Chapters 1.5 and 2.5.2).

Findings

Three main findings were made in this study.

a) Directors serve shareholders' interests ahead of other stakeholders' interests

The legal analysis showed that both company law and takeover law prioritise the interests of shareholders above non-shareholding stakeholders. Despite that, the enlightened shareholder value approach under section 172 of the Companies Act 2006 requires directors to promote the success of the company as whole including shareholders and other stakeholders. Furthermore, directors have no duty to maximise the short-term gains of shareholders during takeovers above the long-term interests of the company and other stakeholders.

Takeover law takes the view that the interests of the company are the same as the shareholders by giving shareholders decision making powers during takeovers. Although this position is not supported by case law or company law principles, in practice, directors would face immense difficulty in recommending a bid based on a criteria other than price. The difficulty lies under Rule 21 of the Takeover Code which does not only hand decision making powers to shareholders, it bars directors from frustrating a takeover bid. This makes the duty to promote the success of the company as whole practically difficult for directors if shareholders who are increasingly driven by the high premium elect to sell their shares to the bidder.

b)   Short-termism has a major influence on the outcome of takeovers

Shareholder primacy under takeover law has a major bearing on the outcome of takeovers. Short-term investors buy the highly inflated shares of the target company during the offer period firm in mind that their vote will determine the fate of the target company. For example, the takeover of Cadbury by Kraft was largely decided by short-term shareholders. By the second bid, the board's resistance had been broken and could no longer find any justification for rejecting the bid because short-term shareholders wanted and would accept any premium price.

The case studies showed that individual shareholders are bought out during the offer period by mainly institutional shareholders such as mutual funds and hedge funds, who are motivated by the prospect of earning a premium price. However, it is not only the individual shareholders that are bought out, institutional shareholders hold most of the equity in the UK public companies thus they also sell to arbitrageurs during takeovers. This throws away the concept of moral consciousness emphasised by pre- twentieth century theorists that would deter individuals from selling their shares if the decision would have a negative effect on society. In the modern economy, institutional shareholders to whom moral consciousness is inapplicable make the decisions that influence corporate policy and it is mostly them that stand to gain during takeovers. Thus, it unlikely that short-term institutional shareholders who buy highly inflated shares during the offer period would accept a loss by rejecting the offer due to non-price related factors such as employee jobs concerns.

In regards to shareholders' earnings, the study proved more or less what was expected. It found that target company shareholders earn a premium. However, it is the manner in which they earned it that raises concern.

c) Takeovers have an adverse impact on the interests of non-shareholding stakeholders

First and foremost, employees suffer a different fate as compared to the highly enriched shareholders following a takeover. On average, 14 per cent of Cadbury and Corus employees lost their jobs. The level of job loss is higher than that found in existing empirical studies. Furthermore, in both takeover cases, there was a failure to provide relevant (as required under Rule 24.2 of the Takeover Code) and meaningful information in relation to employment (Rule 19.1). There is no requirement for the bidder to provide guarantees over any of the promises made towards stakeholders such as employees. Thus, the 2011 Takeover Code reforms have added more layers of information requirements for the bidder and target boards without tackling the main issue of having guarantees. Although companies are willing to provide information, the information normally does not meet the standard required under Rule 19.1. Thus, employees continue to have limited protection against job losses under the Takeover Code.

Second, in both takeover cases, over 60 per cent of senior managers retained their positions following the takeover. In Cadbury, 65 per cent of senior managers retained their positions. On the board of directors, 35 per cent remained. In Corus, 80 per cent of senior managers retained their positions and on the board of directors, 33 per cent remained. The marked difference in the retention of senior managers was largely down to the nature of the takeovers. Corus was engaged in friendly merger negotiations with Tata Steel prior to the takeover. However, Kraft did not have the same relations with the Cadbury senior management and pursued a hostile takeover.

Third, only one supplier in both target companies had their contracts renegotiated. There was no notable termination or renegotiation of supplier contract in Corus following their takeover by Tata Steel. It is possible that the high retention of senior managers contributed to the better protection experienced by Corus' suppliers. This is in line with existing research evidence which shows a strong relationship between managerial turnover and protection of creditors' interests. Cadbury, however, renegotiated Burtons Biscuits' contract leading to the company entering into financial trouble and closing a manufacturing plant. Neither the findings in this study nor the existing research evidence was sufficient to determine the extent to which suppliers' interests are impacted on by takeovers. Thus there is a need for a larger study in order to determine the full extent to which takeovers have a detrimental effect on suppliers.

Fostering a long-term approach instead of regulatory reform

Although scholars and politicians were critical of the manner in which short-term investors drove Cadbury into Kraft's hands, the responses to a Takeover Panel public consultation in 2010 yielded a completely different picture from the business community. They were overwhelmingly opposed to reducing shareholder control over the takeover process or tampering with the right of short-term investors to conduct themselves in such a manner.

a) The board-centric model

It was concluded that even though the board would be permitted to frustrate takeovers, the takeovers that succeed would result in restructurings that would inevitably lead to loss of jobs. A change of company law rules would also be necessary since directors owe their duties to shareholders and other stakeholders come second. The need to overhaul company law rules suggested that the idea of implementing a US takeover model in the UK should remain a theoretical one.

b) Disenfranchisement of short-term shareholders' voting rights

The proposal to disenfranchise the voting rights of short-term shareholders who buy the target company's shareholder during the offer period was rejected because it is largely premised on assumptions on how long-term shareholders would vote without guarantees that non-shareholding stakeholders' interests would be protected. Furthermore, the proposal goes against the principles of the Takeover Code such as equal treatment of all shareholders of the same class. It may even lead to companies being taken over easily given the limited number of shareholders in the company that would have to vote on the takeover decision.

Two variants to this proposal were considered. First, rather than denying all short-term shareholders a casting vote, their votes could be halved. However, this proposal is also based on the assumption that more voting powers would remain in the hands of long-term shareholders who would take a long-term view when voting. The second variant was to halve the voting powers of short-term shareholders who buy over one per cent of the target's stock. This would limit bulk buying of the target's shares by short-term investors. Again, the assumption is that the remaining shareholders would vote in the interest of the company. However, since the long-term shareholders would also be interested in the premium offer, this proposal is unlikely to provide safeguards to non-shareholding stakeholders.

Failure to find a feasible regulatory solution meant that answers had to be sought outside company law and takeover law. The decision was to change the mentality of short-term investors such as hedge funds and even long-term shareholders to prioritise the long-term value of the company rather than short-term gains during takeovers. The solution is to increase obligations on institutional shareholders under the Stewardship Code 2012 to take up a long-term approach within investee companies.

Institutional shareholders would be expected to reduce practices such as assessing the performance of fund managers on short-term financial results. However, given that the Stewardship Code is governed by reputational sanctions and on a voluntary comply or explain basis, it is likely that most institutional shareholders may choose to explain away their non-compliance. Despite the challenges in imposing more duties on institutional shareholders, such a policy move could drive forward a change in investment approach among institutional shareholders.

Theoretical implications

The findings in this study should further our understanding of shareholders' rights under takeover law and how shareholders' actions contribute to the detrimental effect on the interests of non-shareholding stakeholders.

This study has contributed to our existing understanding of three concepts.

First, the extent to which takeovers impact on employee jobs is more defined following this study. The findings in this study are not consistent with those in previous studies. Previous studies used US takeover cases in the twentieth century. This study has provided evidence on the level of impact on employee jobs in the UK by using the twenty-first century takeover cases. It has shown that the level of impact on employees and senior management jobs is higher than previously recorded. However, the results on the impact on suppliers' were not sufficient enough to draw a valid conclusion.

Second, prior to this study, there was no empirical evidence that short-termism during the takeover process contributes to the detrimental effect on non-shareholding stakeholders. The results have shown that concerns by politicians such as Lord Mandelson that UK companies have become easy targets for foreign bidders due to the actions of short-term shareholders were correct and justified. Short-term shareholders pressured Cadbury management to focus on short-term interests and ignore long-term factors. In fact these findings provide the justification for considering the reform proposals. Thus this study links short-termism with a detrimental effect on non-shareholding stakeholders' interests during takeovers.

Third, prior to this study, some scholars had looked into ways of reforming takeover law in the UK to facilitate more protection to non-shareholding stakeholders as well overcome investor and managerial short-termism. Some of the proposals include empowering directors to make takeover decisions. The findings in this study are consistent with Professor Kershaw's findings that a board-centric model that permits directors to frustrate takeovers cannot work in the UK. It has shown that the model would not offer increased protection to non-shareholding stakeholders during takeovers. However, this study has gone a step further by reconsidering the disenfranchisement of short-term shareholders and providing variations to the proposal. The conclusion reached is that the UK takeover system works well for the business community and given the challenges facing the suggested reform proposals, the best solution is to foster a long-term approach among institutional shareholders rather than regulatory reform.

Recommendations for future research

This study encountered three major practical challenges that need to be addressed through future research.

First, the sample size of two takeover cases did not yield enough information to support a change in takeover policy. For example, only one supplier had their contract terminated. If more than two companies had been studied, this figure could have been higher and thus offered a better indication of the level of impact on suppliers' interests.

Furthermore, although the views of the business community were obtained through responses to the Takeover Panel's public consultations, interviews with executive board members would have provided first-hand account on shareholder control and the level of impact on non-shareholding stakeholders. Their views would provide a major contribution to our understanding on how the law should be reformed to safeguard non-shareholding stakeholders' interests while maintaining shareholder primacy. Interviews with fund managers would also provide a first-hand account of their motivations during takeovers. The aim is to find a solution to arbitrage activity during takeovers.

Second, in addition to the three non-shareholding stakeholders, future researchers must study a range of stakeholders including communities and financial creditors. Wider research on how takeovers impact on non-shareholding stakeholders will strengthen the resolve for legal reform and put pressure on policy makers to find solutions.

Furthermore, research should extend to mergers. They were not considered in this study because they are a friendly undertaking and empirical studies have shown that the degree of impact on employee jobs or other non-shareholding stakeholders is minimal. However, future studies on the impact of mergers on a wide range of non-shareholding stakeholders, in the twenty first century and using UK samples, is necessary.

Although this study focused on target company stakeholders, studies on the acquiring company's stakeholders are relevant to this debate. The findings in Chapter 4.1.7 and 4.2.7 showed that the acquiring company suffered financial difficulties following a takeover. Studies on non-stakeholders' interests in the acquiring company post-takeover would highlight the level of impact on their interests and this would reaffirm the need for policy intervention.

Third and lastly, the reform proposals should be subject to further studies. Researchers should explore the possibility of taxation being relied on to encourage long-term investment. The possibility of giving tax breaks to shareholders who invest with a long-term vision should be considered.

Final remarks

Since the late twentieth century, foreign takeovers have been a common occurrence in the UK. Although the economy has benefited from billions that are spent in the UK every year, the impact on employees, in particular, remains a major and ongoing concern. This study has highlighted some of the ongoing concerns over the UK takeover activity. However, since the business community supports shareholder primacy and remains hostile to any reform that interferes with their decision making authority during takeovers, it is likely that this concern, although supported by empirical evidence, may remain a theoretical one for now. Nonetheless, future research that offers a wider account of the impact on non-shareholding interests and the subsequent acquisition of iconic British brands should increase pressure on policy makers to intervene and find a solution to shareholder short-termism, and the detrimental impact on non-shareholding stakeholders during takeovers. In the end, policy makers must recognise that a modern company has a social responsibility and if it cannot be voluntarily achieved then regulatory reform should enter the fray.

BIBILIOGRAPHY

Aga, S. (2010), "A Review and Comparison of Takeover Defences in the US and UK", SSRN Working Paper.

Aghion, P & Bolton, P. (1992), "An Incomplete Contracts Approach to Financial Contracting", Review of Economic Studies, Volume 59, Issue 3, pp.473-494.

Aglietta, M & Reberioux, A. (2005), "Corporate Governance Adrift: A Critique of Shareholder Value", Cheltenham: Edward Elgar.

Agrawal, A. Jaffe, J. F & Mandelker, G. N. (1992), "The Post-Merger Performance of Acquiring Firms: A Re-examination of an Anomaly", Journal of Finance, Volume 47, Issue 4, pp. 1605-1621.

Agrawal, A & Walkling, R. A. (1994), "Executive Careers and Compensation Surrounding Takeover Bids", Journal of Finance, Volume 49, Issue 3, pp. 985-101.

Alazzawi, S. (2004), "Foreign direct investment and knowledge flows: evidence from patent citations", University of California, Davis, 8 January.

Alchian, A. (1969), "Corporate management and property rights", in Manne, H. (ed.), Economic policy and the regulation of corporate securities (Washington, D.C.: American Enterprise Institute); reprinted in Furobotn, E & Pejovic, S. (1974), "The economics of property rights", Cambridge, MA: Ballinger.

Alchian, A. & Demsetz, H. L. (1972), "Production, Information Costs, and Economic Organization," American Economic Review, Volume 62, Issue 5, pp. 777-795.

Alexandridis, G. Petmezas, D & Travlos, N.G. (2010), "Gains from Mergers and Acquisitions Around the World: New Evidence", Journal of Financial Management, Volume 39, Issue 4, pp. 1671–1695.

Allen, G & Dar, A. (2013), "Foreign Direct Investment (FDI)", House of Commons Library briefing paper, SN/EP/1828, London.

Allen, F. Carletti, E & Marquez, R. (2014), "Stakeholder Governance, Competition and Firm Value" Center for Economic studies and ifo institute, Working paper series No. 4652.

Anfara, V. & Mertz, N. (2006), "Theoretical framework in qualitative research", Thousand Oaks, CA: Sage Publications, London.

AP, "Warren Buffet Opposed Kraft-Cadbury Merger", Washington Post, January 6, 2010

Aristotle (2014), "Nicomachean Ethics" (Translated by Reeve C.D. C.), Hackett Publishing Company: USA.

Armour, J & Whincop, M. (2005), "The proprietary foundations of Corporate Law", Cambridge: ERC Centre of Business Research Working Paper No 299.

Armour, J. Deakin, S & Konzelmann, S. (2003), "Shareholder Primacy and Trajectory of UK Corporate Governance", ESRC Centre for Business Research, University of Cambridge working Paper 226.

Armour, J & Skeel D.A. (2007), "Who Writes the Rules for Hostile Takeovers, and Why? -- The Peculiar Divergence of U.S. and U.K. Takeover Regulation" Georgetown Law Journal, Volume 95, pp. 1727-1794.

Atiyah, P & Summers, R. (1987), "Form and Substance in Anglo American Law: A Comparative Study of Legal Reasoning, Legal Theory and Legal Institutions", Oxford: Clarendon Press.

Baer, J. (2010), "Buffet cautions against share issue", Financial Times, January 6.

Bainbridge, S. (2008), "The New Corporate Governance in Theory and Practice", Oxford: Oxford University Press.

Bakan, J. (2004), "The corporation: The pathological pursuit of profit and power", New York: Free Press.

Baker, R. D & Limmack, R. J. (2001), "UK takeovers and acquiring company wealth changes: The impact of survivorship and other potential selection biases on post-outcome performance", Working Paper, University of Stirling.

Baker, H. K & Nofsinger, J. R. (2010), "Behavioral Finance: Investors, Corporations, and Markets", Wiley John & Sons: New Jersey

Barboutis, G.O. (1999), "Takeover defence tactics: Part 1: the general legal framework on takeovers" Company Lawyer, Volume 20, Issue 1, pp. 14-22.

Baumol, W. J. (1959), "Business Behavior, Value, and Growth", New York: Macmillan.

Baums, T. (1993), "Takeovers versus Institutions in Corporate Governance in Germany" in Prentice, D & Holland, P (eds), Contemporary Issues in Corporate Governance, Oxford: Clarendon Press.

Baxter, P & Jack, S. (2008), "Qualitative Case Study Methodology: Study design and implementation for novice researchers", in The Qualitative Report, Volume 13, Issue 4, pp. 544-559.

Bebchuk, L. Coates, J.C & Subramanian, G. (2002), "The Powerful Antitakeover Force of Staggered Boards: Further Findings and a Reply to Symposium Participants", Stanford Law Review, Volume 55, Issue 3, pp. 885-917.

Bebchuk, L. (2002), "The Case Against Board Veto in Corporate Takeovers", The University of Chicago Law Review, Volume 69, Issue 3, pp. 973-1035.

Bebchuk, L. (2005), "The Case for Increasing Shareholder Power", Harvard Law Review, Volume 118, Issue 3, pp. 833-914.

Beckman, T & Forbes, W. (2004), "An examination of takeovers, job loss, and wage decline within the UK Industry", European Financial Management, Volume 10, Issue 1, pp.141–165.

Begum, H. (2005), "Analysis: Theatre of schemes", The Lawyer, May 30.

Berle, A. A & Means, G. C. (1932), "The Modern Corporation and Private Property". New York: Commerce Clearing House.

Berle, A. (1932), "For whom corporate managers are trustees: A Note", Harvard Law Review, Volume 45, Issue 7, pp. 1365–1372.

Bernard, B & Kraakman, R. (1996), "A self-enforcing model of corporate law", Harvard Law Review, Volume 109, Issue 8, pp. 1911-1996.

Bhagat, S, Shleifer A & Vishny, R, (1990), "Hostile Takeovers in the 1980s: The Return to Corporate Specialization" in Bailey M.N & Winston, C (eds) "Brookings Papers on Economic Activity: Microeconomics", Washington, DC: Brookings Institution.

Birchall, J & Baer, J. (2010), "Buffet wades into battle for Cadbury", Financial Times, January 6.

Black, B. S. (1989), "Bidder Overpayment in Takeovers", Stanford Law Review, Volume 41, Issue 3, pp. 625-626.

Black, B. S & Coffee, J. C. (1997), "Hail Britannia? Institutional investor Behavior under limited regulation", Michigan Law Review, Volume 92, Issue 7, pp. 1997-2087.

Black, B. S & Kraakmann, R. (2002), "Delaware's Takeover law: The Uncertain Search for Hidden Value", Northwestern University Law Review, Volume 96, Issue 2, pp. 521-566.

Blair, M. (1995), "Ownership and control: Rethinking corporate governance for the twentieth-first century" Washington DC: Brookings Institution.

Blair, M. & Stout, L. A. (1999), "A team production theory of corporate law", Virginia Law Review, Volume 85, Issue 2, pp. 247-328.

Blair, M. (2003), "Locking in Capital: What Corporate Law Achieved for Business Organizers in the Nineteenth Century", University of California, Los Angeles Review, Volume 51, Issue 2, pp. 387-455.

Blair, M. (1996), "Wealth Creation and Wealth Sharing", Washington, D.C: Brookings.

Blanc, P. L (2008), "Revolution, Democracy, Socialism: Selected Writings of Lenin". (Pluto Press, London)

Blundell, J & Robinson, C. (2000), "Regulation without the State: The Debate Continues", London: Institute of Economic Affairs.

Bolton, P & von Thadden, E. (1998), "Liquidity and Control: A Dynamic Theory of Corporate Ownership Structure", Journal of Institutional and Theoretical Economics, Volume, 154, Issue1, pp. 177-211.

Bratton, W. W. (2002), "Enron and the Dark Side of Shareholder Value", Tulane Law Review, Volume 76, Issue 2, pp. 1275-1361.

Bremmer, B & Lakshman, N. (2007), "Tata Steel bags Corus- but at what price?" Global economics, January 31.

Bromley, D. B. (1990), "Academic contributions to psychological counselling: I. A philosophy of science for the study of individual cases", Counselling Psychology Quarterly, Volume 3, Issue 3, pp. 299-307.

Bruner, C M. (2008), "The Enduring Ambivalence of Corporate Law", Alabama Law Review, Volume 59, Issue , pp. 1385–1449.

Busha, C & Harter, S. (1980), "Research Methods in Librarianship: techniques and Interpretations". Academic Press: New York

Cadbury, D. (2010), "Chocolate Wars", London: Harper Press.

Cadbury, D. (2010), "The Kraft Takeover of Cadbury." Public Lecture, Birmingham Business School, The University of Birmingham, UK. November 18.

Carnes, L. (2013), "Aristotle's Politics", 2nd Edition. Chicago: University of Chicago Press.

Centre for Economics and Business Research (2013), "World Economic League Table 2013", December 26.

Cesar, C. Loayza, N & Serven, L. (2004), "Greenfield foreign direct investment and mergers and acquisitions: feedback and macroeconomic effects", World Bank Policy Research Working Paper 3192, Washington, DC: World Bank, January.

CFA Institute (2006), "Breaking the Short-Term Cycle", Centre for Financial Market Integrity and Business Roundtable Institute for Corporate Ethics.

Cheffins, B. (1999), "Using Theory to Study Law: A Company Law Perspective", Cambridge Law Journal Volume 58, Issue 1, pp. 197- 221.

Chemla, G. (2005), "Hold-up, Stakeholders and Takeover Threats", Journal of Financial Intermediation", Volume, 14, Issue 3, pp. 376-397.

Chiu, I. (2012), "Stewardship as a Force for Governance: Critically Assessing the Aspirations and Weaknesses of the UK Stewardship Code", European Company Law, Volume 9, Issue 1, pp. 5–11.

Chiu, I. (2013), "Turning Institutional Investors into Stewards: Exploring the Meaning and Objectives of Stewardship", Current Legal Problems, Volume 66, Issue 1, pp. 443- 481.

Christiansen, H & Ogutcu, M. (2002), "Foreign Direct Investment for Development: Maximising Benefits, Minimising Costs", OECD Working Paper.

Christman, J. (1994), "The Myth of Property: Towards an Egalitarian Theory of Ownership" Oxford University Press: New York.

Citera, M & Rentsch, J. (1993), "Is There Justice in Organizational Acquisitions? The Role of Distributive and Procedural Fairness in Corporate Acquisitions", in Cropanzano R. (ed), "Justice in the Workplace: Approaching Fairness in Human Resources Management", Lawrence Erlbaum Associates: Hillsdale, NJ.

Clark, R. (1986), "Corporate Law", Boston: Little, Brown Book Group.

Clarke, T. (2007), "International Corporate Governance: A Comparative Approach", Abingdon: Routledge.

Clarke, B. (2011), "Directors' Duties during an Offer Period, Lessons from the Cadbury PLC Takeover" University College Dublin, Working Papers in Law, Criminology & Socio-Legal Studies Research Paper No 44.

Clarke, B. (2006), "Articles 9 and 11 of the Takeover Directive (2004/25) and the Market for Corporate Control", Journal of Business Law, Volume 26, Issue 2, pp. 355- 374.

CLRSG (1999), "Modern Company Law for a Competitive Economy: The Strategic Framework", London: Department of Trade and Industry.

Coates, J.C, (1999), "The Contestability of Corporate Control: A Critique of the Scientific Evidence", Harvard John M Olin Center for Law, Economics and Business Discussion Paper No. 265.

Coffee, J.C. (1984), "Regulating the Market for Corporate Control: A Critical Assessment of the Takeover's Role in Corporate Governance", Columbia Law Review, Volume 84, Issue 5, pp.1145- 1296.

Coffee, J.C. (2001), "The Rise of Dispersed Ownership: The Roles of Law and the State in the Separation of Ownership and Control", Yale Law Journal, Volume 111, I http://www.thetakeoverpanel.org.uk/wp-content/uploads/2008/11/PCP201101response8.pdfssue 1, pp. 1-82.

Coffee, J. (1993), "Institutional Investors as Corporate Monitors: Are Takeovers Obsolete?" in Farrar, J., (ed), "Takeovers Institutional Investors and the Modernization of Corporate Laws", Oxford University Press: Oxford.

Coleman, J. (1984), "Responsibility in corporate action: A sociologists view" in Hopt, K & Teubner, G. "Corporate governance and directors liabilities: Legal, economic and sociological analysis on corporate social responsibilities", Berlin; New York: De Gruyer.

Collison, D. Cross, S. Ferguson, J. Power, D & Stevenson, L. (2011), "Shareholder Primacy in the UK Corporate Law: An Exploration of the Rationale and Evidence", ACCA Research Report 125.

Company Law Committee of the Law Society, Response to the Department of Trade and Industry Consultation (April 1996) on the Thirteenth Directive on Company law concerning takeover bids.

Company Law Review Steering Committee (2001), "Modern Company Law for a Competitive Economy: The Strategic Framework", Final Report, URN 01/942, London: Department of Trade and Industry.

Company Law Review Steering Committee (2000), "Modern Company law for a Competitive Economy: Developing the Framework", URN 00/656, London: Department of Trade and Industry.

Conyon, M. J. Girma, S. Thompson, S & Wright, P. (2001), "Do hostile mergers destroy jobs?", Journal of Economic Behaviour and Organization, Volume 45, Issue 4, pp. 427–440.

Conyon, M. J. Girma, S. Thompson, S & Wright, P. (2002), "The impact of mergers and acquisitions on company employment in the United Kingdom", European Economic Review, Volume 46, Issue 1, pp. 31–49.

Corbett, A & Spender, P. (2009), "Corporate Constitutionalism", Sydney Law. Review, Volume 31, Issue 1, pp. 147-161.

Cosh, A. Hughes, A & Singh, A. (1990), "Takeovers and Short-termism in the UK" (London: Industry Policy Paper No.3).

Cosh, A & Guest, P. (2001), "The Long-run Performance of Hostile Takeovers: UK Evidence", ESRC Centre for Business Research, University of Cambridge Working Paper No.215.

Curtin, M. (2010), "Evolution, Not Revolution, for U.K. Takeover Rules", Wall Street Journal, October 21.

Danielson, M.G & Karpoff, J.M. (2006), "Do pills poison operating performance". Journal of Corporate Finance, Volume 12, Issue 3, pp. 536-599.

Dann, L & DeAngelo, H. (1988), "Corporate Financial Policy and Corporate Control", Journal of Financial Economics, Volume 20, Issue 2, pp. 87- 127.

David, J. (2000), "Cadbury stresses Kraft bid makes no strategic sense" Reuters (London, 25 /09).

Davies, P. Worthington, S & Micheler, E. (2008), "Gower and Davies: Principles of Modern Company Law", 8th Edition, London: Sweet and Maxwell.

Davies, P. (2003), "Gower and Davies' Principles of Modern Company law", 7th Edition, London: Sweet & Maxwell.

Davies, P. (2012), "Gower and Davies' Principles of Modern Company law", 9th Edition, London: Sweet and Maxwell.

Day, J & Taylor, P. (1995), "Evidence on the Practices of UK Bankers in Contracting for Medium-term Debt", Journal of International Banking Law, Volume 10, Issue 9, pp. 394-401.

Deflem, M. (2008), "Sociology of Law: Visions of a scholarly tradition", Cambridge: Cambridge University Press

Delaware "Why incorporate in Delaware" http://corp.delaware.gov/ (Accessed 18/04/2014).

Demsetz, H. (1967), "Toward a theory of property rights", American Economic Review, Volume 57, Issue 2, pp. 347-359.

Department for Business Innovation and Skills (2011), "A Long-term Focus for Corporate Britain, Summary of Responses", March.

Dignam, A & Lowry, J. (2012), "Company Law", Oxford: Oxford University Press.

Dodd, M.E. (1932), "For Whom Are Corporate Managers Trustees?" Harvard Law Review, Volume 45, Issue 7: 1145-1163.

Dodd, M. E. (1941), "The Modern Corporation, Private Property and Recent Federal Legislation", Harvard Law Review, Volume 54, Issue 6, pp. 917- 948.

Donaldson, T & Dunfee, T. W. (1999), "Ties that bind", Boston MA: Harvard Business School Press.

Donaldson, T & Preston, L. E. (1995), "The stakeholder theory of the corporation: concepts, evidence and implications". Academy of Management Review, Volume 20, Issue 1, pp. 85-91.

Douglass N C, (1990) 'Institutions, Institutional Change and Economic Performance', Cambridge University Press: Cambridge.

Driffield, N. Love, J. Lancheros, D & Temouri, Y. (2013), "How attractive is the UK for future manufacturing foreign direct investment", Foresight: Government Office for Science.

Dunsire, A. (1993) "Modes of Governance" in Kooiman, J. (ed), "Modern Governance: New government-society interactions", London: Sage Publication.

Dworkin, R. (1985), "Is wealth a value? In a Matter of Principle", Cambridge, MA: Harvard University Press.

Easterbrook, F. H & Fischel, D. R. (1981), "The Proper Role of a Target's Management in Responding to a Tender Offer", Harvard Law Review, Volume 94, Issue 6, pp.1161-1166.

Easterbrook, F & Fischel, D. (1991), "The economic structure of corporate law", Cambridge MA: Harvard University Press.

Edmonds, T. Webb, D & Long, R. (2011), "The economic crisis: policy responses", House of Commons Library, SN/BT/4968.

Eisenhardt, K. M & Graebner M. E. (2007), "Theory building from cases: opportunities and challenges." Academy of Management Journal, Volume 50, Issue 1, pp. 25-32.

Fama, E. (1970), "Efficient capital markets: a review of theory and empirical work", Journal of Finance, Volume 25, Issue 2, pp. 383–417.

Fama, E & Jensen, M. (1983), "Separation of Ownership & Control", Journal of Law & Economics, Volume 26, Issue 2, pp. 301-326.

Fama, E. F. (1980), "Agency Problems and the Theory of the Firm", Journal of Political Economy, Volume 88, Issue 2, pp. 288-307.

Fama, E & Jensen, M. (1983), "Agency Problems and Residual Claims," Journal of Law and Economics, Volume 26, Issue 2, pp. 327-49.

Farell, G. (2010), "Buffet reduces Kraft holding", Financial Times, May 19.

Ferrarini, G. (2006), "One Share- One Vote: A European Rule?" SSRN Working Paper.

Ferrell, A. (2002), "On Takeover law and Regulatory Competition", Business Lawyer, Volume 57, Issue 3, pp. 1047-1068.

Fisch, J. (2006), "Measuring efficiency in corporate law: The role of shareholder primacy", The Journal of Corporation Law, Volume 31, Issue 3, pp. 637- 674.

Fleischacker, S. (2004), "On Adam Smith's Wealth of Nations", Princeton, NJ: Princeton University Press.

Franks, J & Mayer C. (1996), "Hostile Takeovers and the Correction of Managerial Failure", Journal of Financial Economics, Volume 40, Issue 1, pp. 163-181.

Franks, J. R & Harris, R. S. (2002), "Shareholder Wealth Effects of Corporate Takeovers: The UK Experience 1955-1965", Journal of Financial Economics, Volume 23, Issue 2, pp. 225-249.

Freeman, E & David L. (1983), "Stockholders and Stakeholders: A new perspective on Corporate Governance". California Management Review, Volume 25, Issue 3, pp. 88-106.

Freeman, E. (1984), "Strategic management: A stakeholder approach", New York: Harper Collins.

Freeman, R. E. Wicks, A. C & Parmar, B. (2004), "Stakeholder theory and the corporate objective revisited", Organization Science, Volume 15, Issue 3, pp. 364-369.

Friedman, M. (1962), "Capitalism and Freedom", University of Chicago Press: Chicago.

Galbraith, J.K. (1967), "The New Industrial State" Houghton Mifflin Company: Boston.

Galbraith, J.K. (1998), "The Affluent Society", 4th Edition. Houghton Mifflin Company: New York.

Galpin, T. J & Herndon, M. (2007), "The Complete Guide to Mergers and Acquisitions: Process tools to support M&A integration at every level", 2nd Edition, Wiley John & Sons: New Jersey.

Gamble, A & Kelly, G. (2001) "Shareholder value and the stakeholder debate in the UK", Corporate Governance: An International Review, Volume 9, Issue 2, pp. 110-117.

Garrahan, M. (2005), "Man Utd board to accept Glazer takeover", Financial Times, May 26.

Gerner-Beuerle, C. Kershaw, D & Solinas, M. (2011), "Is the Board Neutrality Rule Trivial? Amnesia about Corporate Law in European Takeover Regulation" (2011) European Business Law Review, Volume 22, Issue 5, pp. 559–622.

Glaser, B. (2002), "Conceptualization: On theory and theorizing using grounded theory". International Journal of Qualitative Methods, Volume 1, Issue 2, pp. 1-30.

Goergen, M & Renneboog, L. (2004), "Shareholder Wealth Effects of European Domestic and Cross-Border Takeover Bids", European Financial Management, Volume 10, Issue 1, pp. 9- 45.

Gompers, P. A. Ishii, J & Metrick, A. (2003), "Corporate Governance and Equity Prices", The Quarterly Journal of Economics, Volume 118, Issue 1, pp. 107- 155.

Gordon, M. (2002), "Takeover Defences Work. Is That Such a Bad Thing?", Stanford Law Review, Volume 55, Issue 3, pp. 819- 837.

Goyder, G.A. (1951), "The Future of Private Enterprise", Oxford: Blackwell.

Goyder, M. (1998), "Living Tomorrow's Company", Aldershot: Gower Publishing Ltd.

Gregory, A. (1997), "An Examination of the Long Run Performance of UK Acquiring Firms", Journal of Business Finance and Accounting, Volume 24, Issue 7, pp.971-1002.

Grinyer, J. Russell, A & Collison, D. (1998), "Evidence of Managerial Short-termism in the UK", British Journal of Management, Volume 9, Issue 1, pp. 13-22.

Gupta A. K. Wakayama, T & Rangan, U. S. (2012), "Global Strategies for Emerging Asia" Wiley, John & Sons: USA.

Gugler, K & Yurtoglu, B. (2004), "The effects of mergers on company employment in the USA and Europe", International Journal of Industrial Organization, Volume 22, Issue 4, pp.481–502

Habermas, J. (1996) "Between facts and norms: Contributions to a discourse on theory or law and democracy", Blackwell Publishing Ltd: London.

Hamel, G & Prahalad, C. (1989), "Strategic Intent", Harvard Business Review, Volume 67, Issue 3, pp. 63-76.

Hambrick, D. C & Cannella, A. A. (1993), "Relative standing: A framework for understanding departures of acquired executives", Academy of Management Journal, Volume 36, Issue 4, pp. 733–762.

Hampel Committee (1998), "The Hampel Report on Corporate Governance-Final Report", London: Gee.

Hansmann, H & Kraakman, R. (2000), "The End of History for Corporate Law," Georgetown U. Law Review, Volume 89, Issue 2, pp. 439-468.

Hansmann, H. (1996), "The Ownership of Enterprise", Cambridge, MA: Harvard University Press.

Harford, J. (2005), "What drives merger waves", Journal of Financial Economics, Volume 77, Issue 3, pp. 529–560.

Hayes, R & Abernathy, W. (1980), "Managing Our Way to Economic Decline", Harvard Business Review, Volume 58, Issue 4, pp. 67-77.

Helen, B. (2009), "Globalisation and the rise of 'economic nationalism': takeovers and regulation within the European Union", International Journal of Economics and Business Research, Volume1, Issue 2. pp. 234-251

Heracleous, L & Murray, J. (2001), "The urge to merge in the pharmaceutical industry", European Management Journal, Volume 19, Issue 4, pp. 430-437.

Heron, R. A & Lie, E. (2006), "On the Use of Poison Pills and Defensive Payouts by Takeover Targets", Journal of Business, Volume 79, Issue 4, pp. 1783- 1808.

Hobbes, T. (1948), "Leviathan", Oxford: Basil Blackwell.

Hollingsworth, Jr & Muller, K. In "Advancing socio-economics: An institutionalist Perspective", Hollingsworth, J.R. Muller, K.H & Hollingsworth, E.J. (2002), Lanham, Maryland: Rowan and Littlefields.

Holmstrom, B & Kaplan, S. N. (2001), "Corporate Governance and Merger Activity in the United States: Making Sense of the 1980s and 1990s", Journal of Economic Perspectives, Volume 15, Issue 2, 121-144.

Homroy, S. (2012), "Effect of Mergers and Acquisitions on CEO Turnover in Large Firms and SMES: A Hazard Analysis", Department of Economics, Lancaster University.

Horrigan, B. (2008), "Corporate Social Responsibility in the 21st Century: Debates, Models and Practices across Government, Law and Business" Cheltenham: Edward Elgar.

House of Commons, Business, Innovation and Skills Committee, Mergers Acquisitions and Takeovers: the Takeover of Cadbury by Kraft, Ninth Report of Session 2009-2010 (HC 234, Published 6 April 2010).

House of Commons, Business, Innovation and Skills Committee. "Is Kraft working for. Cadbury?" Sixth Report of Session 2010-2012.

Hu, H. T. C & Black, B. (2005), "Empty Voting and Hidden 'Morphable' Ownership: Taxonomy, Implications and Reforms" Business Lawyer, Volume 61, Issue 3, pp. 1011- 1070.

Hussain, W. (2012), "Corporations, profit maximisation and the personal sphere", Economics and Philosophy, Volume 28, Issue 3, pp 311-331.

IMAA (2014), "Statistics on Mergers and Acquisitions worldwide" http://www.imaa-institute.org/statistics-mergers-acquisitions. html#MergersAcquisitions_United%20Kingdom (Accessed 17/08/2014)

Institute of Directors (2010) "IoD reacts to review of Takeover Code" Press Release, 21 October.

Intintoli, V. J. Serfling, M.A & Shaikh, S. (2012), "The Negative Spillover Effects of CEO Turnovers: Evidence from Firm-Supplier Relations" SSRN Working Paper Series.

Ireland, P. (2003), "Property and Contract in contemporary Corporate Theory", Legal Studies, Volume 23, Issue 3, pp. 453–509.

Ireland, P. (1999), "Company Law and the Myth of Shareholder Ownership", Modern Law Review, Volume 62, Issue 1, pp.41.

Ireland, P. (2001), "Defending the Rentier: Corporate Theory and the Reprivatization of the Public Company", in Parkinson, J. Gamble, A & Kelly, G. (eds), "The Political Economy of the Company", Oxford: Hart Publishers.

Jannarone, J & Curtin, M. (2010), "Hershey's Chocolate Dreams" Wall Street Journal , 16 January

Jarrell, G. A. Brickley J. A & Netter J. M. (1988), "The Market for Corporate Control: The Empirical Evidence since 1980", Journal of Economic Perspectives, Volume 2, Issue 1, pp. 49-68.

Jeffrey, A. Krug, J. A & Aguilera, R.V. (2005), "Top Management Teams turnover in mergers and acquisitions. Advances in Mergers and Acquisitions", Volume 4, pp.121–149.

Jensen, M & Smith, C. (1985), "Stockholder, Manager and Creditor Interests: Applications of Agency Theory", in Altman, E & Subrahmanyam, M. (Eds),

"Recent Advances in Corporate Finance", Irwin Professional Publishing: Homewood, USA.

Jensen, M. (2001), "Value Maximization, Stakeholder Theory, and the Corporate Objective Function", European Financial Management, Volume 7, Issue 3, p. 297.

Jensen, M. C. (1986), "Agency costs of free cash flow, corporate finance and takeovers", American Economic Review, Volume 76, Issue 2, pp.323-329.

Jensen, M. C & Ruback R. S. (1983), "The Market for Corporate Control", Journal of Financial Economics, Volume 11, Issue 1, pp 5-50.

Jensen, M.C & Meckling, W.H. (1976), 'Theory of the Firm: Managerial Behaviour, Agency Costs and Ownership Structure', Journal of Financial Economics, Volume 3, Issue 4, pp. 305-360.

Jones, S. (2010) "How the Hedge Fund Industry Influences Boardroom Battles", Financial Times, 22 June.

Joseph, F. (2012), "Who Really Drove the Economy into the Ditch?" Algora Publishing: New York.

Kahan, M & Rock, E.B. (2007), "Hedge Funds in Corporate Governance and Corporate Control", University of Pennsylvania Law Review, Volume 155, Issue 5, pp.1021- 1093.

Kang, J.K & Shivdasani, A. (1996), "Does the Japanese Governance System Enhance Shareholder Wealth? Evidence from the Stock-price Effects of Top Management Turnover", Review of Financial Studies, Volume 9, Issue4, pp. 1061-1095.

Kapp, K. W. (1950), "The Social Costs of Private Enterprise", Cambridge, MA: Harvard University Press.

Keay, A. (2011), "Moving Towards Stakeholderism? Participant Statutes, Enlightened Shareholder Value and All That: Much Ado About Little?" SSRN Working Paper Series.

Keay A, (2012) "The Kay Review of UK equity markets and long-term decision making", (July).

Keay, A. (2008), "Ascertaining the Corporate Objectives: An Entity Maximisation and Sustainability Model", Modern Law Review, Volume 71, Issue 5, pp. 663-698.

Kelly, G. Kelly, D & Gamble, A. (1997), "Stakeholder capitalism", London: Macmillan Press.

Kershaw, D. (2007), "The Illusion of Importance: Reconsidering the UK's Takeover Defence Prohibition" International and Comparative Law Quarterly, Volume 56, Issue 2, pp. 267-308.

Kershaw, D. (2012), "Company law in context: Text and Materials", Oxford: Oxford University Press.

Kiarie, S. (2006) "At Crossroads: shareholder value, stakeholder value and enlightened shareholder value: Which road should the United Kingdom take?" International Company and Commercial Law Review, Volume 17, Issue 11, pp. 329-343.

King, I. (2010), "Buyout leaves a bad taste", The Times, September 1.

King, D. R. Dalton, D. R. Daily, C. M & Covin, J. G. (2004), "Meta-analyses of post-acquisition performance: Indications of unidentified moderators", Strategic Management Journal, Volume 25, Issue 2, pp. 187–200.

Koller, T. Goedhart, M & David, W. (2010), "Valuation, Measuring and managing the value of companies", 4th Edition, Wiley John & Sons: New Jersey.

Korten, D. (2005), "When corporations rule the world", West Hartford, Conn and San Francisco: Kumarian Press and Berrett- Koehler Publishers.

Kouloridas, A. (2008), "The Law and Economics of Takeovers", Hart Publishing: Oregon, pp.2-5.

Kriegbaum, C. (1989), "Innovation and Industrial Strength: A study in the UK, West Germany, the United States and Japan", Policy Studies Institutive, London.

Krug, J. A & Aguilera, R.V. (2005), "Top Management Teams turnover in mergers and acquisitions", Advances in Mergers and Acquisitions, Volume 4, Issue 1, pp. 121–149.

Krug, J. A & Shill, W. (2008), "The big exit: executive churn in the wake of M&As", Journal of Business Strategy, Volume 29, Issue 4, pp. 15-21.

Kumar, B. R. (2012), "Mega Mergers and Acquisitions: Case Studies from Key Industries", Basingstoke, Hampshire: Palgrave Macmillan.

Leshem, S & Traford, V. (2007), "Overlooking the conceptual framework", Innovations in Education and Teaching International, Volume 44, Issue 1: 93-105.

Lewin, K. (1952), "Field Theory in Social Science: Selected Theoretical Papers", London: Tavistock.

Lichtenberg, F.R & Siegel, D. (1989), "The Effect of Takeovers on the Employment and Wages of Central Office and Other Personnel", First Boston Working Paper Series, Graduate School of Business: Columbia University.

Lieberman, D & Krantz, M. (2010), "Is Kraft's $19B Cadbury Buy a Sweet Deal? Buffett has Doubts", US Today, January 20.

Lipton, M. (1979), "Takeover Bids in the Target's Boardroom", Business Lawyer, Volume 35, Issue 1, pp.101- 134.

Lord Mandelson, Secretary of State for Business, Innovation and Skills, Speech at the Trade and Industry dinner, Guildhall, the Mansion House, London (March 1, 2010)

Lord Mandelson (2010) "Britain needs investors for the long-term", The Financial Times.   January 13.

Loughran, T & Vijh, A. M. (1997), "Do long-term shareholders benefit from corporate acquisitions?", Journal of Finance, Volume 52, Issue 5, pp. 1765–1790.

Loughrey, J. Keay A & Cerioni L. (2008), "Legal Practitioners, Enlightened Shareholder Value, and the Shaping of Corporate Governance", Journal of Corporate Law Studies, Volume 8, Issue 1, pp.82-87.

Lowenstein, R. (2004), "Origins of the Crash: The Great Bubble and Its Undoing", Penguin Books Press: New York.

Manne, H. G. (1965), "Mergers and the Market for Corporate Control", Journal of Political Economy, Volume 73, Issue 2, pp.110-120.

Manne, H. G. (1967), "Our Two Corporation Systems: Law and Economics", Virginia Law Review, Volume 53, Issue 2, pp. 259-284.

Mariano, C. (2000), "Case study: the method", Chapter 10. In Munhall P. & Boyd C.O, (eds). Nursing Research: A Qualitative Perspective. 2nd Edition, Sudbury, MA: Jones and Bartlett Publishers, pp. 311- 337.

Marris, R. L. (1964), "The Economic Theory of Managerial Capitalism", London: Macmillan.

Martin, S & Partnoy, F, (2005) "Encumbered Shares", University of Illinois Law Review, Volume 30, Issue 3, pp. 775-814.

Martin, K.L & McConnell, J.J. (1991), "Corporate Performance, Corporate Takeovers, and Management Turnover" Journal of Finance, Volume 46, Issue 2, pp. 671-687.

Marx, K. (1867), "Capital: A critique of political economy", Frederick Engels, ed., Moore, S & Aveling, E. Marxist.org.

Marsh, P. (2010), "Tata confident Corus will regain its lustre", Financial Times, 4 May.

Matthew, P. (2013), "Protecting shareholders from themselves: How the United Kingdom's 2011 Takeover Code Amendments hit their mark", Pennsylvania State Journal of Law & International Affairs, Volume 2, Issue 2, pp. 409-446.

Mehra, B. (2001), "Research or personal quest: Dilemmas in studying my own kind". In Merchant B. M & Willis A. I. (Eds.), "Multiple and intersecting identities in qualitative research", Mahwah, NH: Lawrence Erlbaum, pp. 69-82.

Mihir, B. (2007), "Manchester Disunited: Trouble and Takeover at the World's Richest Football Club", London: Aurum Press.

Mikkelson, W. H & Partch, M. M. (1997), "The decline of takeovers and disciplinary managerial turnover", Journal of Financial Economics, Volume 44, Issue 2, pp. 205-228.

Miller, E. L. JR. (2008), "Mergers and Acquisitions: A Step-by-Step Legal and Practical Guide" John Wiley & Sons: Hoboken, New Jersey.

Moeller, T. (2005), "Let's Make a Deal! How Shareholder Control Impacts Merger Payoffs", Journal of Financial Economics, Volume 76, Issue 1, pp. 167-190.

Moeller, S. B. Schlingemann, F. P & Stulz, R. M. (2005), "Wealth destruction on a massive scale, a study of acquiring firm returns in the recent merger wave", Journal of Finance, Volume 60, Issue 2, pp. 757-783

Monks, A. G & Minow, N. (2011), "Corporate Governance", 5th Edition, New York: John, Wiley & Sons.

Morrison, K. (2006), "Marx, Durkheim, Weber Foundations of Modern Thought", 2nd Edition, London: Sage Publications.

Motis, J. (2007), "Mergers and Acquisitions Motives Toulouse School of Economics", University of Crete: Working Paper.

Mumford, M. (2000), "Strategic directions for corporate governance", Lancaster University Management School: Working Paper 024.

Munari, F & Sobrero, M. (2003), "Corporate Governance and Innovation" in Calderini M. Garrone P & Sobrero, M (eds) "Corporate Governance, Market Structure and Innovation", Cheltenham: Edward Elgar.

Myners, P. (2001), "Institutional investment in the United Kingdom: a review", HM Treasury: London.

Notes (1969), Cash Tender Offers, Harvard Law Review, Volume 83, Issue 2: 377-403.

OECD (2009), "Corporate Governance and the Financial Crisis: Key findings and main message" (OECD Corporate Governance Committee.

Office for National Statistics (2012), "Mergers and Acquisitions by foreign companies". Available at statistics.gov.uk.

Office for National Statistics, "Share Ownership: A Report of Ownership on UK Shares" 31 December 2010.

Ogowewo, T. (1997), "Rationalising General Principle 7 of the City Code", Company Financial and Insolvency Law Review, No. 74.

Oesterle, D.A. (2006), "Regulating Hedge Funds", Entrepreneurial Business Law Journal, Volume 1, Issue 1, pp. 1-42

Paddy, I. (1999), "Company law and the Myth of Shareholder Ownership" Modern Law Review, Volume 62, Issue1, pp. 32- 57.

Parker, C. (2010), "The open corporation: effective self regulation and democracy", Cambridge University Press.

Parkinson, J. E. (1996) "The Contractual Theory of the Company and the Protection of Non-Shareholder Interests" in Feldman, D & Miesel, F. (eds.), "Corporate and Commercial Law: Modern Developments", London: Lloyds.

Parkinson, J. (1993), "Corporate Power and Responsibility: Issues in the Theory of Company Law", Oxford: Oxford University Press.

Parantap, B. Chakraborty, C & Reagle, D. (2003), "Liberalization, FDI, and Growth in Developing Countries: A Panel Cointegration Approach." Economic Inquiry, Volume 41, Issue 3, pp. 510-516.

Patrone, M. R. (2011), "Sour Chocolate? Cadbury/Kraft and the 2011 Proposed Amendments to the UK Takeover Code - A Call for Further Research", SSRN Working Paper.

Perotin, V & Robinson, A. (2003), Employee Participation in Profit and Ownership: a Review of the Issues and Evidence, Working paper, Social Affairs Series, Luxembourg Parliament, Directorate- General for Research.

Phillips, M. (1992) "Corporate moral personhood and three conceptions of the corporation", Business Ethics Quarterly, Volume 2, Issue 2, pp. 435-459.

Pilgrim, R. (2010), "UK Takeover Panel Recommends Code Change", Tax News, 26 October.

Pinheiro, M. (2009), "Short-selling restrictions, takeovers and the wealth of long-run shareholders", Journal of Mathematical Economics, Volume 45, Issue 5, pp. 361-375.

Pippard, R. (2011), "A Takeover Too Far Can the UK prohibition on board defensive action be justified any longer?" SSRN Working Paper.

Porta, R.L. Lopez-de-Silanes, F & Shleifer, A. (1999), "Corporate Ownership Around the World", Journal of Finance, Volume 54, Issue 2, pp. 471-517.

Porter, M. (2005) "Capital Choices: Changing the Way America Invest in Industry", Journal of Applied Corporate Finance Volume 5, Issue 2, pp. 4-16.

Post, J. E. Preston L.E & Sachs, S. (2002), "Redefining the Corporation Stakeholder Management and Organizational Wealth", Stanford CA: Stanford University Press.

Posner, R. (1980), "The Present Situation of Legal Scholarship", Yale Law Journal, Volume 90, Issue 5, pp. 1113- 1130.

Prasad, M, (2006) "The Politics of Free Markets: The Rise of Neoliberal Economic Policies in Britain, France, Germany and the United States" University of Chicago Press: Cambridge.

Prentice, D. D & Holland P.R.J. (1993), "Contemporary Issues in Corporate Governance", Clarendon Press, Oxford.

Rajan, R. G & Zingales, L. (1998), "Power in the Theory of the Firm", Quarterly Journal of Economics, Volume 113, Issue 2, pp. 387- 432.

Rapperport, P. (2011), "A bitter Taste" Financial Times, May 23.

Rawls, J. (1999), "A theory of justice" 2nd Edition. Cambridge, MA: Harvard University Press.

Rigby, E. (2014), "Vince Cable plans to toughen up takeover rules" Financial Times, July 13.

Roe, M. J. (1994), "Strong Managers, Weak Owners: The Political Roots of American Corporate", Princeton: Princeton University Press.

Robert, M. (1997), "Aristotle's Criticism of Plato's Republic", Lanham: Rowman & Littlefield.

Robinson, W.S. (2012), "A change in the legal wind- how a new direction for corporate governance could affect takeover regulation", International Company and Commercial Law Review, Volume 23, Issue 9, pp. 292-307.

Roe, M. J. (2002), "Corporate Law's Limits", Journal of Legal Studies, Volume 31, Issue 2, pp. 233-271.

Roe, M. J. (2001), "The Shareholder Wealth Maximization Norm and Industrial Organization", University of Pennsylvania Law Review, Volume 149, Issue 6, pp. 2063-2081.

Roger Carr, "Cadbury: Hostile bids and takeovers" (Saiid Business School, February 15, 2010).

Romano, R. (1992), "A Guide to Takeovers: Theory, Evidence, and Regulation", Yale Journal on Regulation Volume 9, Issue 1, pp. 119- 180.

Rossi, S & Volpin, P. F. (2004), "Cross-Country Determinants of Mergers and Acquisitions", Journal of Financial Economics, Volume 74, Issue 3, 277-304.

Russell, J. (2009), "ABI Leads Attack on Myners Over Reform", Telegraph, August 1.

Salacuse, J. (2004), "Corporate Governance in the New Century'", Company Lawyer, Volume 25, Issue 3, p. 77.

Sanderson, P. Seidl, D & Roberts, J. (2013), "The Limits of Flexible Regulation: Managers' perceptions of corporate governance" Centre for Business Research, University of Cambridge, Working Paper No. 439.

Sants, H. (2009), "The crisis: The role of investors" Speech at the NAFT Investment Conference, March 11 (UK Financial Services Authority).

Scharfstein, D. (1988), "The Disciplinary Role of Takeovers", Review of Economic Studies, Volume 55, Issue 2, pp.185- 199.

Schenk, H. (2011), "Time to protect the public from highly corrosive mergers and acquisitions" 05 October, Public Policy Network.

Schumann, L. (1988), "State Regulation of Takeovers and Shareholder Wealth: The Case of New York's 1985 Takeover Statutes", Rand Journal of Economics, Volume 19, Issue 4, pp. 557-567.

Schwert, G. W. (2000), "Hostility in Takeovers: In the Eyes of the Beholder?", Journal of Finance, Volume 55, Issue 6, pp. 2599-2640.

Shleifer, A & Summers, L. (1988), "Breach of Trust in Hostile Takeovers". In Auerbach A. J., Corporate Takeovers: Causes and Consequences, University of Chicago Press: Chicago.

Shleifer, A & Vishny, R. (1997), "A Survey of Corporate Governance", the Journal of Finance, Volume 52, Issue, 2, pp. 737-783.

Scott, W.R. (2001), "Institutions and Organisations", 2nd Edition, Thousand Oaks: Sage Publications.

Short, K & Keasey, H. (1997), "Institutional Shareholders and Corporate Governance in the United Kingdom", in Keasey, K. Thompson, S & Wright, M (eds) "Corporate Governance: Economic, Management and Financial Issues", Oxford University Press: Oxford.

Smith, A (1987). "Theory of Moral Sentiments", in Heilbroner, R. L. "The Essential Adam Smith", 3rd Edition, New York: WW Norton & Company.

Smith, A. (1976), "An Inquiry into the Nature and Causes of the Wealth of Nations", Oxford: Clarendon Press.

Smith, D (2004), "On values and values", New Jersey, USA: Pearson Education Inc.

Stake, R. E. (2006), "Multiple Case Study Analysis", New York: The Guilford Press.

Sternberg, E. (1997), "The defects of stakeholder theory", Corporate Governance: An international Review, Volume 5, Issue 1, pp. 3-10.

Stone, C. D. (1991), "Where the law ends: The social control of corporate behaviour", Waveland Press Inc: Illinois.

Stout, L.A. (2003),"The Mechanisms of market inefficiency", Journal of Corporation Law, Volume 28, Issue 3, pp. 635-669.

Stout, L. (2002),"Bad and non-so bad arguments for shareholder primacy", Southern California Law Review, Volume 75, Issue 3, pp. 1189-1210.

Subramanian, G. (2003), "Bargaining in the Shadow of Takeover Defenses", Yale Law Journal, Volume 113, Issue 3, pp. 621-686.

Sudarsanam, S. (2006), "Creating value from Mergers and Acquisitions: The challenges", Prentice Hall: New Jersey.

Teubner, G. (1987) "Juridification: Concepts, Aspects, Limits and Solutions" in Teubner, G (ed) "Juridification of social spheres: A comparative analysis of areas of labour, corporate and antitrust and social welfare law", Berlin: Walter de Gruyter.

The High Level Group of Company Law Experts (2002), "Report of the High Level Group of Company Law Experts on a Modern Regulatory Framework for Company Law in Europe" Brussels.

The High Level Group of Company Law Experts (2002), "Report of the High Level Group of Company Law Experts on Issues Relating to Takeover Bids" Brussels.

The Takeover Panel, "Response Statement to the Consultation Paper on Review of Certain Aspects of the Regulation of Takeover Bids" (October 2010).

The Takeover Panel, "Report and accounts for the year ended 31 March" London.

The Takeover Panel, "Consultation Paper Issued by the Code Committee of the Panel: Review of Certain Aspects of the Regulation of Takeover Bids" (21 October 2010).

The Takeover Panel, "A review of the 2011 Amendments to the Takeover Code",26 November, 2012.

The Takeover Panel (2011), "Reviews of Certain Aspects of the Regulation of Takeovers Bids: proposed amendments to the Takeover Code", London.

Tiller, E & Cross, F. (2006), "What is Legal Doctrine", North-Western University Law Review, Volume 100, Issue 1, pp. 517- 534.

Thomas, G. (2011), "A typology for the case study in social science following a review of definition, discourse and structure", Qualitative Inquiry, Volume 17, Issue 6, pp. 511-521.

Thomsen, S. (2007), "International Investment Perspectives: Freedom of investment in a changing world" OECD, Chapter 4.

Treanor, J. (2010), "Cadbury management criticised for caving in to Kraft takeover", The Guardian, January 19.

Triantis, G & Daniels, R. (1995), "The Role of Debt in Interactive Corporate Governance", California Law Review, Volume 83, Issue 4, pp. 1073-1113.

Trimbath, S. Frydman, H & Frydman, R. (2000), "Corporate Inefficiency and The Risk of Takeover", Economic Research Reports from C.V. Starr Center for Applied Economics Working Paper 00-14.

United Nations Conference on Trade and Development, "The Law Applicable to International Investment Disputes", UNCTAD/EDM/Misc.

Vishwanath, S.R. (2009), "Cases in corporate finance" Tata McGraw-Hill Education.

Wallace, J. (2003), "Value Maximisation and Stakeholder Theory: Compatible or Not?" Journal of Applied Corporate Finance, Volume 15, Issue 3, pp. I20-127.

Walter, G & Barney, J. (1990), "Research Notes and Communications: Management Objectives in Mergers and Acquisitions", Strategic Management Journal, Volume11, Issue 1, pp. 79-86.

Ward, A. (2014), "Pfizer admits defeat in AstraZeneca Bid" The Financial Times, May 26

Waton, N. (2010), "Cadbury, Kraft and the politics of making chocolate", BBC News, 19 January.

Webb, T. (2010), "Lord Mandelson call for overhaul of UK takeover rules", The Guardian, March 2.

Wempe, J & Donaldson, T. (2004), "The practicality of pluralism: Redrawing the simple picture of bipolarism and compliance in business ethics" In Brenkert G. G. (ed) "Corporate Integrity and accountability", London: Sage Publications.

Wiggins, J & Saigol, L. (2009), "Hedge fund interest in Cadbury increases", Financial Times, November 10.

Williams, C & Conley, J. (2005), "An Emerging Third Way? The Erosion of the Anglo- American Shareholder Value Construct" Cornell International Law Journal, Volume 38, Issue 2, pp. 493-551.

Williamson, O. E. (1964), "The Economics of Discretionary Behaviour: Managerial Objectives in a Theory of the Firm", Englewood Cliffs, NJ: Prentice-Hall.

Williamson, O. E. (1975), "Markets and Hierarchies: Analysis and Antitrust Implications". New York: The Free Press.

Wood, Z. Treanor, J. (2010), "2m a day cost of Cadbury deal- plus 12m for bosses". The Guardian, 19 January.

Woller, G. M. (1996), "Business ethics, society and Adam Smith: some observations on the liberal business ethos", Journal of Socio Economics, Volume 25, Issue 3, pp. 311- 332.

Wong, S.C.Y. (2010), "Long-Term versus Short-Term Distinction in the UK Takeover Review Misses the Point", The Financial Times, August 23.

Yin, R. K. (2003), "Case study research, design and methods" 3rd Edition, Thousand Oaks: Sage Publications.

Zucker, D. M. (2009), "How to Do Case Study Research", University of Massachusetts: Amherst.

INDEX